Edexcel GCSE

Leisure and Tourism

Written by Pauline Morris, Maureen Kelly, Stella Douglas and Lee Fletcher

Introduction by Peter Mealing

A PEARSON COMPANY

Published by Pearson Education Limited, a company incorporated in England and Wales, having its registered office at Edinburgh Gate, Harlow, Essex, CM20 2JE. Registered company number: 872828

www.heinemann.co.uk

Edexcel is a registered trade mark of Edexcel Limited

First published 2009

13 12 11 10 09
10 9 8 7 6 5 4 3 2 1

British Library Cataloguing in Publication Data
A catalogue record for this book is available from the British Library

ISBN 978 1 846904 11 0

Edited by Rachael Williams and Alyson Jones
Designed by Tek-Art, Crawley Down, West Sussex
Typeset by Tek-Art
Original illustrations © Pearson Education 2009
Illustrated by Tek-Art
Picture research by Helen Reilly
Cover photo/illustration © Edexcel
Printed in Spain by Graficas Estella S.L.

Acknowledgements
Every effort has been made to contact copyright holders of material reproduced in this book. Any omissions will be rectified in subsequent printings if notice is given to the publishers.

Websites
There are links to relevant websites in this book. In order to ensure that the links are up to date, that the links work, and that the sites are not inadvertently linked to sites that could be considered offensive, we have made the links available on the Heinemann website at www.heinemann.co.uk/hotlinks. When you access the site, the express code is 4110P.

Contents

Introduction

Welcome to the Edexcel GCSE Leisure and Tourism qualification, which enables you to learn about the leisure and tourism industry in an interesting and practical way. Leisure and tourism is one of the most important industries both here in the UK and throughout the world. It is one of the fastest growing areas of the economy and one that employs, both directly and indirectly, millions of people. The industry is exciting, dynamic, and responding to economic, cultural and social changes.

This book has been specifically written for students who are preparing for both Edexcel's GCSE Leisure and Tourism Single and Double qualifications. The book, with its associated activities and assessment tasks, will help inform, reinforce and support your learning during this course. You will be able to increase your knowledge and understanding of the leisure and tourism industry, and develop skills to apply in a range of activities and assessments. The book has been written by a group of authors with a wide experience of the industry, or of teaching the subject in schools and colleges.

This introduction has been written to help you understand more about the qualification and how you will be assessed. It also includes information on how to identify your own learning style, and use this to learn more easily and obtain good grades. You will also find tips on how to use this book, as well as a description of the different features it contains for quick and easy reference. These include the special Make the Grade sections that follow each unit, which have been designed to help you prepare effectively for your assessment.

Remember it

GCSE Leisure and Tourism (Double Award) is a **vocational** qualification. The word 'vocational' simply means it is related to the world of work, in this case the world of leisure and tourism.

About the qualification

The GCSE Leisure and Tourism qualification can be studied as a Single Award or as a Double Award.

- The Single Award means you must complete two units successfully to be awarded. You will either study units 1 and 2 or units 1 and 4 to be awarded the Single GCSE.
- The Double Award is equivalent to two GCSEs. You must complete all four of these units successfully to be awarded the Double GCSE.

The book, like the qualification, is divided into four units and all four of these units are covered in this book, so you will find everything you need whether you are taking the Single Award or the Double Award.

Take it further

Talk to your tutor and find out whether you are taking the Single Award or the Double Award. Then find out the order in which you will study the units.

What you will learn

In each unit you will learn about the different aspects of the leisure and tourism industry.

- **Unit 1: The Leisure and Tourism Industry**
  In this unit you will study the different types of leisure and tourism organisations, the products, services and the employment opportunities they offer. You will also study why people make use of leisure facilities, and why and how people travel. You will be expected to research the type of destinations people travel to, and explore the impact of tourism on communities and environments.
- **Unit 2: Sales, Promotion and Operations in Leisure and Tourism**
  You will study how leisure and tourism organisations operate, and how they promote and sell their products and services. You will be asked to comment on how organisations market themselves and on the effectiveness of their methods. You will also look at the impact of new technology and business methods on the operation of leisure and tourism organisations. Your research and investigations in this area will be applied to real organisations in the industry.
- **Unit 3: The Leisure and Tourism Environment**
  This unit looks at the changing nature of the leisure and tourism industry, the appeal of different types of destinations and where these are located within the UK. You will also study both the positive and negative impacts of tourism globally, on local communities and on the environment. You will be asked to consider the issue and importance of sustainability to the leisure and tourism industry, both in the UK and internationally.
- **Unit 4: Customers and Employment in Leisure and Tourism**
  In this unit, you will research and investigate visitor attractions, tourist destinations and leisure facilities both in the UK and internationally. You will explore the factors that influence how people spend their leisure time and the way tourist destinations, leisure facilities and visitor attractions meet customer needs, including different cultural and specific needs. You will also look at the importance of health and safety issues in the industry. Your study will involve looking at opportunities for employment, and the skills and qualities required by those working or wanting to work in the leisure and tourism industry.

Remember: your teacher or tutor will advise you which units you will study if you are taking the Single Award.

Introduction to assessment

You will be assessed for every unit you study. Two units are **internally** assessed and two units are **externally** assessed.

- Units 1 and 3 are externally assessed. After you have completed one of these units you will take a 60-minute written examination worth 50 marks each. The questions will be a mixture of short-answer questions and

Describe it

Internal (controlled) assessment takes place in your school or college and your work is marked by your tutor.

External assessment means your work is sent to Edexcel to be marked.

questions that will allow you to develop your answers more. These units will be worth 40% of the Single GCSE and 20% of the Double GCSE. Both written examination papers can be sat either in January or June. This book will provide you with the essential information you will need for both written papers as well as tips for revision. Use is made throughout of the type of questions you will be asked in both written papers and in the controlled assessments for Units 2 and 4.

- Units 2 and 4 are based on coursework and are internally assessed. For these units you will be involved in research and the collection of information and data. You will then use this to complete the four assessment tasks in each of the controlled assessment units. Controlled assessment will be worth 60% of both Single and Double awards. The assessment tasks will be given to you by your teacher or tutor and have been written by Edexcel. It is important that you follow the instructions you are given carefully, complete each task and make sure that all the work is your own. You will carry out these tasks under controlled conditions. This means that you do the work in school or college, not at home, and a tutor is present when you are doing it. You will leave any partially completed work and research with your tutor until the next controlled assessment session. Your completed work is marked by your tutor and then sent to Edexcel for checking.

Remember it

The time you have to complete your research is limited to a maximum of 30 hours and the time you have to write up your work is limited to 15 hours (per unit). This means you must use your time wisely. You will find helpful guidance in the Make the Grade sections for Units 2 and 4.

Maximising your learning power

The brain is an amazing and complex organ made up of billions of cells that has a capacity much greater than our ability to access all of its potential. The brain allows us to see, hear, smell, taste, feel and move. It also allows us to store new information that we need and can use. We are not always good at storing this information in our memory or recalling it. The brain has different areas that allow us to learn and retain information in different ways. It is made up of two hemispheres – a right and a left side. The left side is more concerned with language, numbers, words and logic. The right side is more focused on creativity, visualisation pictures, music and patterns. Some people use one side of their brain more than they do the other. We need to develop our capacity to use both sides of the brain in order to increase our capacity to study more effectively.

Remember it

If you are worried about your ability to achieve a good grade at your first attempt, there is usually the opportunity to re-sit an assessment if you need to improve your grade.

There are three ways by which the brain receives and processes information:

Visually – through seeing

29% of the population finds this the best method. Methods of learning visually include using pictures, displays, diagrams, textbooks, computers, handouts and videos.

Auditory – through hearing

34% find storing sounds in the brain a more effective form of learning.

Learning methods include group work and discussion, talks, sound recordings, CD-ROMs and computers.

Kinaesthetically – learning through touching, moving and doing

37% prefer to learn using this method. Learning methods involve practical activities, skill demonstrations, and computers. Many people who are attracted to applied subjects prefer this method.

The most efficient use of the brain is to use all three methods to increase your capacity to store, use and make sense of new information. The aim of this book and associated resources is to provide learning activities that can stimulate learning through all three ways – visual, auditory and kinaesthetic – using a range of different methods in every unit.

Take it further

At your next tutorial, talk to your tutor about your own learning style and the way in which you can use this knowledge to help yourself learn more easily.

Applied learning

Applied learning offers you the opportunity to put into action the theory you learn about leisure and tourism by encouraging you to use it in real-world and practical situations. It involves breaking down barriers between theory and practice. It stresses the importance of developing and using the skills, values and knowledge that are necessary in the leisure and tourism industry, in context, and not just theoretically. Applied learning seeks to give equal weighting and value to the vocational as well as the academic, to learning and working, and to theory and practice. Recognition is given to the knowledge students bring to their learning. Applied learning promotes a diversity of learning methods and styles, and values the practical and 'hands-on' approach. It does not see the theoretical as an end in itself.

How to use this book

This book is designed to enable you as a student to acquire the essential concepts and knowledge – and to develop the skills through application and practice – necessary to understand the leisure and tourism industry. This book includes lots of different activity types to help you apply the knowledge you have gained. You will be able to see where the learning fits into the course you are following and how this relates to the leisure and tourism industry.

Throughout the book a specific topic is covered, either over two pages or four. There are four units in this book, each covering all the essential information you will need for that unit. Each section will contain a range of activities, including case studies, exam and coursework tips, and areas where you can do more research and find out more. There are also activities to carry out in groups or as a class, as well as discussion topics.

At the end of each unit you will find a Make the Grade section. This has been specially written to help you to prepare for your assessment. For Units 2 and 4, the Make the Grade section gives you guidance on the type of information you will need to collect for your internal assessment, as well as sample marked answers so you can see the type of responses that are good and not so good! For units 1 and 3, The Make the Grade section focuses on the types of questions you will have to answer in your external assessment, and again gives you examples of excellent responses and those that need some improvement.

Features of this book

This book contains several features to help you find the information you need quickly and easily.

- **Describe it** Key words or concepts that you need to understand are highlighted.
- **Assessment tips** Helpful information for your assessments.
- **Talk about it** The opportunity to discuss and debate relevant topics in class.
- **Research it** The opportunity to investigate certain topics further.
- **Hotlinks** Website details of relevant businesses. You can find links to all the websites mentioned in this book at www.heinemann.co.uk/hotlinks. Just enter the express code 4101P.
- **Remember it** Key concepts that you need to know for your assessments are highlighted.
- **Case studies** These show how the information you have learned applies to actual businesses. There are often questions and activities to complete.
- **Apply it** These features enable you to apply what you have learned.
- **Take it further** These activities are designed to stretch you. You can work on these on your own or in small groups in order to understand even more about a topic.
- **Summaries** At the end of each topic there will be a summary of the main areas covered in the topic and the most important ideas.

And finally...

Studying the leisure and tourism industry we hope will be both stimulating and successful. Leisure and tourism is an industry that is increasingly relevant both as a provider of products and services to its customers, and as a major employer and presence in the UK economy. Hopefully as you make progress through this book you will develop skills, knowledge and confidence that can form the basis for progression, either in education or in the world of work in this exciting sector. Hopefully you will find your studies both enjoyable and stimulating. Following a course of study is like a journey – I hope you travel it well. Good luck with your future!

Peter Mealing
Chair of Examiners for Edexcel GCSE Leisure and Tourism

Remember it | Research it | Take it further | Apply it | Talk about it | Assessment tips

Rambling is a very popular leisure pastime

Remember it

Countryside recreation is 'recreation that uses or is linked in some way to the landscape of the countryside'.

Countryside recreation

Countryside recreation can take place in National Parks, Areas of Outstanding Natural Beauty (AONB), on the coastline, or on the moors. A place is visited not just for its landscape and scenery, which may be mountains, hills, valleys, lakes, sand dunes or even just fields, but also for the many activities that can take place there, such as walking, canoeing, potholing, or skiing.

Talk about it

'The countryside is boring.' Do you agree? In your group, make a list of what is good and not so good about the countryside. Then discuss reasons that you think different types of people visit the countryside.

Research it

Do you know the difference between walking, hiking, rambling and trekking? Is there any?

Some charities, like the Ramblers Association, work to promote walking in the countryside and to improve conditions for all walkers. Walking is generally a free activity. Other free activities in the countryside include photography, landscape painting, picnicking, and cycling. These tend to be 'low'-level activities, suitable for all age groups. However, the countryside increasingly offers highly active recreational activities, such as caving, skiing, snowboarding, climbing, mountain biking, and on the coast, a variety of water sports such as windsurfing and sailing.

Take it further

New recreational activities are being introduced all the time. Have you heard of 'canyoning', 'zorbing', 'coasteering' or 'geocaching'?

You will learn more about these in Unit 3.

Home-based leisure

It is not always necessary to leave your home to take part in leisure activities. Home-based leisure includes:

- Music – including playing and listening
- Television-related entertainment
- Crafts
- Home improvements and gardening
- Internet-based leisure
- Reading
- Games – including interactive games

You will learn more about home-based leisure later in this unit.

14

Play- and activity-based leisure

Play-based leisure is activities that are mainly associated with children. Examples range from 'paint a plate' to bouncy castles for children. Activity-based leisure is a fast-growing component of the leisure industry. Many new activities have been introduced as people are not content to just sunbathe when on holiday or just walk when visiting the countryside. Examples of activity-based leisure include whitewater rafting and aerial adventures like forest adventure courses that involve rope bridges and zip slides for older children, teenagers and adults.

Apply it

Read the newspaper article and answer the questions that follow.

When the wide world was our playground

By Keith Waterhouse, Daily Mail August 7th 2008.

Yesterday was National Playday. It is a pity I was too busy to play marbles or conkers. Playday is supported by Persil under the slogan "Dirt is Good".

Does playtime have to be organised, pasteurised and supervised? One of the most depressing things I have seen lately is the installation of a shiny new climbing frame in a playground. It was the replacement for a gnarled old tree that has stood for years, but was now said to be "dangerous".

In my day, we made our own playgrounds. We chalked hopscotch grids onto the pavement, played marbles with cats eyes from the road, climbed trees, made a den, sneaked into orchards for apples, went picking blackberries in the hedgerows, all without a thought for "health and safety".

1 How old do you think the writer of this article is?
2 Why do you think children do not play outside or in their neighbourhoods as much anymore?
3 How do you think the developments in home-based leisure have affected 'free' play as described above?

Remember that play- and activity-based leisure activities are available in towns, cities and seaside resorts, as well as in the countryside. Many types of leisure in this component are free, such as mother and toddler playgroups, local park playgrounds for younger children, beach activities such as paddling, swimming, or body boarding for older children, and tea dances or power-walking for older people.

Summary

The key components of the leisure industry are: sport and physical recreation, arts and entertainment, countryside recreation, home-based leisure, and play- and activity-based leisure.

Talk about it

In groups, talk about what you did last weekend. How many of these activities took place in your home? Do you think if you were to ask a different age group, e.g. older people or families with small children, the activities listed would be totally different?

Research it

Over £77 million was spent in the UK alone on cookery books in 2007. What are three other popular home-based leisure activities in the UK?

Talk about it

Consider a range of age groups, and think of a possible free play- or activity-based leisure activity for each age group.

Assessment tip

Make sure you know the exact names of each of the five components that make up the leisure industry and that you can describe what is included in each component. You will also need to be able to give examples of activities in each component and match different activities to the correct component.

15

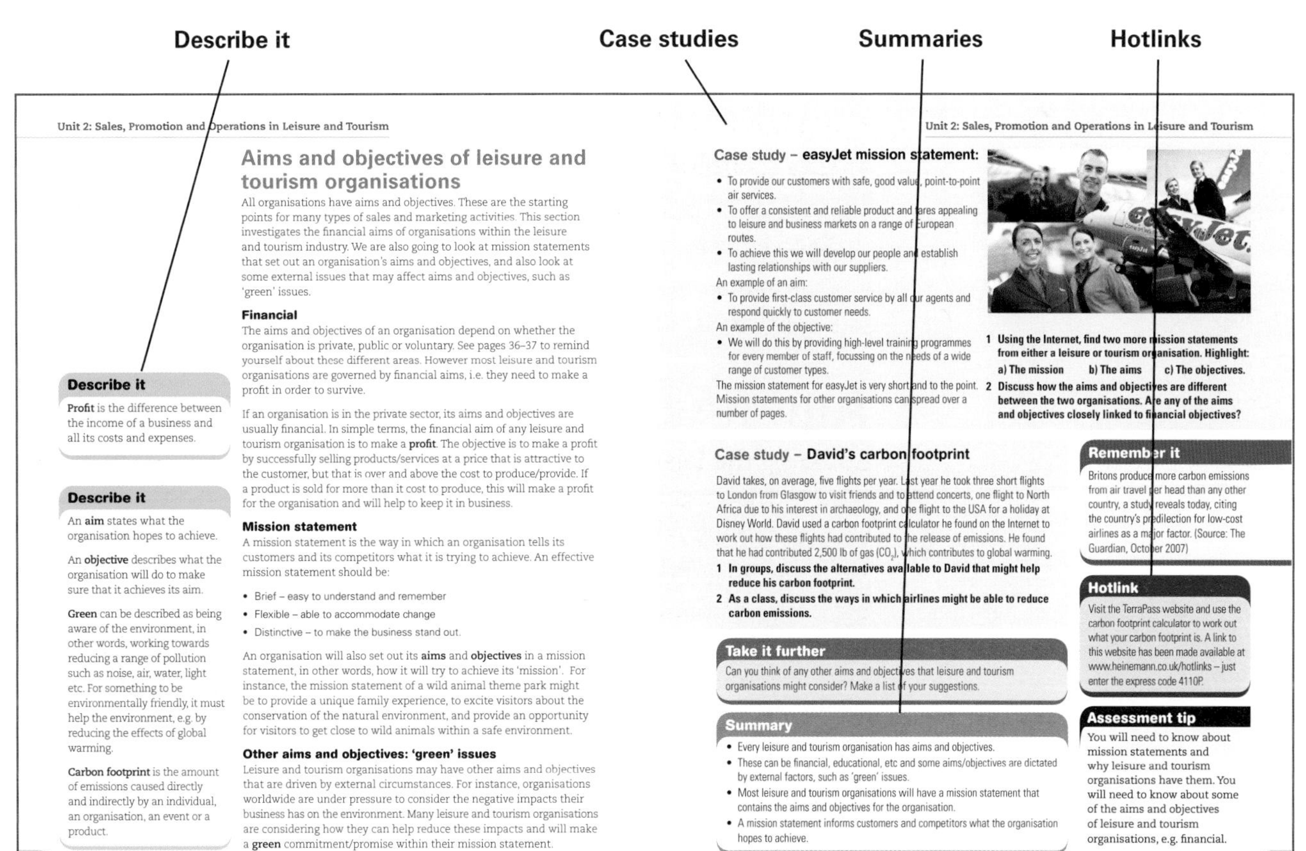

Describe it | Case studies | Summaries | Hotlinks

Unit 2: Sales, Promotion and Operations in Leisure and Tourism

Aims and objectives of leisure and tourism organisations

All organisations have aims and objectives. These are the starting points for many types of sales and marketing activities. This section investigates the financial aims of organisations within the leisure and tourism industry. We are also going to look at mission statements that set out an organisation's aims and objectives, and also look at some external issues that may affect aims and objectives, such as 'green' issues.

Financial

The aims and objectives of an organisation depend on whether the organisation is private, public or voluntary. See pages 36–37 to remind yourself about these different areas. However most leisure and tourism organisations are governed by financial aims, i.e. they need to make a profit in order to survive.

If an organisation is in the private sector, its aims and objectives are usually financial. In simple terms, the financial aim of any leisure and tourism organisation is to make a **profit**. The objective is to make a profit by successfully selling products/services at a price that is attractive to the customer, but that is over and above the cost to produce/provide. If a product is sold for more than it cost to produce, this will make a profit for the organisation and will help to keep it in business.

Mission statement

A mission statement is the way in which an organisation tells its customers and its competitors what it is trying to achieve. An effective mission statement should be:

- Brief – easy to understand and remember
- Flexible – able to accommodate change
- Distinctive – to make the business stand out.

An organisation will also set out its **aims** and **objectives** in a mission statement, in other words, how it will try to achieve its 'mission'. For instance, the mission statement of a wild animal theme park might be to provide a unique family experience, to excite visitors about the conservation of the natural environment, and provide an opportunity for visitors to get close to wild animals within a safe environment.

Other aims and objectives: 'green' issues

Leisure and tourism organisations may have other aims and objectives that are driven by external circumstances. For instance, organisations worldwide are under pressure to consider the negative impacts their business has on the environment. Many leisure and tourism organisations are considering how they can help reduce these impacts and will make a **green** commitment/promise within their mission statement.

Describe it

Profit is the difference between the income of a business and all its costs and expenses.

Describe it

An **aim** states what the organisation hopes to achieve.

An **objective** describes what the organisation will do to make sure that it achieves its aim.

Green can be described as being aware of the environment, in other words, working towards reducing a range of pollution such as noise, air, water, light etc. For something to be environmentally friendly, it must help the environment, e.g. by reducing the effects of global warming.

Carbon footprint is the amount of emissions caused directly and indirectly by an individual, an organisation, an event or a product.

84

Unit 2: Sales, Promotion and Operations in Leisure and Tourism

Case study – easyJet mission statement:

- To provide our customers with safe, good value, point-to-point air services.
- To offer a consistent and reliable product and fares appealing to leisure and business markets on a range of European routes.
- To achieve this we will develop our people and establish lasting relationships with our suppliers.

An example of an aim:

- To provide first-class customer service by all our agents and respond quickly to customer needs.

An example of the objective:

- We will do this by providing high-level training programmes for every member of staff, focussing on the needs of a wide range of customer types.

The mission statement for easyJet is very short and to the point. Mission statements for other organisations can spread over a number of pages.

1 Using the Internet, find two more mission statements from either a leisure or tourism organisation. Highlight: a) The mission b) The aims c) The objectives.
2 Discuss how the aims and objectives are different between the two organisations. Are any of the aims and objectives closely linked to financial objectives?

Case study – David's carbon footprint

David takes, on average, five flights per year. Last year he took three short flights to London from Glasgow to visit friends and to attend concerts, one flight to North Africa due to his interest in archaeology, and one flight to the USA for a holiday at Disney World. David used a carbon footprint calculator he found on the Internet to work out how these flights had contributed to the release of emissions. He found that he had contributed 2,500 lb of gas (CO_2), which contributes to global warming.

1 In groups, discuss the alternatives available to David that might help reduce his carbon footprint.
2 As a class, discuss the ways in which airlines might be able to reduce carbon emissions.

Take it further

Can you think of any other aims and objectives that leisure and tourism organisations might consider? Make a list of your suggestions.

Summary

- Every leisure and tourism organisation has aims and objectives.
- These can be financial, educational, etc and some aims/objectives are dictated by external factors, such as 'green' issues.
- Most leisure and tourism organisations will have a mission statement that contains the aims and objectives for the organisation.
- A mission statement informs customers and competitors what the organisation hopes to achieve.

Remember it

Britons produce more carbon emissions from air travel per head than any other country, a study reveals today, citing the country's predilection for low-cost airlines as a major factor. (Source: The Guardian, October 2007)

Hotlink

Visit the TerraPass website and use the carbon footprint calculator to work out what your carbon footprint is. A link to this website has been made available at www.heinemann.co.uk/hotlinks – just enter the express code 4110P.

Assessment tip

You will need to know about mission statements and why leisure and tourism organisations have them. You will need to know about some of the aims and objectives of leisure and tourism organisations, e.g. financial.

85

Unit 1: The Leisure and Tourism Industry

The leisure and tourism industry is one of the largest and fastest growing sectors in the UK and the world. In the UK in 2008, the tourism industry employed over 1.45 million people.

Talk about it

In groups, how many different types of job can you think of within the leisure and tourism industries? Make a list. Compare your lists as a class discussion.

In this unit you will learn about the key components of the leisure and tourism industries. You will learn about the different types of jobs available within these industries. You will be introduced to the business operations for both and their key aims and objectives. Following an introduction to sales and marketing within the leisure and tourism industries, this unit then covers how leisure and tourism organisations use up-to-date business systems and new technology.

The leisure industry is constantly changing and developing as many new and exciting activities are introduced, such as the Go Ape High Wire Forest Adventure. Similarly the tourism industry is also constantly changing to keep up with new developments and social trends. This unit will explore the reasons why UK leisure and tourism organisations need to adapt to the rapid pace of change.

The Fantasticable ride between two mountains in Châtel, France is an example of a new and exciting leisure and tourism activity

The most important part of any industry is its customers.

- Why would someone choose to visit a health club?
- Why would a businessperson choose to travel by train rather than by car?
- Why is security so important to travellers?

These are just some of the questions you will learn to answer when studying this unit. Health and safety legislation is also explored.

You will also examine some of the different types of leisure activities that people are interested in and you will learn how to identify the different places where leisure activities take place. You will find lots of practical examples of the types of facilities that are needed to support different leisure activities. This unit attempts to answer the question – why do people use leisure facilities?

For the tourism industry, you will discover there are two main types of visitor attractions – natural and built. You will also explore the main types of holidays, different methods of travel and the factors that influence customers' choice of travel method. This unit answers the question – what are the main reasons for travel? It also looks at the different types of tourist destinations. And finally, we need to look after our environment and protect it for the future. Tourism has affected our environment and our communities, and not always in a good way. You will look at examples of this, and explore ways in which tourism can develop using sustainable methods.

This unit covers the following topics:

1.1 The nature of the leisure and tourism industry
1.2 Introduction to business operations in leisure and tourism
1.3 Factors influencing customer choice
1.4 Introduction to destinations, impacts and sustainability.

Remember it

Blackpool is the largest seaside resort in Europe. It has more tourist beds than the whole of Portugal. (Source: blackpooltourism.co.uk)

How you will be assessed

Unit 1 is a compulsory unit for all learners. This unit is assessed by an external examination, which is one hour long. The questions are of three types – multiple choice, short answers, and extended-answer questions. Many of the questions will be based on case study information that will be within the exam paper, but you may also be asked to supplement this with examples from your own studies. You will find lots of useful hints and tips in the Make the Grade section at the end of this unit on pages 72–77.

1.1 The Nature of the Leisure and Tourism Industry

Key components of the leisure industry

What is leisure? One dictionary definition states that leisure is 'time free from the demands of work or duty when you can rest or enjoy hobbies or sports' (source www.dictionary.reference.com).

The leisure industry is divided into five key components:

Talk about it

What is leisure? In small groups, talk about the meaning of the word and decide on a definition in not more than one sentence.

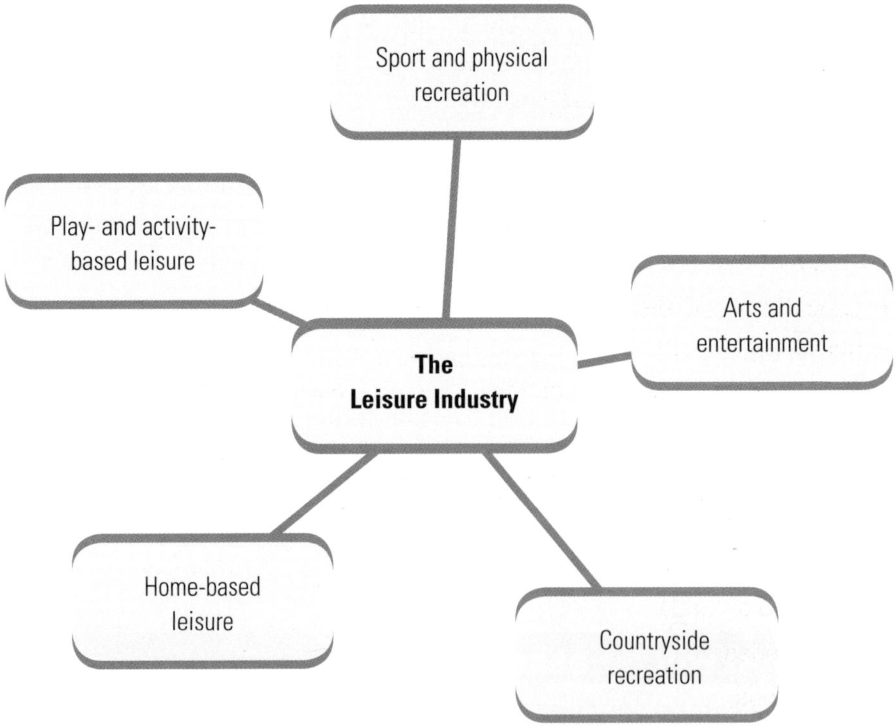

The five key components of the leisure industry

Remember it

Leisure time is the time you have left after work, school, sleep, and household jobs, such as cooking, washing and cleaning.

Sport and physical recreation

Sport is a form of physical activity that usually has some element of competition and is normally governed by a set of rules. Physical recreation is participating in any physical activity that refreshes the body and mind. Some sports can be a physical recreation when the competition is not present, such as cycling, horse riding and sailing. Both sport and physical recreation may be aimed at improving health and fitness.

Sport can be:

- Active or participative, e.g. playing rugby or badminton
- Passive or spectator, e.g. watching a football match.

Some sports you can play/do on your own or with a partner, such as gymnastics or golf; others you play as part of a team, such as cricket or hockey.

Sport and physical recreation can take place indoors, outdoors, on land or on water. However the boundaries can often be blurred, for instance, athletics can be both indoor and outdoor, and some individual recreations can also be played as a team sport, such as playing in a tennis team in the Davis Cup, or sprinting as part of a relay team in athletics.

Talk about it

What sports do different members of your class participate in or watch? Why?

Arts and entertainment

Arts and entertainment refers to things that take place outside your home that 'entertain you'. Again this can include things that you watch, e.g. a musical at a theatre, or things that you can actively take part in, e.g. bingo, youth theatre, dance troops, orchestras, bands, choirs, karaoke, and reading groups.

Included in this component of the leisure industry, you will find:

- Theatre – including musicals and plays
- Opera
- Classical music, orchestral and individual recitals – including fireworks concerts
- Popular music – including bands, individuals, compilation tours, e.g. The X Factor Live
- Dance – including ballet, folk and morris dancing
- Cinema – including IMAX
- Cabaret – including tribute bands
- Stand-up comedy
- Art galleries
- Exhibitions
- Others – including festivals, magic shows, ice shows, children's shows.

Research it

Using a local newspaper or website, find out what entertainment is offered in your local area. What range of productions are offered? What are the ticket prices?

Take it further

Compare the prices of theatre tickets in London's West End to those in your local area. Why do you think there is this difference?

Talk about it

Does your school/college offer any art/entertainment outside your normal lessons?

Rambling is a very popular leisure pastime

Remember it

Countryside recreation is 'recreation that uses or is linked in some way to the landscape of the countryside'.

Countryside recreation

Countryside recreation can take place in National Parks, Areas of Outstanding Natural Beauty (AONB), on the coastline, or on the moors. A place is visited not just for its landscape and scenery, which may be mountains, hills, valleys, lakes, sand dunes or even just fields, but also for the many activities that can take place there, such as walking, canoeing, potholing, or skiing.

Talk about it

'The countryside is boring.' Do you agree? In your group, make a list of what is good and not so good about the countryside. Then discuss reasons that you think different types of people visit the countryside.

Research it

Do you know the difference between walking, hiking, rambling and trekking? Is there any?

Some charities, like the Ramblers Association, work to promote walking in the countryside and to improve conditions for all walkers. Walking is generally a free activity. Other free activities in the countryside include photography, landscape painting, picnicking, and cycling. These tend to be 'low'-level activities, suitable for all age groups. However, the countryside increasingly offers highly active recreational activities, such as caving, skiing, snowboarding, climbing, mountain biking, and on the coast, a variety of water sports such as windsurfing and sailing.

Take it further

New recreational activities are being introduced all the time. Have you heard of 'canyoning', 'zorbing', 'coasteering' or 'geocaching'?

You will learn more about these in Unit 3.

Home-based leisure

It is not always necessary to leave your home to take part in leisure activities. Home-based leisure includes:

- Music – including playing and listening
- Television-related entertainment
- Crafts
- Home improvements and gardening
- Internet-based leisure
- Reading
- Games – including interactive games

You will learn more about home-based leisure later in this unit.

Play- and activity-based leisure

Play-based leisure is activities that are mainly associated with children. Examples range from 'paint a plate' to bouncy castles for children. Activity-based leisure is a fast-growing component of the leisure industry. Many new activities have been introduced as people are not content to just sunbathe when on holiday or just walk when visiting the countryside. Examples of activity-based leisure include whitewater rafting and aerial adventures like forest adventure courses that involve rope bridges and zip slides for older children, teenagers and adults.

Talk about it

In groups, talk about what you did last weekend. How many of these activities took place in your home? Do you think if you were to ask a different age group, e.g. older people or families with small children, the activities listed would be totally different?

Apply it

Read the newspaper article and answer the questions that follow.

When the wide world was our playground

By Keith Waterhouse, Daily Mail August 7th 2008.

Yesterday was National Playday. It is a pity I was too busy to play marbles or conkers. Playday is supported by Persil under the slogan "Dirt is Good".

Does playtime have to be organised, pasteurised and supervised? One of the most depressing things I have seen lately is the installation of a shiny new climbing frame in a playground. It was the replacement for a gnarled old tree that has stood for years, but was now said to be "dangerous".

In my day, we made our own playgrounds. We chalked hopscotch grids onto the pavement, played marbles with cats eyes from the road, climbed trees, made a den, sneaked into orchards for apples, went picking blackberries in the hedgerows, all without a thought for "health and safety".

1 **How old do you think the writer of this article is?**

2 **Why do you think children do not play outside or in their neighbourhoods as much anymore?**

3 **How do you think the developments in home-based leisure have affected 'free' play as described above?**

Research it

Over £77 million was spent in the UK alone on cookery books in 2007. What are three other popular home-based leisure activities in the UK?

Talk about it

Consider a range of age groups, and think of a possible free play- or activity-based leisure activity for each age group.

Remember that play- and activity-based leisure activities are available in towns, cities and seaside resorts, as well as in the countryside. Many types of leisure in this component are free, such as mother and toddler playgroups, local park playgrounds for younger children, beach activities such as paddling, swimming, or body boarding for older children, and tea dances or power-walking for older people.

Assessment tip

Make sure you know the exact names of each of the five components that make up the leisure industry and that you can describe what is included in each component. You will also need to be able to give examples of activities in each component and match different activities to the correct component.

Summary

The key components of the leisure industry are: sport and physical recreation, arts and entertainment, countryside recreation, home-based leisure, and play- and activity-based leisure.

Key components of the tourism industry

Research it

Tourism is defined by Mintel, the market research organisation, as 'any travel which involves an overnight stay away from home'. They classify 'Day trips' to visit attractions for example, as part of the leisure industry.

Tourism is one of the largest industries in the UK. It was worth £85.6 billion in 2006. 1.45 million jobs are directly related to tourism – this accounts for 5% of all people working in the UK.

The tourism industry has six key components:

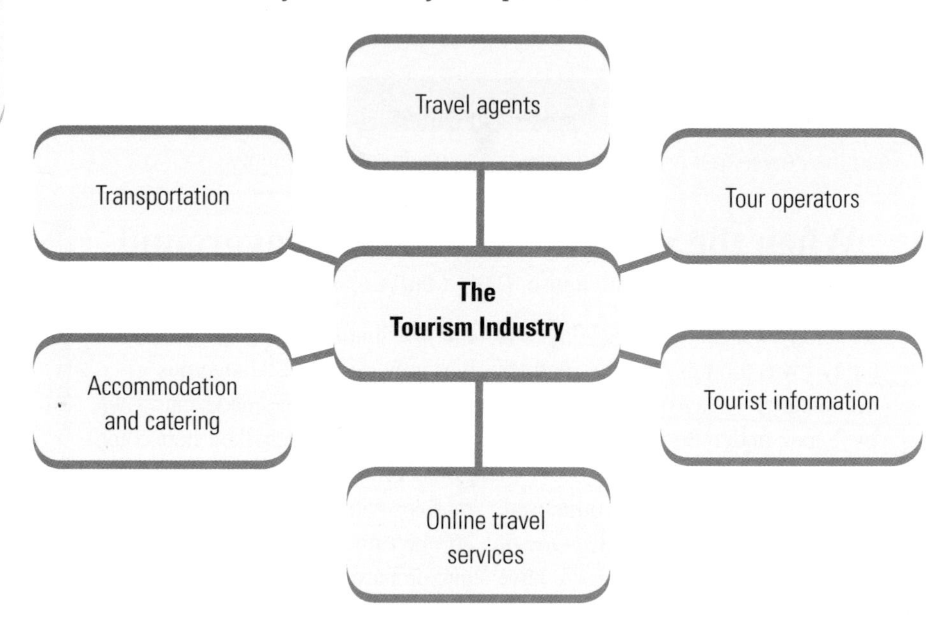

The six key components of the tourism industry

Remember it

A **franchise** is an agreement between two parties that gives a person or group of people (the franchisee) the right to market a product or service using the trademark of another business (the franchiser), e.g. an independent agency can use Global Travel Group's name in their advertisements.

Travel agents

There are three main types of travel agent in the UK, and they all sell holidays not only face to face in the shops, but also online and by phone.

- **Multiples** – a travel agent with hundreds of branches, for example Thomas Cook which also owns Going Places, and Thomson/TUI which also owns First Choice
- **Miniples** – a travel agent with anything from five branches to thirty or more, usually based in a local area, for example Althams
- **Independents** – usually owned and run by one person or a small company and have only up to five branches.

The position in the travel agency sector is always changing, as the smaller miniples and independents are being taken over by the larger multiple travel agencies. Independent agencies are often part of a **franchise**, such as the Global Travel Group.

Home working is also on the increase, where travel clerks work from their own home using the phone and computers to book holidays for individuals. An example of a company of home workers is Travel Counsellors. Business travel is also a part of the travel agency sector. The international company, American Express, is one example.

Talk about it

In groups, make a list of travel agents. Now fit each of the travel agents into one of the three categories above right.

Tour operators

The top tour operators in the UK are also the main travel agents. The difference between a tour operator and a travel agent is that a tour operator puts the holidays (flights, accommodation and sometimes transfers) together and features them in brochures. These holidays are then sold to the customer by the travel agent. This is known as the 'chain of distribution'.

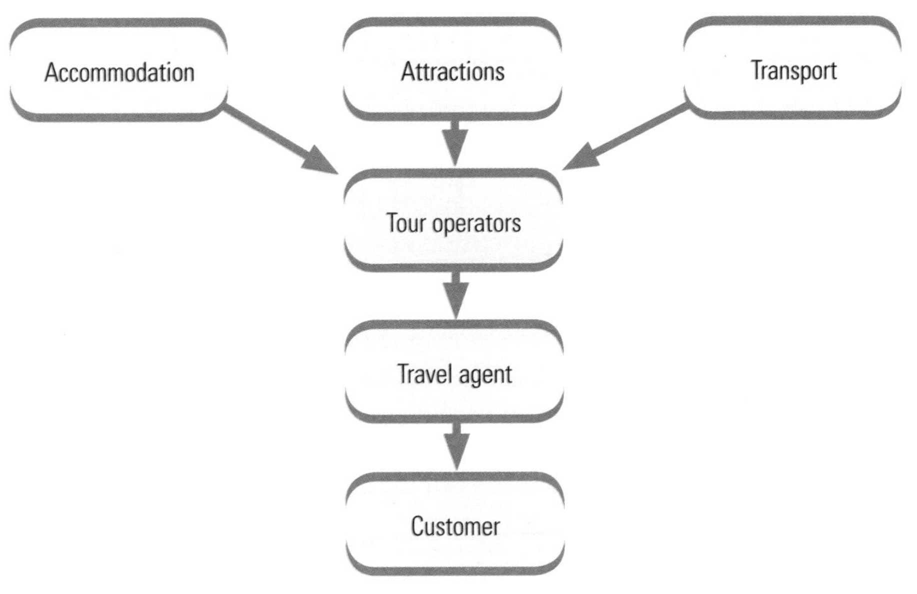

The chain of distribution

With advances in technology and new booking methods, it is likely that travel agents and tour operators may not be needed in the future as more and more customers book their trips directly with the accommodation and transport providers.

Tourist information

There are over 500 tourist information centres in England. They are usually found in town centres, airports, stations or countryside areas such as National Parks. The information centres may be operated by the local council, park authority, or independently, and are usually staffed by local people.

Online travel services

The fifth key component of the tourism industry – online travel services – includes travel companies and airlines that only take bookings online, such as ebookers.com and Expedia.co.uk. Airlines such as easyJet take over 95% of their bookings online and one airline has even named itself after its website: Jet2.com.

Online travel services also include holiday insurance, and other extras that can be booked online which may enhance your holiday. For instance, visiting websites that are provided by a local authority in a

Case study – ABTA

Formed in 1950 by 22 leading travel companies, ABTA – The Travel Association – now represents over 5,500 travel agencies and 900 tour operators throughout the British Isles. Members include small, specialist tour operators and independent travel agencies. All of them carry the ABTA logo.

What are the advantages to the customer of booking a holiday through a travel agent or a tour operator?

Take it further

Visit your local tourist information centre. What sort of services does it offer? How useful is it for: a) local people; b) visitors from other parts of the UK; c) visitors from overseas?

Research it

In your local area, make a list of all the accommodation that is available to visitors. Divide this list into serviced and self catering.

Now think about a contrasting type of destination, such as a seaside resort or large city. What types of accommodation would you find there and why? What type of visitor would stay in each type of accommodation?

Talk about it

Why might a family with very young children choose to stay in self-catering accommodation?

Hotlink

VisitEngland is the official tourist board for England. In addition to marketing the country and being the voice of the industry, VisitEngland is also responsible for ensuring quality across the accommodation sector in England. VisitEngland's portfolio of Quality Assessed Schemes currently include over 24,000 accommodation businesses across nine schemes. The quality rose on a blue background (above) appears at any accommodation that the tourist board has approved for quality. Find out more about VisitEngland by visiting their website. A link to this website has been made available at www.heinemann.co.uk/hotlinks – just enter the express code 4110P.

specific area that you are visiting would provide you with information on walks in the area or sights to visit.

Accommodation and catering

Accommodation and catering is a really large sector of the tourism industry in terms of both employment and amount of money contributed to the economy of the UK.

Accommodation is divided into two main types:

- **Serviced** – where meals are or can be provided, e.g. hotels
- **Non-serviced or self-catering** – where customers can cook for themselves, e.g. self-catering cottages.

The type and cost of accommodation is different if you are in a city centre, a countryside area, or a seaside resort.

Hotels, guest houses and self-catering accommodation in England are graded using a star rating system. Star ratings reflect the level of service, range of facilities and quality of guest care that you can expect. For instance, a one-star rated hotel may offer practical accommodation with a limited range of facilities and services, whereas a five-star hotel may offer the highest quality of accommodation, facilities, services and cuisine within a spacious, luxurious establishment.

Research it

One of the fastest growing types of accommodation is the 'no-frills' hotel, such as Travelodge and Premier Inn. Using the Internet, research one of these hotel companies.

1. **How many hotels do they have? Where are they mainly located?**
2. **What facilities are provided for visitors?**
3. **What is the price of a room? Is this the same all over the country?**

Catering (food and drink) is an important part of any holiday or business trip, and choice would depend on the reason for travel, budget, composition of the group, location, etc. Catering could range from a restaurant in a five-star hotel to a fish and chip van on a caravan site.

Transportation

How are you going to reach your destination? You can choose to travel by air, sea, road, or rail.

- **Air** travel can be by aeroplane or helicopter
- **Sea** transportation includes passenger and car ferries, hovercraft, hydrofoil, catamaran, steamers, and cruise ships
- **Road** transport methods include private car, hired car, coach, bus, bicycle or motorcycle
- **Rail** transport includes trains, trams, and the channel tunnel (Eurotunnel and Eurostar).

You will learn more about travel methods on pages 56–63.

Additional transport methods could be used once you reach your destination. These might include a cable car or chair lift if you are on a skiing holiday, or a 'mini train' if you are in a large seaside resort, or a glass-bottomed boat might enable you to see the beauty under the sea.

A ski lift is an interesting form of transportation

Assessment tip

Make sure that you know the exact names of each of the six components of the tourism industry. Can you describe what is included in each component? Are you able to give examples of companies or organisations in each component? Can you match companies to the correct component?

Summary

The six key components of the tourism industry are: travel agents, tour operators, tourist information, online travel services, accommodation and catering, and transportation.

Visitor attractions

Talk about it

It is said that without visitor attractions, there would be nothing for tourists to do in a destination. Do you agree with this statement? Why?

Key components of both leisure and tourism industry

Visitor attractions are a key component of both the leisure and the tourism industry. A visitor attraction is a place that offers 'amusement, enjoyment, entertainment and education'. Attractions can be visited from a person's home (this makes them part of the leisure industry) or while a person is on holiday in the UK or overseas (this makes them part of the tourism industry).

There are two main types of visitor attractions:

- Natural attractions
- Built attractions.

Natural attractions

Natural attractions include:

- Lakes
- Mountains and hills
- Beaches
- Rivers
- Forests.

Research it

Go online and search for websites of caves that are open to the public (for example, White Scar Cave in Ingleton, North Yorkshire, or Kents Cavern in Torquay, Devon). Find out what the admission fees are and what customers get for their money.

Within this category, there are also individual attractions, such as caves, waterfalls, cliffs, coastline features, islands, headlands, sand dunes, bays, estuaries and natural harbours. Many natural attractions are free, but there are also some that charge admission fees, provide a guide and facilities for the visitor.

Built attractions

Built attractions can sometimes be defined as 'purpose built' or 'built specifically to attract tourists'. However there are many attractions that do not fall into either of these statements.

Built attractions usually fall into one of the following five types:

Historic buildings

- Monuments, ruins, castles, cathedrals, churches, walls, and historic houses are just some of the built attractions included in this category. The Tower of London is an example of a historic 'built attraction'

Museums and galleries

- Museums, e.g. Natural History Museum, London or the Louvre, Paris
- Art galleries, e.g. Walker Art Gallery, Liverpool

Wildlife attractions

- Zoos, e.g. London Zoo
- Safari parks, e.g. Longleat Safari Park, Wiltshire
- Sea Life Centres, e.g. The National Sea Life Centre, Birmingham

Wastwater in the Lake District – Britain's favourite view!

Theme and leisure parks

- Theme and amusement parks, e.g. Alton Towers, Staffordshire
- Leisure parks/swimming/sport complexes, e.g. Blackpool Sandcastle Water Park

Industrial and cultural heritage

- Industry related, e.g. Quarry Bank Mill, Styal and Ironbridge Gorge Museums, Shropshire
- Cultural heritage, e.g. Albert Dock, Liverpool and the Mary Rose (ship), Portsmouth

Research it

Complete the table below by giving an example of each type of built attraction located overseas.

Type of attraction	Overseas example (with location)
Historic building	
Museum or gallery	
Wildlife attraction	
Theme or leisure park	
Industrial or cultural heritage	

Most attractions have some educational value – and not only the museums and galleries. For instance, a zoo, such as Chester Zoo, gives educational talks and presentations on topics ranging from primary school subjects to A-Level Business and Marketing.

Some attractions can be part of more than one category, for example, wildlife attractions that also have a theme park, such as Flamingo Land in North Yorkshire. You will learn more about the different types of attractions and the products/services they offer in Unit 4.

Take it further

Visit the Chester Zoo website and find out what educational value the zoo offers to a range of age groups. A link to the site can be found at www.heinemann.co.uk/hotlinks – just enter the express code 4110P.

Summary

There are two main types of attraction: natural attractions and built attractions. Both types are key components of both the leisure industry and the tourism industry.

Apply it

Can you match each of these UK built attractions to the correct type of historic building it is?

Nelson's Column, London; Stonehenge, Wiltshire; Windsor Castle; Liverpool Cathedral; York Minster; Roman Walls of Chester; Shakespeare's Birthplace, Stratford upon Avon; Chatsworth House, Derbyshire.

Assessment tip

You will need to be able to describe the difference between natural and built attractions, and to give examples of each from within the UK and overseas.

Products and services offered by leisure and tourism organisations

Leisure activities (including home-based leisure)

This section will examine some of the different types of leisure activities that people may be interested in. Leisure activities can be undertaken either outside your home ('out and about') or be part of what is known as 'home-based leisure'. You will find that there are activities that could fit into both categories, for example, listening to music could be done at home, or 'out and about' while you are on the bus or at a concert.

Remember it

Leisure activities are what you actually do in your leisure time. You can either watch or participate in a leisure activity.

Talk about it

Make a list of all the activities you have done in the past seven days. Divide this list into 'out and about' and 'home-based' leisure activities.

Now in small groups, compare your lists. What is the most popular activity in your group?

And finally as a class, discuss what is the most popular activity in your class.

Here are some different types of leisure activity:

Reading

This includes reading books, magazines and newspapers. According to the National Readership Survey (Oct 2007–Sept 2008), the most read newspaper in the UK was *The Sun*, followed by the *Daily Mail*. The most popular free newspaper in the UK was the *Metro*. Books include fiction or non-fiction. Popular non-fiction books include biographies and autobiographies, and books that are linked with TV programmes. New technology also makes it easy to read a book in different ways, for example audio books, eBooks and iBooks.

Research it

What is an iBook? What is an eBook? Find out the names of some famous books available in these formats?

What are the top 10 books currently on sale in your local bookshop or supermarket?

Sport (participating and spectating)

Two of the most popular sports in the UK are walking and fishing. However, football is popular all over the UK and is a good example of a sport that children, men and women can participate in (through playing in local five-a-side teams and competitions), or can spectate (watching either from their home, the local pub, a football stadium such as Anfield (home of Liverpool Football Club), or an international stadium like the Millennium Stadium in Cardiff.

Cinema/home cinema

Publicity and marketing, including releasing trailers on the Internet for large blockbuster films has increased cinema attendance in recent years, and new technology such as IMAX has made watching films in the cinema more exciting. Also, more advanced systems are now available to enable you to watch a film at home with all the sound and special effects of the cinema. DVD rental is still a popular way of viewing a film in your own home, and cinema films are now available on DVD much sooner after cinema release. However, services such as Sky Box Office (a television channel that shows latest films) and Lovefilm.com (with unlimited rentals and no-late fees) have affected the DVD rental market.

Research it

Using your local newspaper or cinema website, find out what films are currently on at your local cinema. What age groups does each of these films appeal to?

Dancing (classes or nightlife)

Dancing is one of the UK's oldest and most popular leisure activities. It is still undertaken today by a vast amount of people across a very large age range, from baby discos and ballet lessons for young children, through nightclubs to tea dances for senior citizens.

The TV programmes *Strictly Come Dancing* and *Dancing on Ice* have increased the popularity of dancing in recent years.

Ballroom and line dancing are just two of many popular dancing leisure activities enjoyed throughout the UK

Research it

In small groups, make a list of different types of dancing. Does anyone in your class dance? Does your school have a dancing group?

Walking

For more about walking, see page 14.

Watching TV/interactive TV

Watching TV is also an extremely popular leisure activity. Programmes are now available 24 hours a day with hundreds of channels to choose from. Sky Plus, Virgin Media and BBC iPlayer have revolutionised the TV schedules – you can watch whatever you want, whenever you want, and even pause live TV. HD (high-definition) televisions and plasma screens have improved viewing technology and the digital TV switchover happening between 2008 and 2012 in the UK (when the old analogue signal currently used to transmit TV and radio programmes will be switched off and replaced with digital) will further enhance this. Interactive TV enables people to vote for their favourite contestant on TV programmes such as *The X Factor*, *Big Brother*, or *Britain's got Talent*, and to enter competitions. People are also now able to pledge money through interactive TV to good causes such as *Comic Relief*.

Some TV programmes, such as *Who Wants to be a Millionaire?* and *Family Fortunes*, have interactive DVD versions available for you to play at home.

Remember it

26.3 million homes in the UK own a TV (source: www.barb.co.uk/tvfacts).

81% of people now have a digital TV service through Sky, Virgin, a Freeview box or other provider (source: Social Trends 2007).

The average person watches TV for 24 hours and 47 minutes a week. How long do you spend watching TV in a week?

Hotlink

Find out more about the most popular UK TV shows and viewing figures by visiting the BARB (Broadcasters' Audience Research Board) website. A link to this website has been made available at www.heinemann.co.uk/hotlinks – just enter the express code 4110P.

What are the most popular TV shows? Are you surprised?

Research it

What are the features of the latest models of iPod or mobile phone?

Listening to music

Cassettes, record players and music videos are a thing of the past. Whether inside or outside your home, there are loads of ways you can listen to music, including CD players, radio, music centres, iPods, and MP3 players. Even your mobile phone can now be used to play music, e.g. the iPhone.

Listening to music live is a very different experience, and music you can listen to live ranges from pop and rock to classical and opera. Some concerts can be combined with a holiday or short break, for example 'See Madonna Live in Paris'.

Eating out

Eating out is becoming more popular, especially since the range of restaurants available in most areas has increased, with places to eat on the high street including gastropubs, Italian, Greek, Indian, Malaysian, Chinese, and Thai restaurants, and fast-food restaurants such as burger bars. In this unit, eating out is only considered a leisure activity when it is linked with tourism. This is because for most people a visit to a fast-food restaurant or a take-away can be a regular occurrence and part of everyday life, i.e. the need for food.

Playing computer games

Technological advances have helped enhance computer video games to now include interactive video gaming. Interactive video gaming means that players can physically participate to influence the characters in the game. Players can compete against one another in physical competition and results are displayed on the game screen. Games, such as 'Dance UK' for Playstation™, include a mat that players step on to keep up with various beats and rhythms. Other systems involve movement-based game play where controls mimic objects used in the game (e.g. swords, tennis racquets, boxing gloves, etc). Current systems such as the Nintendo Wii have been designed to be interactive, with many sports games already available.

Socialising electronically

By far the most important development in recent years is Internet-based leisure. The Internet can be used for communicating via online socialising through sites such as Facebook. People can play games with each other across the Internet, such as online bingo, or bid for items that other people are selling through sites like eBay. There are also more Internet dating sites that encourage people to socialise electronically.

Talk about it

In small groups, discuss how long you spend on the Internet each day. What sites do you use the most?

As a class, compile a list of all the sites used by your class. Which is the most popular and why? Now discuss what you think the future holds for interactive games.

Take it further

Other leisure activities that people undertake include: knitting, sewing, model making, cookery, building, home improvements, gardening (at home or on an allotment), homebrewing/wine making, painting, flower arranging.

Can you think of ten more?

Visitor attractions

For more about visitor attractions, see pages 20–21.

Assessment tip

You need to know about what products/services are included in each of the leisure activities listed in this section. For example, products/services for listening to music might include iPods, portable CD players, etc.

Summary

Leisure activities are what people do in their spare time. Leisure activities can be participative or spectator. Eating out is not considered a leisure activity.

Remember it

A leisure facility is not only a place where leisure activities **take place**, e.g. leisure centres, swimming pools. Leisure facilities are also the organisations that **support or provide equipment** for leisure activities, e.g. DVD rental shops, ski hire shops.

Research it

Identify three different leisure facilities in your local area. Find out what different activities each one has to offer.

Research it

Libraries have changed a lot in recent years. They are no longer places just full of books. When did you last visit your local library? Make a list of all the products/services offered by your library for the following:

- Children aged 3–10 years
- GCSE students
- Senior citizens.

How do you think this is different from 20 years ago? Ask your parent/guardian or the library assistant for their thoughts.

Talk about it

In groups, make a list of each type of shop in the UK that supports leisure activities. Are there any other shops in your local area that support leisure activities? What are they?

Leisure facilities (where leisure activities take place)

This section will help you to identify the different places where leisure activities take place, and think about some examples of what facilities are needed to support leisure activities. Leisure facilities include:

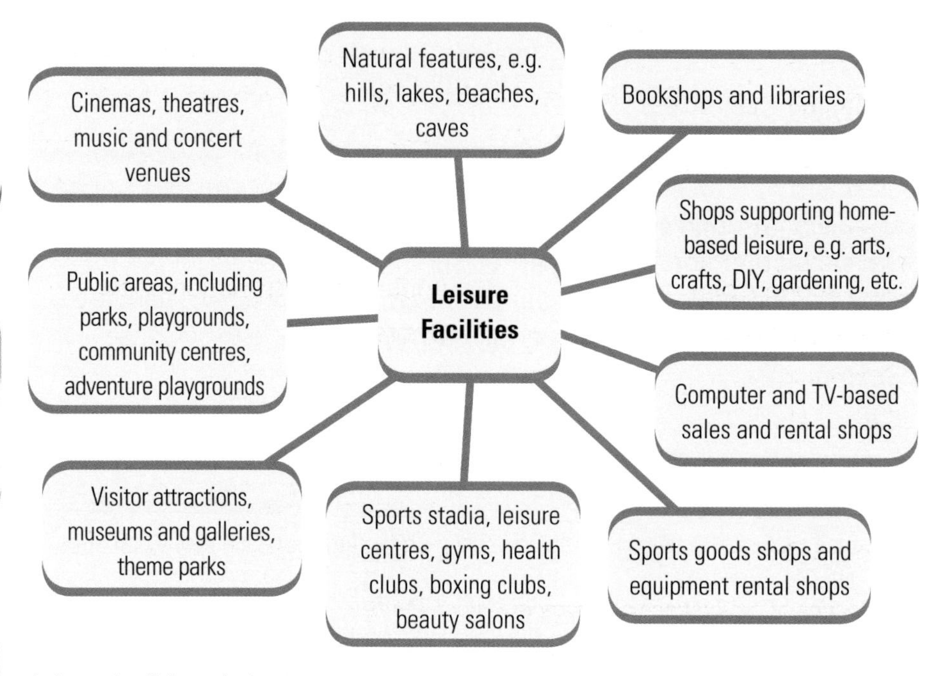

Leisure facilities mind map

You will see that this mindmap also includes the organisations that support or provide equipment for leisure activities, such as libraries and craft shops.

Leisure facilities where leisure activities take place include:

- **Purpose-built** buildings, e.g. ice rinks or velodromes
- **Multi-purpose** buildings e.g. community centres
- **Natural landscapes,** e.g. rivers, caves or cliffs.

The availability of leisure facilities depends on where you live. If you live in the countryside, there will be lots of facilities for outdoors activities. However if you live in a town there will be many more purpose-built or multi-purpose facilities. Many leisure facilities are now indoors to cater for the British weather. For instance, very few swimming pools are outdoors now compared to those built 40 years ago.

Facilities that support leisure services

Facilities are needed to support leisure activities. People often need to eat after taking part in a sports activity or on a day trip to a country park. People may like to have a drink while at a music concert. The growth in the leisure industry provides income and employment in a range of different shops. For instance, people need to be able to buy or rent the equipment they need to take part in the leisure activity of their choice, or to research it at their local bookshop or library.

Products/services offered by leisure facilities

Leisure facilities often offer a range of products/services to appeal to as many different types of customer as possible. A theatre, for example, may try to attract more customers by having a range of different types of show, including pantomimes at Christmas, kids shows in the school holidays, and a variety of plays, musicals, dance shows, and live acts. It may also have a licensed bar and/or coffee bar. It will sell sweets, ice cream, and children's toys to suit the programme, such as magic wands and swords during a pantomime.

Production	Type
Sing-a-long Abba	Audience participation show
Tosca/Carmen	Opera
Cinderella	Pantomime
Swan Lake	Ballet
Joseph	Musical
Cinderella on Ice	Ice spectacular
Scooby Doo	Children's show

A selection of productions at Liverpool Empire Theatre

Increasingly, many leisure facilities offer non-typical activities. For instance, some sports venues have a licence for civil weddings, such as Manchester United Football Club and Lancashire Cricket Club. You can even get married in a cave, such as the White Scar Cave, Ingleton, Yorkshire.

Take it further

Why do you think that many leisure facilities offer food and drink to their customers?

Assessment tip

You will need to be able to identify the different types of leisure facility and give examples. Also to evaluate the range of products/services offered by different facilities. The information for this may be given to you in a case study in the exam.

Summary

- Leisure facilities are places where leisure activities take place. They also include shops and organisations that support leisure activities, by selling or renting equipment etc.
- Leisure facilities will offer a range of products/services to appeal to as many different types of customer as possible.

Case study – **Xscape, Milton Keynes**

Xscape is an indoor leisure facility that can be found in Milton Keynes, Castleford, and Braehead. The Milton Keynes facility was built in 2005 and has had over 25 million visitors. Xscape Milton Keynes offers an indoor snow slope, rock-climbing walls, bowling, a cinema, gym and fitness centre, numerous bars and restaurants, and a shopping complex.

1 Evaluate the range of products/services offered by Xscape for a range of customer types, including:

- **Families**
- **Teenagers**
- **Couples**
- **Senior citizens.**

Remember it

Package holidays are defined as a pre-arranged combination of transport and accommodation, advertised and sold together at an inclusive price by a tour operator. Other tourist services, such as rental car hire or outings during the holiday, may also be included/sold. In addition, the length of stay must be 24 hours or more/must include overnight accommodation.

Research it

The package holiday industry is governed by the Package Travel, Package Holidays and Package Tours Regulations, 1992.

Undertake some research to find out more about how this – and other systems, such as ATOL – are used to protect a customer's money.

Talk about it

What do you think are the advantages to the customer of 'dynamic packaging'?

Holiday types

Holidays can be classified by:

- Booking method – **package** or independent
- Destination – domestic, inbound or outbound
- Length of flight – short haul or long haul
- Purpose of travel – holiday, **short break**, special interest, business trip, etc.

You will learn about all these different types of holiday in this section.

Package

Traditionally, **package holidays** were put together by a tour operator, and sold through the high-street shops of a travel agent. (See page 17 for more on the chain of distribution.) Nowadays, however, many customers are booking direct with either tour operators, or accommodation and transport providers. The travel agency sector has responded by 'dynamic packaging' – putting together for the customer exactly what they want in terms of flights, accommodation, car hire, etc – rather than the customer being tied to a pre-defined package. To be a package holiday provider, a travel agency needs an ATOL (Air Travel Organisers' Licence).

Independent

Independent holidays have always been common in the UK domestic market. They are when the customer chooses to book everything themselves, either by phone or on the Internet. So, for example, an independent holiday would involve booking a caravan site in Wales directly with the caravan site owner and then driving there in the customer's own car.

Independent holidays overseas are increasing in popularity. However, by booking everything themselves, the customer may not always be protected against companies they are dealing with going bankrupt, for instance.

Research it

The XL travel group collapsed in September 2008.

1 How many customers lost both their holiday and their money? Why?

Domestic

A domestic holiday is when a traveller/customer books a holiday in the same country in which they live. For example, when someone who lives in London books a holiday to Cornwall.

Inbound

An inbound holiday is when a tourist comes IN to a country from outside it for a holiday. For example, when someone who lives in France comes to visit Cardiff for a holiday.

Outbound

An outbound holiday is when a tourist leaves the country in which they live and travels OUT to another country for a holiday. For example, when someone who lives in Newcastle goes on holiday to Majorca.

Short haul

A short haul is a holiday to a destination where the flight time is less than six hours. Short-haul destinations from the UK include all of Europe, the Canary Islands, North Africa, and all countries bordering the Mediterranean Sea.

Long haul

A long haul is a holiday to a destination where the flight is six hours or more. Examples of popular long-haul destinations from the UK include Florida, Jamaica, South Africa and Thailand.

Special interest

Special-interest holidays can take place anywhere around the world and are often closely linked with a particular activity or activities. They range from cookery in Italy, to photography in Iceland, to sailing in Greece.

Short breaks

Short breaks are one of the fastest growing holiday types. Many people are choosing to take a short break as well as their main summer holiday. Short breaks don't necessarily need to be taken overseas. For instance, Center Parcs UK sell more short breaks than they do full-week holidays. The top European city for short breaks is Paris, but some people choose to go as far away as New York for a shopping trip.

Research it

Using a selection of holiday brochures, find out the flight time to each of the following places:

Ibiza; Cyprus (Larnaca); Tenerife; New York; Sydney; Barbados; Rome.

Then say whether the holiday would be short haul or long haul from the UK.

Research it

Many large hotel chains, such as Hilton Hotels, offer a range of short-break holidays at their hotels. Many short breaks are themed or linked to a special interest. Using the Internet, research one type of short break available. Produce a poster for this short break in your group.

Remember it

A **short break** is defined as a holiday that involves one to three nights away from home.

Assessment tip

Make sure that you know the definition of all the holiday types mentioned in this section. You will need to know the difference between domestic, inbound and outbound holidays, and give examples of each.

Summary

- Holiday types can be broken down into package or independently booked, short or long haul, and purpose of travel.
- There are overlaps between holiday types, for example, a couple from Oxford on a three-day painting holiday to Italy would be classed as going on an outgoing, short-haul, short-break, special-interest holiday!

Taking a short break to New York can be a perfect holiday solution

Remember it

Over 50% of jobs in the health and fitness industry are part-time, according to a 2006 survey by the Register of Exercise Professionals.
The majority of part-time positions are held by women between the age range of 18–34.

Talk about it

In groups, consider all the facilities you have learned about on pages 26–27. How many different jobs can you think of that exist within these facilities?

Leisure jobs

The leisure industry is a large employer. According to the Institute for Sport, Parks and Leisure (ISPAL):

- Leisure has been one of the fastest-growing industries in the 21st century
- One in four new jobs are created in this sector
- Sport and recreation alone employs 621,000 people.

Just thinking back to the leisure facilities mentioned on pages 26–27, and imagining the number of different jobs that exist within those facilities makes you realise how many different leisure jobs there are. However in this section we will concentrate on five main leisure jobs.

Leisure centre assistants

Here are some of the skills and knowledge that are needed to work in a leisure centre:

- A keen interest in sport and fitness activities
- Awareness of health and safety
- Good communication skills
- Flexibility
- Willingness to do routine tasks
- Physical fitness and stamina.

Apply it

Look at this mind map about jobs in a leisure centre.

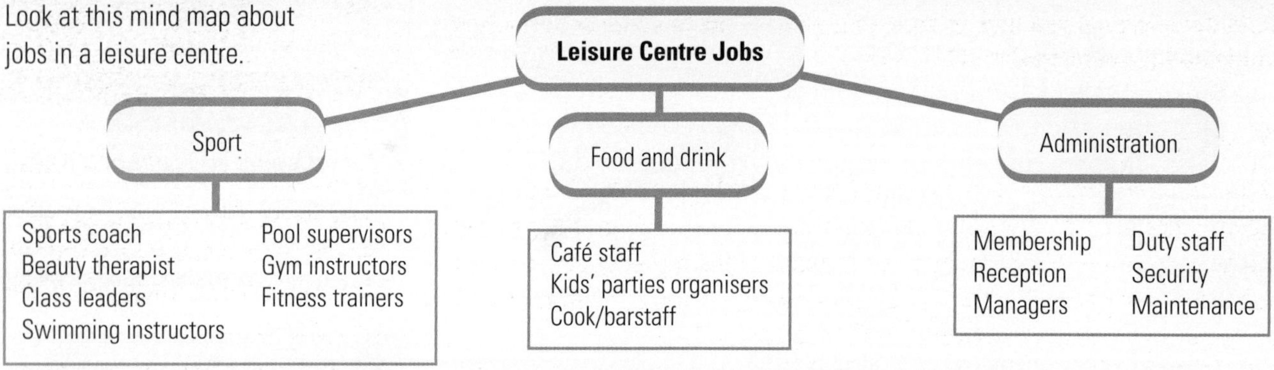

Leisure Centre Jobs

Sport
- Sports coach
- Beauty therapist
- Class leaders
- Swimming instructors
- Pool supervisors
- Gym instructors
- Fitness trainers

Food and drink
- Café staff
- Kids' parties organisers
- Cook/barstaff

Administration
- Membership
- Reception
- Managers
- Duty staff
- Security
- Maintenance

Choose two of the jobs on the mind map and decide what you think would be the main duties for those jobs.

Hotlink

Find out more about fitness instructors by visiting Directgov (the official government website for citizens). A link to this website has been made available at www.heinemann.co.uk/hotlinks – just enter the express code 4110P.

Fitness instructors

The main duties of a fitness instructor are to teach and train people to do exercises that will improve their tone, shape, fitness or general health. Fitness instructors can be based in a leisure centre, but they can also be based in a health club, work from home, or even work in hospitals.

Some health clubs may call their fitness instructors 'personal trainers'. Both do a similar job and are qualified one-to-one instructors, although most people associate personal trainers as just being employed by famous Hollywood stars. However this is not the case, and often sports people, or those recovering from serious injury or illness, or just wanting to get into shape may use a fitness instructor/personal trainer to help them.

Lifeguards

Lifeguards are not only found in pool complexes, leisure centres and attractions such as water-parks, but also on the beaches of the UK and the world.

Case study – Being a lifeguard

Brian (20) is a lifeguard on a beach in Devon. He is a university student, working for the summer months. He has always been a keen swimmer and surfer, and before university he studied leisure and tourism at his local college.

To be employed as a lifeguard, Brian had to pass lifesaving qualifications before attending an intensive two-week course run by the RNLI. He received training in the use of specialist equipment such as inflatable rescue boats, rescue watercraft (jet skis) and quad bikes.

His main duties are:

- To 'zone' the beach into separate safe areas for swimmers and surfers
- To monitor the safety of all beach users, both in and out of the sea
- To rescue those in difficulties in the water
- To administer emergency first aid
- To liaise with emergency services such as the coastguard whenever necessary.

1 What is the RNLI?

2 What personal skills do you think a lifeguard would need?

3 What advice would you give to someone who wants to swim or surf when there is no lifeguard on patrol?

Park rangers

Rangers can be employed in local, country and national parks. They manage the conservation and use of resources in the park, as well as often serving as community workers and customer service representatives. Park rangers are also responsible for the safety and education of visitors, enforcing safety laws and providing aid when needed.

Cinema staff

Depending on the size of the cinema there will be a range of different jobs available, including ticket desk staff, and refreshment staff in bars, coffee bars, popcorn stands, pick 'n' mix counters, etc. There are also jobs as film technicians and projectionists.

Research it

Using the website of your local park, country park or national park, find out what events and activities are on offer to the public.

Considering your findings, what do you think the role of the park ranger will be?

More information on jobs in leisure together with their roles and responsibilities can be found on career advice websites.

Apply it

You work as a refreshment sales person in a cinema. The manager has asked you to plan and supervise a party for fifteen 8–9 year olds as the usual party supervisor is off sick.

1 Make a list of everything you would need to check and do before and during the party.

2 What personal skills do you think you will need to complete this job?

Summary

- There is a wide range of jobs in the leisure industry. Five main jobs have been covered in this section.
- Job roles and responsibilities will vary depending on the location and size of the organisation you work for.

Tourism jobs

As with the leisure industry, there are a wide variety of tourism jobs. In this section we will concentrate on six main tourism jobs. People who choose to work in tourism could be based in either the UK or overseas.

Travel clerk

Traditionally travel clerks always used to work in a travel agency in the main street of a town or city, or a travel office at a station or airport. Although many still do, there are other types of travel clerk who now work from home. For example, the independent travel agency Travel Counsellors employs home-based travel agents.

Alternatively, travel clerks work in a call centre, taking bookings by phone and answering customer queries by email.

The main duties of a travel clerk would include:

- Helping customers to find a suitable package holiday or to plan independent travel, booking transport and accommodation
- Checking availability of the chosen holiday by telephone or computer and making bookings
- Collecting deposits, filling in booking forms and collecting final payments
- Checking and issuing tickets
- Informing customers of any changes such as cancelled flights, and arranging alternatives.

Talk about it

What skills do you think you need to be a travel clerk?

Would these be different if you worked in a call centre?

What skills would you need if working overseas?

Coach driver/courier

Some holiday companies, for example, Shearings, employ drivers on their UK holidays who also act as couriers. The role of the courier is to look after the passengers' every need, whether this is information, assistance on and off the coach, advice on departure and arrival times, or details about places of interest.

Some coach companies employ travel couriers in addition to their drivers. Travel couriers are responsible for luggage transfers and deal with problems such as lost luggage or illness. They are also the main liaison with people such as coach drivers, ferry and hotel staff, and customs and immigration.

Take it further

Using the list of services offered by tourist information centres you researched on page 17, what do you think is the main duty and role of someone who works in tourist information?

Tourist information centre staff

Staff that work in a tourist information centre have a wide range of duties and responsibilities. Refer back to the research you did on the services offered by tourist information centres on page 17.

Air cabin crew

All airlines employ cabin crew and their prime function is to ensure passenger safety. However, most airlines will also use their cabin crew to increase revenue by selling tax-free and duty-free goods and refreshments.

Case study – Ryanair cabin crew advertisement

This extract is taken from an actual advert for cabin crew positions for Ryanair.

Ryanair recruitment are currently recruiting for exciting cabin crew positions to operate on Ryanair aircraft.

We are looking for enthusiastic, friendly and outgoing people to join our winning team. This is an ideal opportunity for someone who wants to begin a career in aviation or maybe you just want to try a job that's different every day!

Requirements

You need to be:

- Experienced in dealing with the public and comfortable in a selling role
- Physically fit with a good attendance record in your current position
- Hard working, flexible & willing to operate on a shift roster
- Over 5'2 (1.57m) in height with weight in proportion
- Of normal vision (contact lenses acceptable)
- Able to swim well
- Ready to meet the challenge of dealing with people and demanding situations
- Friendly and outgoing with a lively personality

There is a difference between skills and qualities. Skills are what you can do or learn to do. Qualities are what you are like as a person and how you behave.

1 **Choose two skills from the list on the left. For each one explain why you think that they are important for a cabin crew member.**

2 **Which are the most important personal qualities needed by a member of cabin crew on an aircraft? Why do you think this?**

Resort representatives

Holiday representatives, also known as reps, look after guests at resorts, usually abroad. They ensure that guests' holidays are enjoyable and safe. Duties can include:

- Meeting guests at the airport and taking them to their hotel
- Holding welcome meetings to give out information
- Selling the travel company's day trips and other excursions
- Answering questions and helping with problems, such as lost passports or illness.

Hotlink

Research the skills and qualities needed by a resort representative by visiting the Connections Direct Jobs4U careers database. A link to this website has been made available at www.heinemann.co.uk/hotlinks – just enter the express code 4110P.

In addition, there are some specialist representative jobs, such as children's reps, ski reps and campsite reps.

Guides

Guides are usually found in major tourist cities, where they may conduct walking tours around places of local interest or enhance a visit to a destination through providing guided themed tours, such as historic walks or 'ghost walks'. Guides also work in museums, galleries and places of local interest. They may also give information to tourists about the destination they are visiting from open-top-buses or coach sight-seeing tours. Blue Badge Guides are those who have qualified as 'experts' in their own local area.

Talk about it

In groups, discuss what you think would be the main differences in the duties and the role of a representative working for the following:

- Club 18-30 in Ibiza
- Canvas Holidays on a campsite in France
- Thomson Ski in Austria.

Research it

Using the Internet, find out about ghost walks offered to tourists in cities such as York or Edinburgh. What is the role of a guide on one of these walks? What skills and qualities do you think a ghost walk guide needs?

Summary

- There are many jobs in tourism. Six of the main jobs have been covered in this section.
- Roles and responsibilities will vary depending on the travel company you are working for, and whether you work in the UK or overseas.
- More information on jobs in tourism, together with roles and responsibilities, can be found on career websites on the Internet.

1.2 Introduction to Business Operations in Leisure and Tourism

Functional areas of leisure and tourism organisations

In this section, leisure and tourism organisations will be subdivided into functional areas or departments, and you will explore what each of these departments is responsible for. In small organisations with only a few employees, the manager may undertake these roles, but in large organisations there may be a separate department for each of these main areas of work.

In most organisations, the functional departments will have to work together. For example, marketing and sales will have to work with finance as there will be a limit to the budget available to spend on advertising a product.

Talk about it

Can you think of any other departments that would work together? How?

Human resources (HR)

Human resources, or HR, is the department that looks after the staff. Formerly known as 'personnel', this area is responsible for recruiting and monitoring staff. Some HR departments may also be responsible for induction (training for new employees), staff training, and paying salaries and wages.

Information technology (IT)

Duties of staff in this area include:

- Maintenance of all the technology used in the organisation
- Training staff to use IT systems
- Updating materials on websites
- Maintaining servers and booking technology
- Troubleshooting any problems, including providing a helpline service.

Some IT departments are also responsible for designing and installing software for the organisation to use.

Research it

Some websites are more effective than others. Choose one good example of a website.

What is it that makes it a good website? List your reasons.

Take it further

How do you think the IT department has contributed to the website you researched above?

Finance

Most leisure and tourism organisations have to work within a budget. Expenditure cannot exceed income, otherwise the company may go into liquidation. The finance department has a vital role in **budgeting**, **forecasting future turnover** and **income.** They must also keep informed about external influences on the business, for example the price of oil/petrol/diesel is vital to a transport company, and the fluctuation in the exchange rate (dollars to pounds) would be critical for a UK tour operator offering holidays to the USA.

Sales and marketing

Marketing involves several stages:

- Research and evaluating findings of research
- Developing products to match customers' needs
- Informing potential customers about the products by advertising and promotion.

Sales will become involved once the product is researched, developed and advertised. They will be responsible for actually selling it. This may be:

- Face to face (e.g. a cinema ticket sold at a box office)
- Over the telephone/through a call centre (e.g. a flight sold over the phone)
- On the Internet (e.g. a new computer game sold online).

Research it

Using a local newspaper, find an advert for a leisure product/service, for example membership of a health and fitness club. How effective do you think this advert is in attracting people? How could it be improved?

Describe it

Budgeting is the creation of a list of all planned expenses and revenues for a company.

Revenue is the income that a company receives from its normal business activities, usually from the sale of goods and services to customers.

Turnover is another word for income.

Income is the money businesses receive from customers and other sources such as bank interest.

Administration

The role of administration is to ensure that everything runs smoothly and the customer receives the correct product/service at the correct price. The admin department will produce invoices, receipts, tickets, and deal with complaints and refunds.

Case study – Administration

Jasmine works for a coach tour operator in the administration department. She says, 'It is a really interesting job, as I do lots of different things in a day. First, I open all the post. Customers will have sent cheques for their holiday payments and I will have to process these and send them receipts. Also in the post there may be letters from customers with special requests, such as requiring a room on a low floor at the hotel, or special dietary requirements such as a vegetarian menu. I have to pass these on to the hotel concerned. Some customers send emails with queries on their holiday, and I reply to these. If people have not paid up on time, I have to send them reminder invoices. About two weeks before they are due to go, I send out joining instructions, which are the details of when and where they will be picked up by their coach, along with tickets and labels for their luggage. The worst part of the job is dealing with complaints, but fortunately there are not many of these!'

1 **Make a list of the different administrative jobs Jasmine has to do each day, and beside each job, write what skills she will need to be able to do this role.**

Summary

There are five main functional areas in leisure and tourism organisations: Human resources (HR); Information technology (IT); Finance; Sales and marketing; Administration (usually shortened to Admin).

Assessment tip

For each of the functional areas in this topic, i.e. HR, IT, etc, you will need to understand what each area is responsible for.

Aims and objectives of leisure and tourism organisations

All organisations have aims and objectives. No one starts up a company without knowing what they aim to achieve. Aims and objectives are also the starting point for many types of marketing activities.

The aims and objectives of a company can be:

- Financial, e.g. to increase sales/profits
- Not for profit, e.g. improving health
- Or a combination of the two, e.g. some private sector organisations are also committed to supporting government initiatives or not-for-profit objectives, for instance Fitness First works closely with the Fitness Industry Association (FIA).

Remember it

An organisation's aims and objectives are usually referred to in their mission statement. For example, the National Trust, a voluntary sector organisation, has a mission statement of 'To look after special places for ever, for everyone', which reflects its aim of preserving the countryside and its buildings for the future.

Financial

Whether the aims and objectives are financial or not sometimes depends on whether the organisation is private, public, or voluntary.

Private sector

These companies usually have aims and objectives that are financial, i.e. linked to increased profits, turnover, income or sales. This is because they have to keep in profit otherwise they would go out of business.

Public sector

These organisations are usually linked to the government, which may be local, regional or national. Examples of leisure and tourism organisations in the public sector include local swimming pools, community leisure centres, and libraries. Typical objectives for organisations in this sector may be:

- Generating benefit for the local community
- Targeting under-represented or disadvantaged community groups, e.g. youth groups.

However, the public sector still has to try and gain some income so they can pay staff, as the money they get from the government in the form of grants, etc, will not always cover this. That is why libraries, for example, may charge for renting DVDs or for ordering publications, and people are charged a fine for the late return of books.

Research it

Find out more about your local swimming pool. Is it owned by your local council? Does it offer free swimming and if so, for which age groups? What other evidence of the Legacy Action Plan can you find?

Case study – The 2012 Legacy Action Plan

The 2012 Legacy Action Plan was launched by the government in 2008. This plan sets out an ambitious target to get two million people more active by 2012. It includes plans to increase the number of people who swim regularly, with £140 million being invested in the scheme. It is designed to encourage as many local authorities as possible to make swimming free for those aged 60 and over, and those aged 16 and under. It also includes other initiatives such as free lessons for adults who cannot swim and hopes to provide free swimming for all in the future.

Not for profit

Voluntary sector

This sector is sometimes known as 'not for profit' or the charity sector. This means that although many charities receive government grants, membership fees, donations and hold fund-raising activities to raise money, the money is not used to make more money. It goes towards paying staff, research, raising awareness, etc. The term 'voluntary' can be misleading and people often think that those who work in this sector don't get paid. However although voluntary organisations rely on occasional or regular volunteers for help, many voluntary organisations have paid staff.

Case study – The National Trust

The National Trust is an example of a large organisation in the voluntary sector. The Trust owns and manages over 300 historic houses and gardens, 600,000 acres of countryside and 705 miles of coastline within the UK. It has many employees.

Visit the National Trust website, and find out about its aims and objectives. A link to this website has been made available at www.heinemann.co.uk/hotlinks – just enter the express code 4110P.

1 If you had to put the National Trust's aims and objectives in order, which do you think are the most important? Give reasons for your choice.

Summary

- Aims and objectives are vital to all organisations.
- They vary depending on whether an organisation is in the private, public or voluntary sector.
- Aims and objectives are used as the starting point for marketing activities.

Assessment tip

Make sure that your know the difference between aims and objectives that are financial and those that are 'not for profit'. You will need to be able to give examples of each type of objective.

The marketing mix

Describe it

Marketing is 'Getting the right **product** to the right people in the right **place** at the right time, at the right **price**, using the right **promotion**.' (Source: Outhart et al, 2000)

Describe it

Tangible is something you can touch or pick up.

Intangible is something you can't touch or pick up.

Talk about it

What other products/services in the leisure industry are:

a) Tangible?

b) Intangible?

Make two lists in your group, then compare your list with others in your class.

Introduction to sales and marketing

You have already seen that the sales and marketing department of a leisure and tourism organisation has a vital role in not only helping the organisation to strive towards its mission/goal, but also to achieve its objectives. The most important concept in sales and marketing is the 'marketing mix'.

Marketing mix

Marketing mix is the way the following **4 Ps** work together:

- **P**roduct
- **P**rice
- **P**lace
- **P**romotion.

Product

In marketing, the word 'product' always refers to both the products and the services that an organisation may offer.

In the leisure industry, products may refer to either:

- **Tangible** products, such as sports equipment or DVDs
- **Intangible** products/services, such as a coaching session or sauna.

In the tourism industry, most of the products and services are intangible, i.e. you can't touch or pick up a holiday.

Product also refers to the facilities offered by both leisure and tourism organisations. For instance, a visitor attraction offering rides, or a golf complex offering two 18-hole courses and golf lessons are all products.

Price

The 'price' charged for a product/service always has to be seen by the customer as 'value for money'. That is not necessarily to say the product is cheap, but that it's worth what you pay for it.

For instance, if you were buying a CD you might be wary if it was too cheap, as it could be a copy and the sound quality may not be good. But if you wanted a pair of branded trainers, such as Nike, you would be prepared to pay more than for unbranded ones.

Similarly, a customer booking a room in a 5-star hotel would expect it to have high quality furniture, service and food, and they would be willing to pay a higher price than they would for a guest house or a hotel with a lower-star rating.

Many leisure and tourism organisations use special offer prices to tempt customers to visit or to buy. For example, they may offer reduced price family tickets for zoos, early booking bargain train fares, or reduced price off-peak membership of a health club.

Place

There are two aspects to 'place':

- The actual **location** of the facility – and linked to this, its accessibility
- The way that the products/services are **sold** or **distributed** to the customer, e.g. through a travel agent, direct, through the Internet, by phone, etc.

Promotion

A special-offer pricing strategy, as described in 'price', is linked very closely with 'promotion' – you need to tell customers about it – this is what promotion is all about. The choice of promotional technique will depend on who the customer is and how much money the organisation has to spend.

Promotional techniques are the ways that companies use to market their products/services. Promotional materials are the actual materials they design and use to promote these products/services. Examples of each are shown in the table below.

Promotional techniques	Promotional materials
Advertising	Adverts in newspapers, magazines, on TV or radio, websites/**pop-ups**, DVDs
Direct Marketing	**Mailshot** letters, phone calls
Public Relations (PR)	Press releases, celebrity openings or visits
Displays	Posters, leaflets, billboards
Sponsorship	Football team shirts, TV programmes
Demonstrations	Cookery, sports coaching
Sales Promotions	Special offers, discounts

Summary

- Sales and marketing is a vital function for all leisure and tourism organisations
- The 4 Ps work together as the marketing mix
- Product also refers to services offered
- Place is where the facility is located plus how it is sold
- Price is not always cheap!
- Promotion is how organisations use different techniques and materials to encourage customers to purchase their goods
- You will learn more about sales and marketing in Unit 2.

Research it

Airlines, such as British Airways, offer at least three different classes of travel on their long-haul flights e.g. from London to Sydney. Using the Internet, find out the differences in the fare for a first class and an economy class ticket. What different products/ services do you get for your money? Is it worth it?

Describe it

Pop-up ads or **pop-ups** are a form of online advertising. A pop-up window containing an advertisement can appear on screen when certain websites open a new web browser window.

Mailshots (or **Mail shots**) are bulk mail advertising sent through the mail in the UK to potential customers to advertise goods or services.

Talk about it

The airline Emirates sponsors the UK football team Arsenal. Even the Arsenal football stadium is named after them!

1. **What other examples of sponsorship can you think of in the leisure and tourism industry?**
2. **Now think of some PR techniques used within the leisure and tourism industry.**

Assessment tip

Make sure that you know what each of the 4 Ps stands for. You will need to understand how the 4 Ps combine together in the marketing mix. You will need to be able to apply information about each of the 4 Ps to a case study, which may be presented in the examination.

Remember it

According to an Omnibus Survey carried out for the Office for National Statistics in 2007, 49% of all people surveyed had used the Internet to book travel, accommodation or holidays. Over 40% had used the Internet to book tickets for events, and 40% had used it to purchase film or music DVDs.

The use of up-to-date business systems and new technology

In recent years the massive advances in all types of technology have changed the way we book holidays, watch sport, go shopping, pay for things, and travel around. It has also changed the way that businesses operate. In most cases this is for the better, e.g. better communication, easier record keeping and faster ways of researching information. This section is about just some of the ways leisure and tourism organisations use up-to-date business systems and new technology.

Internet/broadband/email

The Internet and its email facility, particularly since the introduction of broadband, has revolutionised business communication, both within organisations, and externally with customers and suppliers. For instance, the customer can now book virtually any type of travel and leisure service on the Internet, either the whole package or separate components. Internet shopping for leisure products – from books, DVDs and CDs to computers and digital cameras – has also rapidly increased in recent years using websites such as Amazon.

New technology is also clearly linked with advertising. For instance, virtual tours of attractions and hotels, web-cams in resorts, e-brochures, and DVDs of destinations are now very common methods of promotion for the leisure and tourism industry.

Describe it

WAP stands for Wireless Application Protocol and it allows a person to access the Internet from a mobile phone or laptop computer.

Bluetooth is a method of exchanging data over short distances using fixed and mobile devices, such as phones, and wireless technology.

Handsfree describes equipment that can be used without the use of hands (for example via voice commands).

Research it

Find out more about the following: virtual tours, web-cams, e-brochures.

Which do you think is the most effective method of promotion and why?

Remember it

From 1997–2006, the proportion of households with a mobile phone increased from 20% to 80% while ownership of home computers increased from 29% to 67%. (Source: Social Trends 38)

Mobile phones/WAP

The use of mobile phones, pagers and wireless Internet has enabled communication to continue even when people are not in the office at their desks. People can still work on a train, a plane, at the station or airport, using **WAP** or **Bluetooth**. **Handsfree** equipment is now available for mobile phones, which means that people can even work from their car. Availability and speed are the main advantages of these systems for the leisure and tourism industry.

Computerised records/electronic databases

Computerised Reservations Systems (CRS) have been used since the 1970s and have evolved into Global Distribution Systems (GDS), making the booking of air tickets, hotel rooms, car hire and other travel and tourism products exceptionally easy for travel agents.

Computerised records also help with security. For instance, membership cards for leisure and tourist facilities have become much more sophisticated. Many have a barcode that can be read by a machine. In a gym, for example, this enables the computer to recognise your face when you swipe your card on entry to the gym. The computer can also use this barcode to create a record of how many times you have visited the gym or to find out when your subscription is due for renewal and automatically send you a letter.

An electronic database, such as the one used by hotels, can be used to quickly produce a list of customers that a mailshot letter could be sent to, or to create a list of rooms that are available. Systems such as these can also produce a bill or invoice very quickly.

Other new technologies that have influenced the way leisure and tourism organisations operate includes advances in hardware (PCs, printers, photocopiers, scanners etc.) and associated software such as Publisher and Photoshop.

Electronic security/identification measures

Security is also vital to every customer. New identification measures, such as iris recognition technology at airports, are just one example of how new technology is being used to make air travel safer. Many leisure and tourist facilities have installed CCTV cameras to ensure the safety of visitors and that the facilities themselves remain protected.

See later in this unit for more detail on security systems.

Booking and payments

Credit and debit cards have made booking leisure and travel much simpler. These cards can be used over the phone, on the Internet or at the point of sale. The use of debit cards especially has grown rapidly. Between 1991 and 2006 there was a substantial increase in the number of payments by debit card in the UK. The use of cheques to pay for items in 2006 was less than half the number used in 1991.

Research it

What are the advantages of paying by credit or debit card:

a) To customers?

b) To organisations?

Use of new technology

New technology and the customer

Leisure and tourism organisations have made use of new technology to increase and improve the facilities and services they offer to the customer. For instance, online check-in, e-tickets and e-vouchers make going on holiday much less stressful. New technology used by visitor attractions, such as Alton Towers to let customers know how long they will have to queue for a ride, is a helpful way to manage visitor flows and visitor expectations. Technology is also being used to enhance the visitors' experience, including using the latest in ride technology to make knuckles even whiter on theme park rides.

Technology has made rides more exciting

In the sport and recreation sector, examples include exercise machines in a gym or health club that can now tell you how many calories you have burned, as well as average speed and distance covered, while some have an individual TV screen so you can watch your favourite programme while exercising.

New technology and sport

'Hawk-Eye' technology is a ball-tracking system that uses sensors. It is used on the lines of the tennis courts at Wimbledon to tell whether a ball is in or out, or within cricket stumps to indicate whether they have been hit or not.

Improvements in video technology have led to the 'video referee' in rugby, when a sports official is called upon to help give a verdict on a referee decision in a sports match using television footage. There are now also highlight functions on TV that can track the ball and movement of players.

Talk about it

Why does football not use a video referee system?

Can you think of any other sports that use new technology to improve things for either those participating or the spectator?

Research it

Nike have a range of trainers available that have a built-in pedometer to enable you to see how far you have walked, jogged or sprinted. Find out all about them. Are there any other sports products that offer similar things?

New technology and transport

New technology in transport includes:

- Building of the Eurotunnel/use of Eurostar
- Pendolino tilting trains
- Metrolink trams in major cities
- Super-ferries, high-speed hydrofoils
- Larger aircraft e.g. A380 Airbus, or Boeing Dreamliner
- Satellite navigation and GPS systems.

Technology also enhances the products and services that are now offered on different types of transport. For example, there are now beds on planes, laptop points on trains, and even a wave machine on a cruise ship!

Take it further

New technology in transport has changed the way we travel forever. Only 100 years ago, hardly anyone owned a car. In 1971, 52% of the eligible population owned a car. This increased to 77% in 2006.

International air travel has also increased significantly – from 43 million passengers in 1971 to over 186 million passengers in 2008. (Source: Social Trends 38)

What do you think a disadvantage of the use of new technology might be?

Assessment tip

You will need to understand how different leisure and tourism organisations use new technology. You will need to be able to explain the advantages and disadvantages of using new technology for customers and organisations

Summary

- Business systems and new technology benefit both customers and organisations.
- Communication technology has advanced significantly in recent years.
- You will study the impacts of business technology in more detail in Unit 2.

Why the leisure and tourism industry needs to adapt to the rapid pace of change

To understand why the leisure and tourism industry needs to adapt, we need to know more about the historical development of the industry.

It could be said that tourism and leisure began in ancient times, when gladiators travelled around Italy, or when the first Olympic Games were held in Greece. The industry as we know it probably started in the 1800s.

Important dates include:

1830	First passenger train service
1841	First 'holiday' offered by Thomas Cook
1860	Invention of the bicycle
1871	Bank Holidays Act (4 days)
1936	First Butlin's Holiday Camp opened at Skegness
1938	Holidays with Pay Act
1952	First Jet airliner introduced – the Comet
1965	Thomson Holidays, largest tour operator, was founded
1968	Countryside Act
1969	Concorde's first commercial flight (ceased in 2006)
1994	The Eurotunnel between Britain and France opens
2012	London hosts the Olympic Games.

Looking at the table below, we can also see the rapid increase in the number of days' holiday people are entitled to. With customers now entitled to more days' holiday, there is the increasing need for the leisure and tourism industry to adapt.

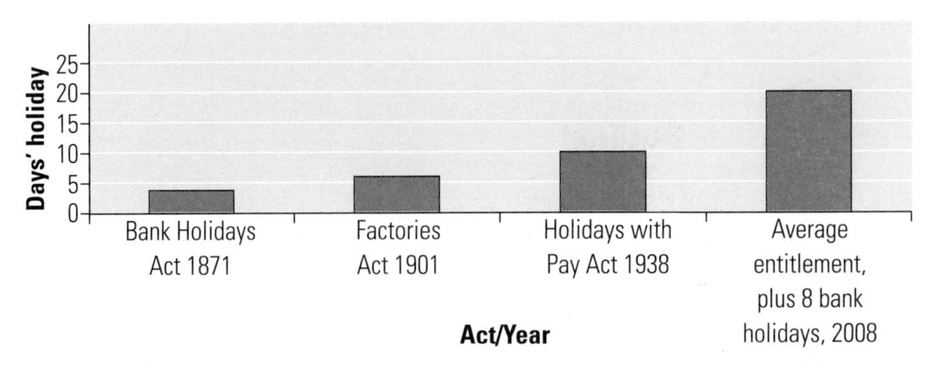

Chart showing the increase in holidays since 1871

Some other reasons why the leisure and tourism industry needs to adapt to the rapid pace of change include:

- To keep existing customers
- To attract new customers
- Increasing competition
- External influences.

To keep existing customers

Customers are always expecting companies to keep up to date with trends, offer popular destinations, and new types of activity.

Some of the ways that leisure and tourism organisations do this are:

- A theme park introduces new rides each year, to encourage repeat visitors from one year to the next
- A theatre that offers a pantomime will do a different one each year, so that the same families will still come year after year
- A cruise operator will change the itinerary or cruising location of its ships from one year/season to the next, so that those who like that ship can still book with them and see new destinations
- A hotel may offer themed short-break packages to tempt business customers to return with their partners at the weekend.

Take it further

Think of some more real life examples of how an organisation or attraction has introduced new products or services to keep existing customers.

To attract new customers

Some of the methods the leisure and tourism industry uses to keep existing customers may also attract new ones. But generally it is introducing a new or upgraded product/service that will attract new customers.

Income from new tourism is vital to many destinations both in the UK and overseas. Exciting activities are now being offered by destinations across the world to cater for and tempt the adventurous tourist, from bungee jumping in New Zealand and whale watching in Alaska to white-water rafting in Wales.

The sales and marketing team of the organisation plays the most important part in attracting new customers. However it is the customer service that a new customer receives that will influence whether that customer will return or not. As the chef Raymond Blanc admits, 'If a customer has a bad experience, he will tell 20 others, but a customer who has a good experience will tell only seven others.'

Case study – Butlins

Butlins has changed beyond recognition in the last 30 years. Traditionally, customers stayed in self-catering chalets, or accommodation where they were provided with meals in a huge, self-service dining room.

Customers have become much more demanding and want a higher standard of accommodation. The accommodation now offered at Butlins ranges from Gold 5-star accommodation with TV, DVD players, microwaves etc, to the more modest standard apartment.

1 Find out more about the different types of accommodation now on offer at Butlins. Do you think Butlins has succeeded in keeping up with the rapid pace of change? Give your reasons.

Butlins now offers modern and stylish accommodation

Increasing competition

Competition between tour operators, travel agents and destinations overseas is immense. Similarly, there are now more visitor attractions and leisure facilities than ever before, all competing for customers.

Increased competition means that again, marketing and sales has a vital role. One way to market an organisation is to use its Unique Selling Point (USP). Examples of USPs in the leisure industry can be features like 'the only one', or the 'largest', 'biggest, 'fastest', etc. For instance:

- 'The only IMAX cinema in Belfast'
- 'The largest pool complex in England'
- 'The largest collection of working steam trains in the UK'.

In the tourism industry, the same rules apply and USPs are used, e.g. 'Bala, the largest natural lake in Wales', or 'Ben Nevis, the highest mountain in the UK'. TV and media can play a part in promoting USPs and can be a great marketing tool for the destinations nominated.

Remember it

UK residents made a record 45.3 million holiday trips abroad in 2006. In 1971 there were only 6.7 million trips abroad. (Social Trends 38)

External influences

No matter how good the marketing or the service, there will still be occasions when things beyond the control of leisure and tourism organisations will influence their development.

The three main external influences on the leisure and tourism industry are:

- Price of oil
- Credit crunch
- Terrorism.

Research it

Think of examples of leisure and tourism in your local area. What USP's are used to promote these organisations? Can you think of any other USP's that could be used?

How do you think TV and media could help with promoting these USP's?

Price of oil

In 2008 the price of oil increased significantly. This forced many airlines and some tour operators to go out of business. Over 30 airlines worldwide went into liquidation in the first eight months of 2008, including the UK carriers Zoom Airlines Ltd and XL Travel Group. Ryanair spends £1.2 billion pounds on aviation fuel in a year, so you can see how a big rise in the price of oil will affect their income and profits.

One of the ways that airlines responded to the high price of oil was to impose fuel surcharges on top of the price of the air ticket. Others closed down routes that were unpopular or not very heavily booked, such as Gatwick to Seville, and others tried to increase revenue in different ways, e.g. easyJet started charging passengers to board the plane first.

The price of oil also affects the cost of goods, especially food that has to be transported long distances. These increased costs that have to be met by the accommodation providers would then be passed on to the customer. For example, the cost of a holiday that included meals in its price would increase.

Talk about it

Make a list of ways the increase in the price of oil affects the leisure and tourism industry. Should increased costs be passed on to the customer? Discuss in groups.

Credit crunch

The credit crunch is the name given to the downturn in the global economy and recession conditions in many developed countries, including the UK. It is linked with interest rates, the stock market and share prices falling, and the financial problems being experienced by banks and other financial institutions. This will have a two-fold impact on the leisure and tourism industry:

- The organisations themselves will find it hard to pay bills, get more credit, or pay off loans
- The customer will have less disposable income (money left after paying bills, food, etc) so will have less money to spend on leisure activities and holidays, meaning less income for the organisations.

Terrorism

The increased threat of terrorism since the attacks of 11 September 2001 in New York, the London bombings of July 2005 and the 2008 Mumbai attacks in India have affected the way that the leisure and tourism industry considers the security of its customers. To find out more about this, see page 133.

Natural disasters

Another external factor, beyond the control of the leisure and tourism industry, is natural disasters. Examples of this are the Indian Ocean tsunami of 2004, or one of the many hurricanes that hit places like the Caribbean islands or the USA each year, e.g. Hurricane Ike in 2008.

Talk about it

In groups, discuss how the credit crunch may affect leisure and tourism in your local area. What signs can you already see that this is happening?

Assessment tips

You will need to be able to identify and describe examples of how organisations have responded to the rapid pace of change.

Remember some examples of how organisations have adapted, changed or increased their product/services over the years.

Know the three main external influences on the industry, and be able to give examples of these.

Take it further

Can you think of any other terrorist attacks or natural disasters in either the UK or overseas that have had an impact on the leisure and tourism industry?

Summary

- The main reason why organisations need to adapt to the rapid pace of change is that if they do not, they will go out of business.
- The most effective way of retaining existing customers is by giving good customer service and introducing new products each year.
- External influences play a vital, though sometimes uncontrollable, role in the way organisations operate.
- The three main external influences are: credit crunch, price of oil, and terrorism, although natural disasters may also may have an impact, especially if they occur in tourist areas.

Health and safety legislation

Health and safety legislation are laws that apply to the workplace. For the exam, you do not need to know details of the content of the legislation, or the dates it became law. You will, however, need to be able to understand and use extracts from legislation and know how these could apply to different organisations in the leisure and tourism industry.

The legislation you need to know is that affecting:

- Employees
- Customers
- Property
- Health and hygiene.

Employees

Health and safety at work is the responsibility of both the employer and employee. These responsibilities are laid down in the Health and Safety at Work Act 1974.

Employers have a responsibility for the working conditions of their employees with regard to lighting, temperature, ventilation, washing and toilet facilities, and rest areas.

Training is important, especially if machinery is used, and employees may also have a right to be provided with protective equipment such as steel toe boots, ear defenders or eye shields. In an office environment, computer desks and chairs must be the correct height so as to avoid injuries such as back problems, eye strain or repetitive strain injury.

An Accident Report form or book must be used by law – no matter how minor the accident is. By recording any accident, this ensures that it never happens again, informs others about safe working practices and maintains a record in case the employee claims **compensation**.

It is also the responsibility of the employer to maintain records of fire alarm checks/drills, locate first aid boxes and fire extinguishers at appropriate points and to **induct** new staff in all aspects of health and safety.

Other legislation that protects employees in the workplace include COSHH (Control Of Substances Hazardous to Health) and RIDDOR (Reporting of Injuries, Diseases and Dangerous Occurrences Regulations).

Research it

Research and briefly describe what the following two pieces of legislation cover:

- COSHH
- RIDDOR

In what ways do they protect the employee?

Hotlink

Find out more about the Health and Safety at Work Act 1974 by visiting the Directgov website. A link to this website has been made available at www.heinemann.co.uk/hotlinks – just enter the express code 4110P.

Describe it

Compensation is money that is awarded to an employee due to a failure of the employer to comply with health and safety laws at work.

Induction is to provide support and guidance to a new employee.

Customers

Health and safety legislation also affects customers. There is a requirement for all organisations to carry out **risk** assessments to ensure the safety of anyone who visits their facility. So for instance, when your school/college goes on a trip or visit, the risks have to be assessed. There is usually a standard form for this. Risk assessment forms will also contain information on what could be done to prevent the risk from happening and how severe the impact would be.

Many leisure and tourism organisations will already have a risk assessment completed, and you can get these from the Internet in advance of your visit.

Posters and notices are another way in which the customer can be informed of the rules of an organisation. Rules are usually made to help the organisation to minimise the risks.

Describe it

Risk is the likelihood of something happening. When something is 'low risk', if it actually happened it would have only minor consequences. However when something is 'high risk' there is a risk of serious injury or even death.

Rules help keep customers who are visiting an attraction or leisure facility safe

Research it

On your next visit to an attraction or leisure facility, find out what measures are in place to maintain the safety of the customer, e.g. what notices do they have on the walls? Is there any protective clothing available?

How will these measures minimise the risk to customers?

Research it

Research either:

a) A visitor attraction, such as an amusement or wildlife park, where you think there may be a 'high risk' factor, or

b) An activity centre offering a 'high risk' activity, such as quad-biking or rock climbing.

Make a list using two columns: 'high risk' and 'low risk'. Decide what you would put under each heading.

Is there a risk assessment on the facility's website? If not, use your list to create one.

Booking forms with conditions can also be used if an activity is considered as high risk. The customer may be asked to sign to say that they accept this risk when taking part in the activity. This is to cover the organisation and protect them against legal action by a customer.

Take it further

What would be the implications if the attraction or leisure facility did not comply with legislation to keep the customer safe?

The customer should expect a safe and healthy environment with suitable clean toilets, safe parking, an acceptable level of supervision and protective clothing if necessary. For example, on a visit to White Scar Caves in the Yorkshire Dales National Park, you will be given a safety helmet to wear as parts of the cave roof are low and the rock is sharp.

Safety whilst travelling is also vital, whether it be by train, coach, air, car, or boat. Transport companies have a responsibility to provide equipment, such as lifeboats on ferries, and instructions to customers as to what they should do and how they should behave in case of an accident or incident.

Talk about it

Why does an airline do a safety briefing before each flight? What is included in this briefing?

Property

The property of both employees and customers needs to be protected, though not usually using legislation. In the workplace and at some facilities, lockers and other methods of secure storage, such as cycle lockers, can be used. CCTV cameras are used to monitor car parks, grounds and entrances, and lighting and alarm systems also help with security.

The property, i.e. baggage of customers when travelling, should be the responsibility of the transport company, i.e. the airline, coach company, etc. In cases of loss or damage to property, you can claim compensation or replacement from the company, as long as you complete the correct form.

A travel insurance policy is the best way for customers to ensure that their property is protected whilst travelling overseas. Specialist insurance cover may be needed for expensive valuables, for example golf clubs or a surfboard, as a standard policy will have a maximum amount you can claim for if those items are lost or damaged, and this may be less than the items are worth.

Health and hygiene

Places that offer food to the public must comply with strict health and hygiene regulations. This is vital when food or drink is involved and includes examples such as food served in holiday accommodation, at an attraction or event, or whilst travelling, e.g. on a ferry, cruise ship or aeroplane.

The most important legislation affecting food is Food Hygiene Regulations 2006, General Food Regulations 2004, and the Food Safety Act of 1990. In the UK, food hygiene legislation is very well monitored. Inspectors visit regularly to check whether food being served is safe to eat, the cleanliness of the premises serving food, and that working practices are being followed. Consequences of failing to comply with the main requirements for good health, e.g. washing hands regularly, can lead to outbreaks of disease.

Research it

Norovirus is a serious illness causing acute sickness and diarrhoea. It sometimes occurs on cruise ships, as this is a very confined environment.

1. **Find out about an outbreak of Norovirus on a ship in recent years.**
2. **How did it affect the passengers?**
3. **What precautions were taken to stop it spreading?**
4. **What precautions do cruise ships take to prevent it from breaking out?**

Summary

- Health and safety is the responsibility of both employers and employees.
- Risk assessments must be carried out to protect both employees and customers.
- Property may be insured against risk of loss or damage.
- Health and hygiene applies mainly in the food industry – in leisure and tourism, any organisation that serves food is covered by this legislation.

1.3 Factors Influencing Customer Choice

In this section, we will look at why people use leisure facilities and why people travel. We will explore the different methods of transport available, and assess some of the advantages and disadvantages of each. We will also examine some of the factors that influence a customer's choice of travel method, as well as other considerations when choosing the most appropriate method of transport.

Why do people use leisure facilities?

There are seven main reasons why people use leisure facilities:

- Health
- Fitness
- Relaxation
- Entertainment
- Spiritual wellbeing
- Challenge
- Social opportunities.

Health

The term 'health' refers to the health of the person participating in the leisure activity. Health problems can include obesity, heart problems, birth defects or mobility problems. A health problem can be something that you were born with or something that develops later in life, e.g. following a car accident or illness. Leisure activities can help people to improve their health and maybe even to prolong their life. Diet clubs, such as Weight Watchers and Slimming World, could also be included in this category, and some may fall into both health and fitness, e.g. Rosemary Conley Diet and Fitness Club.

Fitness

The aim of health clubs and gyms in the UK is to improve the fitness of the clubs' members. New government guidelines released in 2007 are that people should undertake 30 minutes of moderate exercise a day as the minimum. Days of moderate exercise should also be combined with days of vigorous exercise. People should also do two weight-training sessions a week and adults over 65 should also do balancing exercises. Exercise reduces the risk of heart disease, diabetes and some cancers. Therefore people often use leisure facilities to improve their fitness.

Relaxation

In these days of stressful and busy lives, relaxation is a high priority. People use leisure facilities to help relieve some of the stress and to relax.

Some people find that a walk in the countryside is enough to relieve stress and to escape from their busy lives at work. Others use strenuous activities such as boxing to 'take out' their anxiety and aggression in a different way. However, relaxation is usually associated with hobbies and interests that are less strenuous, such as painting, reading or cookery.

Talk about it

In small groups or pairs, discuss why you choose to take part in a leisure activity or visit a leisure facility.

Take it further

Produce a graph of the main reasons given by your entire group in the activity above. Which is the most popular reason? How do these reasons match up to the list of seven reasons we are going to cover in this section?

Research it

Find out more about diet clubs.

What are the main differences between the different types of diet club?

Which do you think would be most successful in improving health and fitness? Why?

Describe it

Light exercise (e.g. a short walk, gardening, DIY) generally allows you to talk at the same time.

Moderate exercise (e.g. a brisk walk, carrying heavy bags) makes you slightly breathless.

Vigorous exercise (e.g. aerobics, playing football or running) makes you breathe rapidly.

Talk about it

How many minutes of exercise do you do a day? A week?

Is it enough? How can you do more?

Entertainment

Entertainment is probably the most popular reason for visiting leisure facilities. You will have already identified the different sorts of entertainment available in Topic 1.1, pages 12–15. The wide range of facilities for entertainment, from theatres to theme parks, means that there is plenty of choice for all types of customer.

Entertainment is another form of relaxation, and for many young people it's a great social opportunity, i.e. many 'first dates' take place in the cinema!

Spiritual wellbeing

Spiritual wellbeing is very closely linked with relaxation and this reason to use leisure facilities is probably more mental than physical. Some of the relaxation activities, such as swimming or walking, when completed leave the participant feeling mentally refreshed as well as physically tired. Yoga or a gentle martial art like Tai Chi could be an example of mild physical activity, but are also closely linked with spiritual wellbeing.

Challenge

People may use leisure facilities for the 'challenge'. The challenge can be personal, for example to lose weight, build up a 'six pack', climb a mountain, run a faster time, get into a sports team, or to win!

The challenge can not only be personal but can also be to benefit others. The London Marathon is a good example of how a challenge encourages people to take part in leisure activities, as most runners are sponsored for their participation and this raises money for a wide range of charities.

Similar, but shorter events, such as the 5K Cancer Research Race for Life or the Sport Relief Mile, which are held annually at venues all over the UK and have many participants who have never run in a race before, are good examples of a challenge undertaken by a wide cross-section of the British public.

Social opportunities

Social opportunities are not just limited to young people who want to get together to chat, listen to music or meet new people. Many of the typical leisure activities we have studied already could also be used to socialise.

Summary

- Reasons why people use leisure facilities depends on age, gender, where a person lives, how much money they have, and how much time they have.
- Many people have more than one reason for participating in leisure.
- Health and fitness are closely linked.
- Challenge can be personal or to benefit others.

Hotlink

Motorcise Healthy Living Centres are a new sort of gym. Find out more about them by visiting their website. A link to this website has been made available at www.heinemann.co.uk/hotlinks – just enter the express code 4110P.

1. **What sort of people would visit a Motorcise centre?**
2. **What are their aims?**
3. **How many centres are there in the UK?**
4. **Do you think that this is a good idea?**

Research it

Find out about your local health club, gym, beauty therapy centre and local evening classes. Make a list of the products/services that each provide. Which of these link with spiritual wellbeing?

Research it

Have a look at a charity that offers a range of challenges and events to raise money. Using their website, produce a table of the different types of event available and give an example of each.

Assessment tips

You will need to be able to identify the seven main reasons why people use leisure facilities. These may be the subject of a multiple-choice question.

You will need to understand how these reasons are linked together.

You will need to be able to give examples of facilities and activities that are linked to each of the seven reasons.

Reasons why people travel

Travel is defined as 'to go from place to place or visit places and countries for business or pleasure' (Encarta World Dictionary 1999). Travel may be:

- Within a local area
- Within a country (domestic)
- International (outbound or inbound).

This definition implies that there must be some purpose for travel. We are now going to explore six main reasons why people travel.

Holidays

'Everybody needs a holiday from time to time. A change of air, a different environment, meeting new people or simply taking time for yourself, can really be of benefit' (RNIB). A holiday is a form of travel that includes an overnight stay, and can range from a weekend break in your own country to a round-the-world trip.

The reasons for people taking different types of holiday are extremely varied and can include:

- For a special occasion e.g. birthday, anniversary, wedding, honeymoon, stag/hen party, etc
- Rest and relaxation e.g. spa weekend, a week/fortnight in the sun, viewing scenery
- Sport/activity/special interest/adventure e.g. golf holiday, ski holiday, trekking, watching a sporting event such as a motor-racing Grand Prix, etc.

It is not always simple to put holidays into a category. For example, an overnight stay in Blackpool could be a special occasion (hen or stag party) or it could be linked with rest and relaxation (a weekend break). There could be a combination of reasons for travel, depending on customer type, time of year, length of stay, etc.

Sightseeing

Sightseeing basically means going out to look at places of interest. This can be either in your local area or while you are on holiday. Places of interest range from natural, such as the scenic Lake District, Loch Ness in Scotland or the Giants Causeway in Ireland, to places with historic interest, such as the city of Chester with its Roman walls. Sightseeing is often associated with a 'tour'. For instance a popular way of seeing the sights of a town or city is on an open-top bus tour. Overseas visitors to the UK will often go on a longer sightseeing tour. They want to visit all the major destinations in the UK in a short time.

Sightseeing can also include travelling around a destination or country by car, public transport, bicycle or on foot, using a guidebook to identify the major sights.

Research it

In groups, remind yourselves of the definitions for each of the following:

- Domestic
- Outbound
- Inbound.

Write a short description of each.

Take it further

Can you think of any other reasons why people may take a holiday? In groups make a list and then compare those reasons in a class discussion.

Hotlink

Find out more about open-top bus tours in the UK and also overseas by visiting the City Sightseeing Worldwide website. A link to this website has been made available at www.heinemann.co.uk/hotlinks – just enter the express code 4110P.

Find out what other cities in the UK have open-top bus tours. How do the prices vary?

Research it

What do you think are the most popular sightseeing tours in the UK? Conduct some research. A link to the VisitBritain website has been made available at www.heinemann.co.uk/hotlinks – just enter the express code 4110P. It is a great resource for itineraries for tours in regions and countries of the UK.

Are you surprised by what you discover?

Visiting tourist attractions

We looked at different types of tourist attraction on pages 20–21. People may choose to visit attractions in their local area or while they are on holiday.

The reasons why people travel to visitor attractions may include:

- Amusement/enjoyment e.g. swimming pools
- Thrill or excitement e.g. extreme rides at a theme park
- Entertainment e.g. watching a show at a water park
- Education/conservation e.g. a zoo, heritage centre or garden attraction, such as the Eden Project in Cornwall.

Visiting friends and relatives/relations

Visiting friends and relatives/relations is also known as VFR and could include anything from visiting for a few hours to a day trip, a weekend or an extended stay. The length of stay often depends on the distance people have to travel, for instance from the UK, visiting a family in India could be a two-week trip, but visiting a friend in another city in the UK could be for a weekend or less.

The difference between VFR and other types of travel is that you would not need accommodation as you could stay with your family or friends, so you would need less spending money.

Business travel

Business travel generally involves travelling from your normal place of employment for the purpose of work. It does not include travelling from home to the workplace. Volunteering or working abroad as part of a 'gap year' is also not classed as business travel as you would probably not have a usual place of employment.

People who travel for business may be away from home for as little as a day, e.g. for a meeting in London, or working away from home for months or more, e.g. on an engineering contract in Dubai.

Business travel includes:

- Meetings
- Conferences and seminars
- Trade fairs and exhibitions
- Maintenance – of machinery and equipment
- Training courses

Educational purposes

This type of travel involves travelling, either domestically or internationally, to be educated or to learn something, not simply just travelling to school or college. There are many overseas students who come to the UK to study at the colleges and universities, and many UK students study overseas as part of their UK course, for example language students often spend some time in the country they are learning the language of.

Curriculum-related school trips, such as to Stratford-upon-Avon to see a Shakespeare play, to the Peak District for a geography trip, or a trip to the WW2 battlefields of northern France are also good examples of travel for educational purposes.

Research it

Using the four categories (amusement, thrill, entertainment, education), think of an attraction for each category. The attractions can be either in or outside the UK.

Then explore what each attraction has to offer. Find out information on the accommodation offered, the types of visitor who may be attracted and their length of stay.

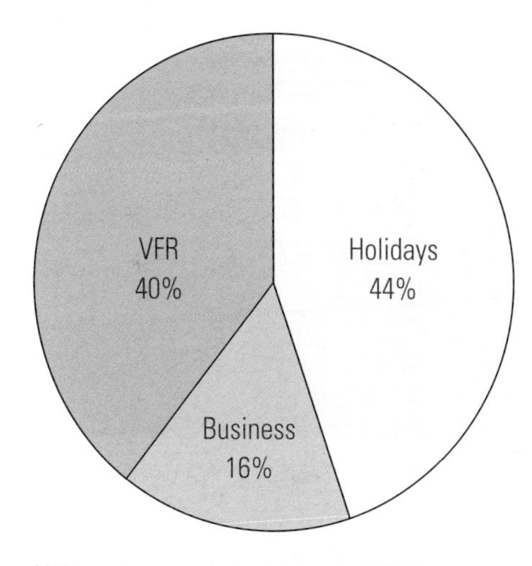

UK tourism overnight trips in 2007

Summary

- There are six main reasons why people travel.
- Reasons for travel will vary with age.

Assessment tips

You need to know the six main reasons why people travel. Being able to provide examples of each of the six reasons for travel will also be useful for the exam.

You will need to be able to apply this information to a case study, which may be presented in the examination.

Methods of travel

Travel is a major part of both the tourism industry and the leisure industry. Travel can be subdivided into three types:

- Travel **to** (and from) a destination, attraction or leisure facility e.g. flight, train, coach, etc
- Travel **around** a destination e.g. taxi, tube, tram, etc
- Travel methods as a **type** of tourism e.g. a cruise, flotilla sailing, motorhome tour, etc.

We are going to explore the four main methods of travel – air, rail, sea and road. Each of the methods has advantages and disadvantages. These will depend on the person travelling and how much time they have to travel.

A Seacat ferry

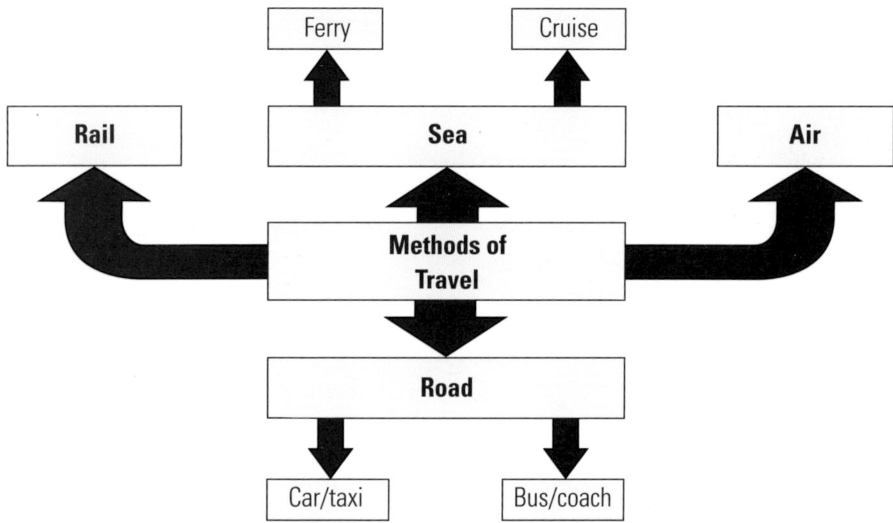

Different methods of travel

Air

The UK has both large international airports, such as London Heathrow and Manchester, and smaller international airports, such as Exeter, Marshall Airport Cambridge, and Leeds Bradford.

There are two main types of air travel:

- Scheduled flights
- Charter flights.

Most airports will receive a mixture of the two.

Scheduled flights

Scheduled flights are flights operated by airlines that fly specific routes, at specific times, on a regular basis – daily, weekly, etc. They will fly whether the plane is full or if there are only a few people on board. Scheduled flights will operate to major cities in Europe and the rest of the world, and the timetables will offer flights throughout the year. The major scheduled airlines in the UK include British Airways and Virgin Atlantic.

Remember it

75% of visitors to the UK arrive by air.

81% of all visits abroad by UK residents are by air. (Source Travel Trends 2006)

Charter flights

Charter flights also operate to regular schedules, however a charter flight takes place as the result of a hiring agreement. Tickets are not usually sold directly to the customer. Instead major tour operators, such as Thomas Cook and TUI Travel will hire (charter) a plane. Travel agents will then sell tickets on the plane as part of a package holiday, in which the price includes flights, accommodation and other services. Charter flights therefore usually fly to holiday destinations. However, this is changing as many tour operators now offer 'flight onlys', not just package holidays, on their charter flights.

Charter airlines often use small- and medium-sized airports in the UK, who rely on charter flights for their survival. The airports make money from the airline landing fee they receive from the charter companies.

Budget flights

No-frills or **budget flights** are short-haul flights on routes traditionally served by scheduled airlines, e.g. flights to major cities and popular holiday, short-break and ski-resort airports. Budget airlines include easyJet, Jet2, bmibaby and Ryanair. Tickets do not have to be bought as part of a package holiday and costs/prices are kept to a minimum, for instance, in-flight meals are only available at a cost, etc.

Here are some of the advantages and disadvantages of air travel.

Advantages	Disadvantages
• Flights can be very cheap if booked in advance. • Actual journey time is shorter than other transport methods. • More destinations served now than ever before, especially by budget/no-frills airlines.	• Airports are not usually near the city centre, so other transport/transfers will be needed. • Check-in and baggage reclaim adds time to the journey. • Many regional destinations are not served by direct flights, so transfers or connecting flights may be needed. • Limited baggage allowance.

Describe it

A **scheduled flight** is one that operates to a published timetable, like a bus, and will operate whether it is full or not.

A **charter flight** is organised by a tour operator and is usually linked to a package holiday. It operates at times agreed with the operator, and if not full, can be cancelled or merged with another (this is known as consolidation).

A **no-frills** or **budget** airline also operates scheduled flights.

Talk about it

In groups, discuss travelling by air. How many in your group have travelled by air? What airline? What features/facilities were available on board i.e. entertainment, food and drink, reserved seats, etc?

Look at the advantages and disadvantages of air travel. Can you add any more advantages or disadvantages to the list?

Rail

Rail travel in the UK includes the intercity, regional and cross-country services, and also light railways like the Metrolink, Greater Manchester's light-railway network, and the Docklands Light Railway in London.

Business people frequently use rail travel. On longer journeys, first-class service is often offered so that people can be served breakfast, drinks and snacks whilst working on their laptop.

Railways can also be used as a visitor attraction. There are numerous functioning steam railways throughout the UK that offer journeys through scenic areas, for example the Ffestiniog Railway in North Wales.

Remember it

Rail travel increased by 8% between 2006 and 2007, and passenger numbers are now the highest since 1961.

Talk about it

Rail travel in the UK is actually increasing at present. Is this because the roads are too busy or because the train service is faster, cheaper and more punctual? What other reasons can you think of that might explain this increase?

Here are some of the advantages and disadvantages of train travel.

Advantages	Disadvantages
• It is comfortable and very fast between major towns/cities. • Most large towns have a station, usually in the centre. • Some cheap tickets are available. • First class is available (business). • Less environmental impact.	• If travelling at peak times it is very expensive. • Some trains in commuter areas, e.g. London, are very busy. • Overseas visitors find fares complex. • For smaller destinations, journeys may have many changes. • Luggage restrictions.

Case study – Eurotunnel and Eurostar

The Channel Tunnel connects the UK to France. The fastest journey time on Eurostar from London to Brussels – a journey of 232 miles – was recorded on 4 Sept 2007 as 1 hour 43 minutes. The fastest journey time from London to Paris is 2 hours 3 minutes, travelling at up to 202 miles per hour!

There are two different types of service that use the Channel Tunnel – Eurotunnel and Eurostar.

Find out the following:

1. **What is the difference between Eurostar and Eurotunnel?**
2. **Who might use each type of service and why?**
3. **Can you think of any advantages and disadvantages of this method of travel?**

Sea

Because the UK is an island (only Northern Ireland shares a land border with the Republic of Ireland), travel by sea is an important part of the travel industry in the UK. There are many offshore islands, including the Isle of Man and the Orkney Islands, which rely on ferries to transport goods and people. Ferries can be either:

- Passenger-only ferries – on shorter crossings, up to 1 hour
- Car ferries, which will also take lorries and caravans – on longer routes

Regular ferry services operate between the UK and Ireland, France, Belgium, the Netherlands, Denmark and Spain. Most ferries will have cafes and shops on board, and accommodation is offered on longer or overnight routes.

Cruises are another method of sea transport used by tourists. Crossing the Atlantic Ocean by ship used to be the only way of reaching the USA.

Cruising is a fast-growing market in the travel and tourism industry, but is really a type of holiday rather than a method of transport.

Research it

There are many different ferry routes from England, Scotland and Wales to ports in both The Republic of Ireland and Northern Ireland. How many different routes can you find? Mark the routes on a map. How long does each crossing take? How many different types of ferry operate these routes?

Advantages	Disadvantages
• The ferry crossing is seen as part of the holiday. • It is relatively cheap. • Many ferries nowadays have great facilities, shops, cinemas, etc.	• The journey takes a long time. • The English Sea can be rough across The English Channel, North Sea etc. • You will need to drive or connect with your destination from the port.

Road

The extensive UK motorway network connects all the major cities and even some of the natural attractions, such as the Lake District. The main motorways are linked by A and B roads, so nowhere is difficult to access. Cars, buses and coaches all use roads to transport leisure passengers and tourists to their destinations.

Car travel

Car travel can be:

- Private car
- Hired car – through international companies such as Avis, Budget or Hertz
- Taxi or chauffeur-driven car.

	Advantages	Disadvantages
ROAD (Car)	• The UK has an extensive road network with very few toll roads. • There is a plentiful supply of petrol stations and services. • The signposting is good. • You can take lots of luggage. • It is convenient if you have children/babies. • You can stop off wherever you want. • It is economical if the car is full. • You can tow a caravan or trailer tent.	• Roads can be very congested. • Inbound tourists are not used to driving on the left. • Parking is difficult, expensive and controlled in some towns and cities. • Increased fuel prices and congestion charges in London (and other cities in the future) makes this an expensive method of travel.

Bus and coach travel

Bus and coach travel includes the following:

- Scheduled coach services, for example those operated by National Express and Megabus
- Coach tours that include accommodation, such as those operated by Shearings Holidays and National Holidays
- Sightseeing/excursion bus tours (see page 54)
- Airport transfer coaches
- Private hire coaches
- Local bus services.

Summary

- There are four main methods of travel: air, rail, sea and road.
- These are subdivided again, for example road travel into car/taxi and bus and coach.
- Each of the methods has advantages and disadvantages. These will depend on who you are, how much time you have to travel and how much money you have to spend.

Research it

To ease congestion, a toll road has been constructed to bypass Birmingham, known as the M6 Toll. A toll road is a road on which you are required to pay a fixed amount to travel. Find out how much it costs to travel on the M6 Toll? Does this price vary with time of day? Why is this? In small groups, discuss the advantages/disadvantages of a toll road.

Remember it

Domestic tourists are more likely to travel by car than any other method – 73% of domestic travellers use their car.

Talk about it

Chauffeur-driven cars are used for tourism, for instance there are general tours, e.g. around London and the UK, or specific tours, e.g. chauffeur-driven wine tours in California. Find out about other chauffeur-driven tours, then discuss the advantages and disadvantages of this method of travel.

Assessment tip

You need to know the different methods of travel available, with examples of companies in each sector. You will also need to know the definition of scheduled and charter flights, and no-frills airlines.

Talk about it

A married couple, who run their own successful publishing business, are travelling to central London from Sheffield for a one day meeting with potential clients.

A college student, Amir, is going from Leicester to visit his mate in South London for the weekend.

1 Which of these would travel first class by train, and which on a late night coach? Why?

Factors influencing customer choice of travel method

We have seen how different methods of travel have advantages and disadvantages. There are also many factors that will influence customers' choice of travel method, including:

- Who they are – their age, occupation and how much money they have
- Who they are travelling with, e.g. family, colleagues or alone
- Why they are travelling.

Cost/fares

How much money a person has will influence their choice of travel method. If someone has more money they are more likely to pay for first-class travel, whereas a person with less money, for instance a student, would consider a lower-budget method of travel, such as an overnight coach. Rail and coach operators offer a range of different ticket prices and it is usually more expensive to travel on their services at peak times. Ferry companies often offer cheaper fares on sailings that are at more inconvenient times, such as 2 am. Airlines offer cheaper flights the earlier you book and a range of fares to appeal to customers with different financial circumstances.

Convenience

The convenience of the method of travel is also a factor. Will the train take you directly to the city centre or will you need to catch a bus? What facilities are on board the method of transport? For instance, laptop points provided on some trains would enable people to work whilst travelling, which may be a consideration. Alternatively, someone may prefer to sleep on their journey so an overnight train or coach would be more convenient.

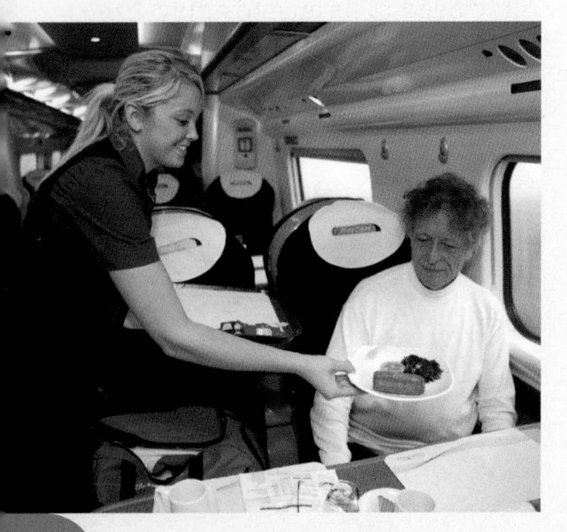

Case study – **Virgin Trains**

Most Virgin train services on the UK West Coast mainline are operated by state-of-the-art Pendolino trains. These trains have on-board facilities including at-seat audio entertainment and a walk-in shop selling a range of hot, cold and alcoholic drinks, sandwiches, hot snacks and magazines. All first-class customers have extra leg room, comfy reclining seats, complimentary newspapers and at-seat power points for charging laptops and mobile phones. Depending on the time of day, first-class customers also receive a choice of breakfast dishes or deli-style snacks that are served at-seat. Complimentary alcoholic drinks are offered to all first-class passengers except at breakfast.

1 Make a list of the key factors that may influence a customer to choose to travel by Virgin trains. Explain your choices.

Availability

Availability of service – how often it runs and at what times – can be another factor that influences a person's choice of transport method. For instance, trains take more passengers than coaches, so a train may be a better choice if you have to book your transport at the last minute.

Frequency

How often a service runs is another important factor. For instance, if there is a chance that a meeting might run over, a method of transport that has more frequent services would be a better choice for a business person.

Accessibility

Accessibility of the method of transport is another consideration. Will a customer need to drive to the train station? Will there be somewhere to leave their car? Will it be expensive? How far is the bus station from the airport? Will the bus take a customer directly into town? Answers to these types of questions can affect the customer's choice of travel method.

Special offers/discounts

Special offers and discounted travel fares can act as an incentive to determine choice of travel method. This is often related to how much money a customer has to pay for travel.

Suitable timetables

Having suitable timetables for a method of transport is closely related to frequency of the service. Business people are less likely to want to travel at night (when they are not getting paid) and safety issues are often a concern for the single traveller, who may not want to arrive at their destination very late at night.

Destination routes

Destination routes influence a customer's choice of travel method and are closely linked with accessibility. Business people are more likely to want direct services to ensure they get to their meetings as quickly and as easily as possible. Train services are obviously restricted to the cities and towns that have a rail link. As there are more roads throughout the UK, buses and coaches are able to go to a wider variety of places, for example.

Summary

- The factors that affect choice of travel method depend on personal circumstances, such as income, age, and purpose of the journey.
- Most transport organisations offer a range of fares, and classes with different services, to cater for a wide range of different customer types.

Research it

Imagine you have a customer, Jo, who wants to travel from Preston to Glasgow any weekday next month. She is totally flexible with her travel times, she just want the cheapest fare, preferably in first class.

Use the Internet to find out the answers to the following questions:

What is the cheapest fare available to Jo?

What times would she have to travel?

What are the main factors that are influencing her choice?

Assessment tip

You need to understand the main reasons for a customer's choice of travel method. You may need to be able to apply these factors to a case study in the examination.

Other considerations that affect travel choices

The main reasons people travel are leisure, business or VFR. If people are travelling on business or visiting friends and relations, their choice of destination is usually made for them, i.e. it is determined by where the company sends them or where the friends live. However, when travelling on holiday, the tourists make the choice of destination themselves, although there are a number of considerations that could influence their choice.

Health

The health of the person travelling is one consideration. For instance, if a person is elderly or has difficulty with mobility, their choice of travel destination will reflect this. For instance, they may choose a destination that has a good local transport system and healthcare services that could be used should the visitor run into any difficulties while on holiday.

The hygiene of the country to be visited sometimes influences the tourist's choice as to whether to visit or not. In many countries, the tap water is not safe to drink and can cause diarrhoea, gastroenteritis, and in serious cases dysentery. The simple advice is, 'Boil it, cook it, peel it or forget it.'

Diseases and precautions

There are still many countries in the world where diseases such as cholera, yellow fever, typhoid and hepatitis are common. A tourist may need to have **inoculations** against these diseases in advance. This would be a major consideration to someone planning a trip at short notice to one of the countries where inoculations are needed.

Insect bites are another potential health problem. In countries with tropical climates, a bite from an infected mosquito can cause malaria. Travellers would need to take precautions when visiting these countries and often travellers may choose locations where this doesn't have to be a consideration.

Take it further

One in five tourists on a package holiday overseas falls ill, most with stomach upsets. The NHS has issued some Healthy Eating Tips to travellers, which include:

- Wash your hands thoroughly before eating food.
- Wash your hands with soap and hot water after using the toilet.
- Drink water from sealed bottles. Hot tea and coffee, fizzy drinks, beer and wine should be OK.
- Avoid local dairy products, particularly ice cream and cheese.
- Fish and shellfish may be hazardous even if well cooked.
- Eat only cooked vegetables and avoid salads, which will have been washed in tap water or not at all.
- Avoid freshly cut fruit, and peel all fruit.
- Avoid food that has flies buzzing around it.

1 Discuss each of the points above and explain why each is important.

2 Create a poster to inform people of this advice.

Describe it

Inoculation is an injection of a serum or vaccine that produces or boosts immunity to a specific disease.

Research it

Because of the risk of diseases, having access to healthcare is an important consideration when travelling overseas. An EHIC card enables you to obtain emergency healthcare in most European countries.

1 What does EHIC stand for?

2 In which countries can you use it?

3 What for?

Apply it

The Foreign and Commonwealth Office (FCO) website has loads of information on diseases, health and how to protect yourself while travelling or living overseas. A link to this website has been made available at www.heinemann.co.uk/hotlinks – just enter the express code 4110P.

1 See if you can find out how you can protect yourself against malaria.

Security at airports is of vital importance to the traveller

Security

Security at passenger transport terminals

Security is of vital importance to all travellers, especially since the attack on the World Trade Centre in New York on 11 September 2001. Airlines immediately took security precautions, such as restrictions on hand luggage and undertaking very strict security checks of both people and luggage. Following the threat of a liquid bomb to blow up another transatlantic flight a few years later, airlines restricted liquids, creams and gels in hand luggage to 100ml containers that need to be carried in a transparent resealable bag.

There has also been increased security at passenger transport terminals. For instance, the extra security at airports has increased check-in times.

Passports and visas

Passports and visas are other measures that help with security when travelling. If you want to leave the UK you will need to have a valid ten-year passport. Passports have now become much more sophisticated to prevent them being forged easily and they provide an added security for airlines to know who is on each flight. Retinal scanning at major airports is also helping to improve security.

A visa is an official 'stamp' or form in a passport that entitles the holder to enter a country. The purpose of a visa is to prevent illegal immigration, to track criminals and to help maintain security.

Security on public transport

In the UK in the aftermath of the London tube and bus bombings of July 2005, security on all other forms of transport was also taken more seriously. 'Unattended baggage will be removed' is a frequent announcement at rail and coach stations. However, it would be impossible to search every passenger on public transport.

Summary

- Everyone needs a passport when travelling abroad.
- You must check if you need any inoculations or protection against diseases when travelling overseas.
- Airport and transport security is of vital importance to the traveller.

Remember it

According to the Home Office Identity and Passport Services (IPS), 38 million adults and 9 million children held a UK passport in 2008.

Hotlink

Find out more about passports by visiting the Home Office Identity and Passport Service (IPS) website. A link to this website has been made available at www.heinemann.co.uk/hotlinks – just enter the express code 4110P.

What is the current price of a ten-year passport?

What is a 'biometric' passport?

How does a biometric passport help to maintain our security?

Talk about it

How safe do you think our public transport is?

What more could be done to ensure our security when travelling?

Assessment tips

You need to know about current security procedures at UK passenger transport terminals and on public transport. You may be asked to interpret information about passports, visas, health and diseases.

1.4 Introduction to Destinations, Impacts and Sustainability

The different types of tourist destinations in the UK

The UK has many different types of tourist destinations. In this section they have been divided into six major types:

- Seaside resorts
- Countryside areas
- Tourist towns and cities
- Business travel destinations
- Purpose-built destinations
- Historical and cultural destinations.

Talk about it

How many seaside resorts can you think of in the UK?

Are they small or large?

What features do they have?

Seaside resorts

Located by the sea/on the coast of the UK, seaside resorts range from small, sheltered fishing villages, such as Mousehole in Cornwall, which may just have a harbour, a stony beach, a pub and holiday cottages. In comparison there are the larger seaside resorts, such as Blackpool, which may have a beach, a promenade, a pier (or three!), tourist facilities such as shops, fast-food consortiums, amusements and a range of accommodation. What they both have in common is the sea.

Whitby in North Yorkshire is an example of a small seaside resort

Countryside areas

This type of holiday destination includes:

- National Parks
- Areas of outstanding natural beauty (AONB)
- Heritage coasts.

National parks

There are 14 National Parks in the UK and each one is looked after by its own National Park Authority. A National Park is an area of land that is designated and funded partly by the government to protect the landscape, and to offer people the chance to experience fresh air, beautiful views, and peace and quiet. The scenery within the National Parks is different, from the moors of Dartmoor and the mountains of Snowdonia, to the Yorkshire Dales, Pembrokeshire coast and the New Forest.

Areas of outstanding natural beauty (AONB)

Like the National Parks, AONB are also parts of the countryside that are protected. There are 35 in England, 4 in Wales, one that straddles the English/Welsh border, and nine in Northern Ireland. Examples of AONB in England include the Forest of Bowland, Cannock Chase, and the Cotswolds, which is the largest.

Take it further

The Natural England website has a list of all the AONBs in England. A link has been made available at www.heinemann.co.uk/hotlinks – just enter the express code 4110P.

1 Are there any AONB in your local area? How do AONB differ from National Parks?

Heritage coasts

A heritage coast is an area of coastline that has environmental or historical significance. A good example of a heritage coast is the East Devon and Dorset Coast, which has many fossils and rocks over 185 million years old. This is now known as the Jurassic Coast and is also England's first natural World Heritage Site.

Tourist towns and cities

Tourist towns and cities are built-up areas that have a variety of accommodation, shopping, attractions, entertainment, and food and drink facilities to choose from. They will also have good transport links from most other parts of the UK, a rail/coach station, and larger ones will also have an airport. The large cities of the UK, such as London and Edinburgh, are popular destinations for weekend breaks with both domestic and inbound visitors. Smaller cities such as Oxford or Newcastle, and towns like Llangollen are also becoming popular.

Remember it

The Welsh National Parks cover 20% of the land area of Wales.

Hotlink

Find out more about the Welsh National Parks by visiting their website. A link has been made available at www.heinemann.co.uk/hotlinks – just enter the express code 4110P.

Can you find a map of all the National Parks? What is the aim of the National Parks?

How many are there in England, Scotland and Wales? What are they like?

Talk about it

In groups, refresh your memory about what you learned about business travel on page 55.

Research it

The largest business travel destinations in the UK are London, Birmingham, Belfast, Cardiff, Manchester and Glasgow.

1 In your group find out:

- **The name of the main conference venue in each city.**
- **The facilities at each venue.**
- **The transport connections that make each one ideal for business.**

Research it

Historical and cultural destinations often attract overseas visitors. Research the features of one historical/cultural destination. Create a poster aimed at attracting overseas visitors that shows these features.

Business travel destinations

Business destinations in the UK have to have excellent facilities, especially if they offer conferences. Excellent transport to the destination is essential. There must be a mainline station and preferably an airport. Accommodation in usually large 4- and 5-star hotels, and availability of conference and meeting rooms are also important.

Purpose-built destinations

These are destinations that have been purposely built for tourism. Unlike the other destination types we have just explored, if it were not for tourists, purpose-built destinations would not exist. Each will have all necessary facilities, such as accommodation, entertainment, attractions and catering all on one site or in one area, which is managed by one organisation. Examples of these include the UK Center Parcs resorts, the Butlins holiday centres, and the Alton Towers Resort, which now has hotels on site.

Historical and cultural destinations

The buildings and architecture of these destinations will reflect their past, and there will be attractions associated with their history, for example Warwick Castle and Caernarfon Castle. Historical and cultural destinations in the UK may also be associated with the past due to a person, such as Shakespeare and Stratford-upon-Avon, or with a historical period, such as the Vikings in York. Both types of destinations reflect the way we used to live and the UK's industrial heritage is included as part of the country's culture. Ironbridge in Shropshire and Beamish near Durham are examples of this.

Warwick Castle was built in 1068 and overlooks the River Avon

Take it further

For each of the places listed below, match it to one of the six major types of tourist destination. You will need to be able to justify your decision.

Place	Type of tourist destination
Leeds	
Scarborough	
Hull	
Cambridge	
Brighton	
Llandudno	
Center Parcs Whinfell Forest	
South Downs	
York	

Assessment tips

You will need to learn the six major destination types and be able to describe each type. You will also have to match examples to each of the different types of tourist destination.

Summary

- There are six types of tourist destination in the UK.
- Each type has specific features.
- There may be some overlap, e.g. London is a tourist city, but could also be a business destination, or even a historical destination.

Impacts of tourism on communities and environments

Tourism not only often affects the destinations travelled to and their environments, but also the people who live in the location and their communities. **Impacts** on destinations can be both positive and negative. In this section you will be introduced to some of these impacts and this subject will be studied further in Unit 3.

Describe it

Impact means how something affects either the community or the environment.

Remember it

33% of all employed residents in the Lake District National Park are dependent on tourism. (Source: 2001 Census)

Talk about it

In groups, make a list of jobs in a National Park in the UK that you think are dependent on tourism.

Take it further

Would there be a different range of jobs in tourism if you were thinking about a Caribbean island instead of a UK National Park? What would these be?

Research it

Compare the price of a similar sized house in a popular seaside resort near the beach to one in the centre of your local town/city.

Impacts of tourism on communities

Positive impacts

Tourism is seen as a good source of employment. New tourism developments can create jobs in destinations. Many developing countries, such as the Caribbean islands of Jamaica and Trinidad, rely heavily on tourism. It also brings with it income. This can be spent on improving facilities, for example roads, power and water supplies, for local people as well as tourists.

Negative impacts

Although employment is a good thing, it can also be restrictive, as many tourism jobs are seasonal. The problems that tourists bring to communities will vary by destination. In the Lake District, 89% of visitors arrive by car. This makes the roads busy and fills local car parks.

In a seaside resort in the UK on a sunny day, there will be traffic congestion on roads to the beach. This will affect locals on their way to/from work. Hostility between locals and visitors can occur anywhere, for instance, between farmers and walkers with dogs in the countryside.

In an overseas destination with a poor standard of living, the influx of wealthy tourists can lead to crime and even prostitution. Popular tourist destinations overseas and in the UK are often desirable locations for holiday homes for the rich. This pushes house prices up beyond the budget of local people and may lead to them having to leave the area. In Salcombe in Devon, over 70% of the properties are holiday homes.

Impacts of tourism on environments

Positive impacts

The development of tourism can often change the appearance of a destination for the better. A good example of this is the re-development of city centres, such as Castlefield in Manchester, or the waterfront and docklands of Cardiff Bay.

In countryside areas, the creation of national parks, nature reserves, SSSI (sites of special scientific interest) and AONB's has helped to protect the environment.

Many tourist destinations try to educate the tourists who visit, using information centres, display boards, and ranger walks and talks. This all contributes toward helping the environment to be protected for the future.

Thousands of walkers a year cause footpath erosion

Research it

Find out what the Countryside Code is. Can you think of ways that this code can be promoted to tourists?

Negative impacts

One of the most serious effects of tourism is pollution. Pollution includes:

- Air pollution – caused by transport
- Visual pollution – inappropriate buildings for area
- Noise pollution – pubs, clubs, traffic, people, aircraft
- Litter and sewage – on both land and sea.

The numbers of tourists to an area can also affect the wildlife. It may lead to the destruction of their habitats or nesting sites, for example the disturbance of an endangered species of turtles in Zakynthos, Greece. An increase in tourist activity could even lead to disappearance of certain wildlife from an area altogether. **Erosion** of footpaths, beaches, buildings and monuments is also another major concern in tourist areas.

Remember it

It costs £100 per metre to repair an eroded path in the Lake District with stone. (Source: Lake District National Park Authority Education Service Factsheet on Path Erosion and Management 2005)

Research it

What sorts of pollution would you expect to find caused by tourism in the following places:

a) The countryside of the UK?

b) An island in the Mediterranean?

c) A large city such as Paris?

Describe it

Erosion means wearing away. It can apply to not only footpaths, but also lake shores, beaches, riverbanks, and even buildings and monuments.

Summary

- Examples of positive impacts of tourism on communities are job creation, increased income to the local area, and improved facilities.
- Examples of negative impacts on communities include traffic congestion, crime, prostitution and hostility.
- Examples of positive impacts of tourism on the environment are regeneration of run-down areas, and improvements to educate locals and visitors about the area.
- Examples of negative impacts on the environment are all forms of pollution, and disturbance of wildlife.

Assessment tips

You will need to be able to identify the impact of tourism on both communities, their people and the environment. You should be able to give positive and negative examples of each.

Introduction to ecotourism and sustainable development

In the previous section, you will have learned that tourism is not always good for communities and environments. To protect these for future generations, it is essential that tourism is developed in a sustainable way.

This section will introduce ecotourism and the important concept of sustainable tourism development.

What is ecotourism?

The Ecotourism Society defines ecotourism as 'responsible travel to natural areas that conserves the environment and improves the welfare of the local people'. A walk in a rainforest in Borneo is not ecotourism unless that particular walk somehow benefits that environment and the people who live there. For it to be ecotourism, it would have to employ local guides, and maybe put some of the money charged for the walk back into a conservation project.

What is sustainable development?

Sustainable development thinks about the future and according to The Pocket Green Guide for England, it is 'development that meets the needs of the present without compromising the ability of future generations to meet their own needs'. The principles of sustainable tourism are:

- Respecting local culture and the natural environment
- Recognising that water and energy are precious resources that we need to use carefully
- Helping to protect endangered wildlife and preserve the natural and cultural heritage of the places we visit
- Protecting and enhancing favourite destinations for the future enjoyment of visitors and the people who live there
- Buying local – giving a fair income to local families
- Having enjoyment, but taking responsibility for our actions.

Research it

Research one example of a sustainable tourism project that can be found on the Travel Foundation website. A link to this website has been made available at www.heinemann.co.uk/hotlinks – just enter the express code 4110P.

How does the project follow the principles above?

The Travel Foundation website has lots more advice regarding sustainable development for both individuals and travel organisations. Make a list of some of this advice.

Importance of sustainable development at international leisure and tourist destinations

International hotels, tour operators, transport companies and holiday destinations can contribute positively to sustainable tourism. Every individual holidaymaker can contribute, too. Some examples are shown below:

- Holidaymakers on average use 400 litres of water per person per day – twice as much as local residents. If local people use water carefully, so should tourists.
- Don't give gifts, money or sweets directly to small children. This encourages begging and it is much better make a contribution towards a local project. Ask your holiday representative or at your accommodation to find out how best to do this.

- Don't have your photograph taken with any 'wild' animals used as photographic props on the beach. Many of these animals live in appalling conditions and are often mistreated and disposed of when they get too large or difficult to handle.
- When you're buying gifts and souvenirs, look for local goods. Buying local crafts and produce – particularly in small villages – will help local families make a decent living out of tourism.

Importance of sustainable development at UK leisure and tourist destinations

UK destinations also need to develop tourism in a sustainable way, particularly in the countryside. Center Parcs is an example of an accommodation provider that is very sensitive to this and even has a water management policy.

Ways in which the environment can be protected include sustainable transport to reduce congestion and pollution, such as park-and-ride facilities and city-centre trams.

There are strict planning controls on new developments in the UK, especially in rural areas such as National Parks, where there is a requirement to build using only local materials.

Organisations and regions of the UK have set up projects designed to help sustainability of both businesses and tourists. One example of this is the Cornwall Sustainable Tourism Project (CoaST).

Assessment tips

You need to know the definition of ecotourism and sustainable development.

Try to think of the principles of sustainable tourism in terms of both the UK and overseas, in both cities and the countryside.

You may need to be able to apply these principles to a case study given to you in the examination.

Summary

- Ecotourism is just one sort of sustainable development.
- Sustainable development is important for both communities and environments for the future.
- Sustainable development needs to be implemented in both overseas destinations and in the UK.
- Sustainable development includes buildings, transport, resources and way of life.
- Everyone can play a part in sustainable tourism.

Take it further

One of the ways in which leisure and tourism organisations can try to be sustainable in their operations is by using the 3 Rs principle: Reduce, Reuse, Recycle. For example, a theme park could use recyclable plastic trays for their fast food.

1 Can you think of other ways in which (a) a hotel and (b) a leisure centre could apply the 3 Rs to the way they operate?

Research it

Find out more about the Cornwall Sustainable Tourism Project. What five principles do they have? Can you find a local sustainable tourism project near you?

Unit 1 Make the Grade

Now you have completed all of the topics in Unit 1, it is time to check that you understand everything you have learned and that you are ready to sit your examination.

Firstly, don't panic! You should already have a good understanding of what you need to learn. The Summary features at the end of each section give you, in brief, what you need to know, for example:

Summary

The key components of the leisure industry are:

- Sport and physical recreation
- Arts and entertainment
- Countryside recreation
- Home-based leisure
- Play- and activity-based leisure.

In addition, the Assessment tips in each section will help you to focus on what is important for each part of the unit. For example:

Assessment tips

You will need to learn the main job roles and responsibilities for each of the following jobs:

Leisure centre assistant; fitness instructor; lifeguard; park ranger; cinema staff.

The exam paper is one hour long and will have four sections, one for each topic in the unit, so it is a good idea to revise one topic at a time. Each section will have different types of questions. It will usually start with a multiple-choice or one-word answer question, then a short-answer question, and then maybe an extended-answer question. In this Make the Grade section you will be able to practise all the different types of question.

Revision tips

- Use the revision checklists provided in this section to make a revision timetable, and allocate a few sessions a week to your leisure and tourism course.
- Don't make revision sessions too long. A short, focused half-hour is much better than an unproductive hour.
- Use different methods of revision. Don't just re-read your class notes or this book. Try having a quiz with your friends, drawing a mind map or spider diagram if you are a visual leaner, get your parent/guardian to test you, or you could try some of the practice questions.
- Find a quiet place to revise, away from distractions of TV, Internet or family members.

Question styles

Multiple-choice questions

These are questions where you are given a number of answers to choose from. Eliminate all the wrong answers immediately. The correct answer will usually be one of the key terms or ideas from the topic, so make sure you know these exactly, e.g. the key components of the tourism industry. Use the Summary features at the end of each topic in this book to help you.

Short-answer questions

Look at how many marks are allocated to a question and try to put that many points in your answer, e.g. two marks means that you need to cover two separate points.

Extended-answer questions

Watch out for your spelling and grammar, as these will be tested in the longer questions. Even if you do not understand the question very well, attempt it anyway as there will be some marks given for basic descriptions or the correct information taken from a case study. You need to do well in these questions if you want a high grade.

Understanding assessment language

For both short- and extended-answer questions, you need to watch out for the **verb** in the question. It will probably be one of the following:

Verb	What do I write?
Identify, list, name e.g. **Name** a scheduled airline. (1 mark)	Give an example or make one or more points briefly, e.g. British Airways.
Describe e.g. **Describe** the duties of a fitness instructor. (2 marks)	Say what something is like, using adjectives and a little more detail about it. More detail = more marks. E.g. A fitness instructor is responsible for teaching members of a gym how to use the machines (1) and designing a fitness programme for them (1).
Explain e.g. **Explain** why a hotel uses a computer at reception. (2 marks)	Say why something is like it is, why it is needed, what it is used for. E.g. A computer is used to enter customers' details. This is so that the hotel can easily see how many rooms are sold and how many are free (1), and when the customer leaves they can use it to issue his or her bill quickly and easily (1).
Analyse, evaluate, assess e.g. **Assess** the safety measures at UK railway stations. (3 marks)	Is something any good? What are its advantages, disadvantages, good points, bad points? Is it useful or not? E.g. Large railway stations have security on patrol looking for unattended bags and this is a good thing as it makes people feel more secure (1). But at smaller stations there is no security at all, so it would be easy for a terrorist to leave a bomb in a bag there (1). There is no searching of bags as there is at airports so the public may not feel as safe as they would if travelling by air (1).

Assessment tips

- Attempt all questions and don't forget to leave time at the end to check what you have written.
- Read questions carefully to make sure you are answering in the right way.
- Manage your time well. You should spend no longer than 15 minutes on each section.
- If you cross an answer out, replace it with another. Otherwise leave it in, you may get some marks for it anyway.
- Make sure you turn over to the last page in the paper so you don't miss any questions.

Unit 1.1 revision checklist and practice questions

Revision checklist – Unit 1.1	Tick
The five key components of the leisure industry	
The six key components of the tourism industry	
The two main types of visitor attraction and examples of each	
Leisure activities and their products and services	
Leisure facilities with examples	
The different types of holiday people can take and examples of each	
Job roles and main duties of the five main leisure jobs	
Job roles and main duties of the six main tourism jobs	

Practice questions

Q1a Which of these is a key component of **both** the leisure industry and the tourism industry? (1 mark)

☐ Art and entertainment

☐ Visitor attractions

☐ Tour operators

☐ Countryside recreation

Jamilla answers:

☑ Visitor attractions

Comments on Jamilla's answer:

This is the right answer and gets Jamilla one mark.

Q1b Long haul and short haul are two types of flight. Define the terms long haul and short haul and give an example of each. (4 marks)

Jamilla answers:

A long haul flight is over six hours. London to New York is long haul. Manchester to Majorca is short haul.

Comments on Jamilla's answer:

The marks are broken down as follows: two marks for defining short-haul and long-haul flights, and two marks for giving an example of each. Unfortunately Jamilla only got three marks out of four for her answer as she didn't give a definition of short-haul flights. If she had said that short-haul flights were under six hours, or from the UK to destinations in Europe or North Africa bordering the Mediterranean, she would have got full marks.

Unit 1.2 revision checklist and practice questions

Revision checklist – Unit 1.2	Tick
The five main functional areas of leisure and tourism organisations and what each area does	
Aims and objectives of organisations, financial, and not-for-profit organisations	
The four Ps: product, place, price, promotion	
Examples of business systems and new technology, and examples of how these are used by leisure and tourism organisations	
Examples of how the leisure and tourism industry is changing rapidly	
Health and safety of employees, customers, property, and health and hygiene	

Practice questions

Q2a Name the functional department in a swimming pool complex that would be responsible for deciding the admission prices for next year. (1 mark)

Jamilla answers:

Sales and marketing.

Comments on Jamilla's answer:

This is not the right answer so Jamilla doesn't pick up any points here. Anything that concerns an organisation's income or money is the responsibility of the finance department.

Q2b It is important that leisure and tourism organisations use up-to-date business systems. Describe how a health club or gym could use new technology for its administration systems. (3 marks)

Jamilla answers:

A gym could use a computer to keep details of its customers, such as their names and addresses. They could also use computerised membership cards so that when someone swipes their card on entry, their picture appears on the computer at the reception desk and the receptionist knows who it is. They could also use computers to automatically send bills to people for their subscriptions and to produce a mailing list to send out any new information, such as events that are happening or new machines that have been introduced.

Comments on Jamilla's answer:

This is a really good answer. You can see that there are three marks available and Jamilla has actually described more than three uses of technology in a gym: record keeping, swiping in and out, identifying customers, sending out bills, and mailshots for marketing. Well done Jamilla.

Unit 1.3 revision checklist and practice questions

Revision checklist – Unit 1.3	Tick
Reasons why people use leisure facilities	
Reasons why people travel	
Methods of travel, and examples of advantages and disadvantages of each	
Factors affecting choice of travel method	
Factors affecting choice of travel, including health, diseases, precautions and security	

Practice questions

Q3a VFR is one of the reasons why people travel.

(i) What do these initials stand for? (1 mark)

(ii) Give an example of VFR. (1 mark)

Jamilla answers:

(i) Visiting Family and Relations.

(ii) I live in Exeter and go to see my auntie in Bournemouth.

Comments on Jamilla's answers:

(i) Jamilla would not get a mark for this answer as VFR stands for Visiting Friends and Relatives/Relations – family and relations are the same thing!

(ii) Jamilla gave a good example as she named a relative and identified the fact that they live quite a long distance away. Jamilla would get the mark here.

Q3b There are many factors that influence a customer's choice of travel method. One of these is **convenience.** Explain why a direct train service would be more convenient for a mum with two children aged 2 and 4. (4 marks)

Jamilla answers:

I think that they need to travel direct because it would be very difficult for her to change trains with two small children. They might have to go to a different platform or up stairs, and the youngest child will probably be in a pushchair.

Comments on Jamilla's answer:

Jamilla's answer is good but she has only made one point about the difficulty of changing trains. Because of the level of detail in Jamilla's answer she would gain two marks, however the question is worth four marks and Jamilla needs to give more reasons to get the full marks. Other points might include the length of the journey, the length of the wait at stations where they change trains, or the lack of facilities at some stations for things like changing and feeding.

Unit 1.4 revision checklist and practice questions

Revision checklist – Unit 1.4	Tick
The **six** different types of tourist destination in the UK, and some examples of each	
The **two** main impacts of tourism on communities and environments, and some positive and negative examples of each	
Definition of sustainable tourism and ecotourism, why sustainable tourism is important in the UK and overseas, and examples of both	

Practice questions

Q4a Name **two** examples of seaside resorts in the UK. (2 marks)

Jamilla answers:

Newquay and Blackpool.

Comments on Jamilla's answers:

Well done Jamilla. You would be awarded two marks for this answer. You will need to learn at least two examples of each type of destination for this topic.

Q4b Identify **two** features of historical/cultural destinations. (2 marks)

Jamilla answers:

Historical destinations are full of history, like castles, and cultural destinations have lots of culture in them.

Comments on Jamilla's answer:

You should not really repeat the words from the question in your answer! However, as Jamilla also stated that castles are to be found in historical destinations she would get one mark. Jamilla would get no marks for the culture part of the answer. Learn the features of each of the six different types of tourist destination in the UK (see pages 64–66) and you will find this type of question easy. A good answer to this question would be something like:

A historical destination is linked with the past and may have buildings or attractions that are part of it, for example castles or Roman walls. A cultural destination is linked with the way we used to live and will often have information about this displayed in a museum, for example. Cultural destinations may also include industrial heritage sites, such as mills or mines.

Q5 Case study: The Eden Project

The Eden Project is a visitor attraction in the UK, including the world's largest greenhouse. It was built on a barren, exhausted china clay pit and opened in 2001. Now its massive biomes contain millions of plants from all over the world. The Eden Project is solely owned by The Eden Trust, which is an educational charity. It uses exhibits, events, workshops and educational programmes to remind people what nature gives to us and to help people to learn how to look after nature in return.

Climate Revolution is just one of The Eden Project's programmes of work. It includes educational projects with schools, the exploration of new technologies for a low-carbon world, and public events such as the Sexy Green Car Show, which includes a showcase for cars run on new fuels that are safer for the environment.

The Eden Project is a sustainable development project.

(i) Define the term sustainable development.
(2 marks)

(ii) Analyse the effects of the programme Climate Revolution on improving the environment.
(6 marks)

Jamilla answers:

(i) Sustainable development is when the natural environment is being protected and there is recognition of the need to conserve natural resources.

(ii) The Climate Revolution is good as it involves schools children. It also involes the public with the Green Car Show.

Comments on Jamilla's answers

(i) This is quite a good answer. It covers two aspects (the environment and resources) so both marks would be awarded.

(ii) The question asked Jamilla to 'analyse' something and there were six marks on offer. As this is an extended-answer question, Jamilla also needed to be careful with her spelling and grammar. Saying the Climate Revolution 'is good' is not enough – she needed to say why. Although Jamilla referred to both children and the public, she could have just copied this from the case study text. To gain higher marks Jamilla needed to use the case study, not copy it. There are also some spelling and grammar errors, which would prevent Jamilla from getting high marks. Jamilla got only two marks for this answer.

A better response to this question would be along the lines of:

The Eden Project has realised that the climate is going to affect the environment in the future. It is addressing this by offering educational programmes for schools, which is great, as the education of future generations is vital to the future of our planet. The Climate Revolution is looking at technology improvements, and this includes a Green Car Show, which is a good idea as more and more people own cars now and a lot of the pollution of our planet comes from them. The Climate Revolution programme of work will therefore be getting both children and parents involved in the project.

A final assessment tip

Don't panic! Revise well, attempt all the questions and good luck!

Unit 2: Sales, Promotion and Operations in Leisure and Tourism

This unit will introduce you to the ways in which leisure and tourism organisations promote and sell their products and services to customers. In addition, the unit will look at the impact of new technology and advances in business systems on the operations of leisure and tourism organisations.

Through your study, you will identify different **selling situations** and which departments within an organisation support sales. Every leisure and tourism organisation will have its own aims and objectives, and you will look at how these affect the **marketing mix**.

Different promotional techniques and materials are used by leisure and tourism organisations, and you will look at these in detail in order to understand how and why they are effective.

Through the development of your investigation and research skills, you will be encouraged to apply your knowledge to real examples of organisations from key components of the leisure and tourism industry.

Describe it

Selling situations are when customers pay for a product/service from an organisation.

The **marketing mix** is made up of four key parts: product, price, place and promotion. These are also known as the 4 Ps.

Travel agents promote and sell leisure and tourism products and services

Take it further

As a class, choose two different types of leisure and tourism organisations from the lists you have compiled, e.g. a travel agency and a tourist information centre. Discuss what a customer would go to these organisations for, e.g. to book train tickets, look for accommodation, etc, and list each activity under each organisation. You may need to refer to this information later in this section.

Research it

In small groups, make a list of the different leisure and tourism organisations in your local area.

This unit covers the following topics:

2.1 Sales in leisure and tourism contexts
2.2 Promotion in leisure and tourism contexts
2.3 Promotional techniques and materials in leisure and tourism
2.4 Operations used in leisure and tourism organisations.

How you will be assessed

Unit 2 will be internally assessed in your centre and then by an Edexcel moderator. You will be given a task covering the content of the unit, and apart from any research and preparation that you will need to do, all other work will be carried out under informal supervision. Your teacher will supervise the assessment process and will also mark your work. Research and investigation will include visits to real leisure and tourism organisations to collect research and data, which you will keep in a research folder.

You will be able to work and build your knowledge with others during your study, but you will have to provide your own answers to the tasks in the assessment.

All of the work you produce must be your own. Quotes or examples can be used to support your own response or argument, but you will need to provide details of where you obtained them.

Face-to-face selling

2.1 Sales in Leisure and Tourism Contexts

There are a number of key selling situations available to leisure and tourism organisations. These include:

- Face-to-face selling
- Telephone
- Online.

In this section we are going to explore selling situations for the following:

- Travel agent
- Leisure centre reception
- Telephone/online cinema booking systems.

Selling situations

A selling situation is when a customer pays for a product/service from an organisation. For many leisure and tourism organisations they need to sell their products/services in order to increase profits. If they don't make a profit, they could go out of business. Money is also needed to pay staff and to improve facilities.

Travel agent

The purpose of a travel agent is to promote and sell the products and services of a range of leisure and tourism organisations. The products and services that they sell can be package holidays, flights, accommodation, train/bus tickets and travel insurance. Many travel agents will also provide a currency exchange service.

There are a number of ways a travel agent can sell goods to a customer, including in store (face to face), on the telephone or online.

Case study – Travel agent

Mary is looking to book her honeymoon and pays a visit to her local travel agency to pick up a number of brochures that have honeymoon packages. Mary also wants to ask advice from one of the staff as she is working on a specific budget and wants to be sure that she is getting good value for money.

1 **What other services could be offered to Mary by the travel agent that would be useful for her holiday?**

Leisure centre reception

The purpose of the leisure centre reception is to sell tickets and or membership packages to customers in order to use the facilities. The leisure centre reception will quite often have a range of products that the customer can buy to help them with their activities.

Take it further

In small groups, think about your local leisure centre/swimming pool. Consider the selling opportunities that exist within the reception area of the centre.

Case study – Leisure centre reception

John is paying a visit to his local leisure centre to go for his regular swim. At the reception, John pays for his ticket to swim and also buys a pair of goggles as his last pair has broken.

1 What other goods/services could the leisure centre receptionist offer John that he might be interested in?

Telephone/online cinema booking systems

For convenience, cinema bookings can be made over the telephone or through an online booking system. The customer will usually have to pay an additional amount for this convenience. Whilst making their booking, customers will get to see/hear promotions for other films, encouraging them to spend more money.

Research it

Using the Internet, find your local cinema's online booking system. See how many selling opportunities you can find and discuss this as a group.

1 Can you think of any other examples of leisure or tourism organisations that use either telephone or online booking systems? Make a list.

Case study – Telephone/online cinema booking systems

Rafiya and Amir want to arrange a night out at the cinema and decide to book the tickets using the online booking system. Amir logs on to the internet and finds the details of what is on at the local cinema. They choose the film they want to see and click on the button that will allow them to book and pay for their tickets online. Rafiya and Amir will pick up their tickets on arrival at the cinema. If they had wanted to, Rafiya and Amir could have booked their tickets over the telephone using an automated service. This would have meant that once their call had been accepted, they would have been guided through a series of options which would have eventually led to them paying for their tickets by using the key pad on their phone. Tickets would be waiting for them on arrival at the cinema.

1 What are the advantages for the customer of using an online booking system?

2 Can you think of a disadvantage?

Assessment tip

Make sure that you know the exact details of different selling situations within the leisure and tourism industry and be able to supply an example for each.

Remember it

In 2007, Alton Towers sold over two million tickets making it the most visited theme park in the UK and the 11th most visited in Europe. Many of the tickets were purchased using either the telephone or internet booking system.

Summary

There are three main selling situations within the travel and tourism industry:

- Face to face/in store
- Telephone
- Online.

You will need to be able to give examples of each selling situation.

Departments that support sales

There are a number of departments within leisure and tourism organisations that support sales. In this section we are going to look at four key departments:

- Administration
- Finance
- Human resources (HR)
- Regional offices.

Other departments that support sales include IT and sales and marketing.

Administration

The role of the administration department is to ensure that everything runs smoothly and the customer receives the correct product/service at the correct price. The administration department within a leisure and tourism organisation will support sales through the production of reports, letters, statements, invoices, tickets, and also through dealing with complaints and refunds.

Finance

Most leisure and tourism organisations have to work within a **budget**. The finance department will support sales by agreeing the budget available for any sales activity. This department will also provide regular information on how much of the budget has been spent.

The finance department controls the amount of money a sales team has to spend

Human resources (HR)

The human resources department (HR) is the department that looks after staff. However it will support sales by making sure that the people with the right skills and experience are recruited to any jobs available. Once the right people are in place, the HR department will make sure that members of staff are given the right level of training and support to be an effective member of the sales team.

Describe it

Administrative duties include typing correspondence, keeping records, arranging travel and/or room bookings for meetings, managing budgets, maintaining websites, dealing with complaints and refunds, etc.

Talk about it

In groups, make a list of administrative tasks you think would be carried out to support sales, e.g. what types of letters or statements would need to be produced.

Describe it

A **budget** is an amount of money that an organisation will set aside to spend on a certain activity, e.g. advertising. The manager who is responsible for the activity will have to show how they have spent the budget and to make sure they don't over-spend.

Travel Consultant Required

Mercer's Travel Agency

Are you an experienced Travel Consultant?

Mercer's Travel Agency chain are looking to recruit an experienced Travel Consultant for their Huddersfield Branch. The new recruit will join their highly professional team providing excellent levels of customer care and assisting in the creation of exciting holiday itineraries that meet the needs of our customers.

The successful candidate will have at least two years previous experience and travel qualifications are desirable.

In return, Mercer's will provide you with a competitive salary with commission and incentives, as well as regular educational visits to enhance your customer service.

Please send your up-to-date CV and covering letter to Miss Amy Strong, HR Manager, Mercer's Travel Agency, 311 High Street, Huddersfield, Yorkshire.

All applications to be received by 10th May 2009.

An advertisement for a sales assistant

Apply it

Carry out some research on the types of sales jobs available in the leisure and tourism industry. What qualities, skills and experience might an HR department look for in someone applying for a job to work in sales? Make a list.

Regional offices

Many tourism and leisure organisations have regional offices. Regional offices are offices spread out over different regions/parts of the UK. They are usually in addition to one central head office. The regional offices will support sales by providing a wide support system for the sales team as they cover different parts of the UK. A regional office may provide the sales team with the organisation's aims and objectives, and also provide information about which products and services have been chosen to be promoted for the next season/months ahead. This would give the sales team clear objectives for the year ahead and would help it to determine targets and methods of selling.

Take it further

Find out where the regional offices are for a number of large leisure or tourism organisations. Do you notice a pattern for where these offices are based?

Summary

There are a number of departments within a leisure and tourism organisation that support sales, including:

- Administration
- Finance
- Human resources (HR)
- Regional offices.

You will need to be able to give examples of how each department supports the sales team.

Assessment tip

You will need to understand the different departments within a leisure and tourism organisation that support the sales team. You will need to explain how these departments support sales and to give examples to support your answers.

Aims and objectives of leisure and tourism organisations

All organisations have aims and objectives. These are the starting points for many types of sales and marketing activities. This section investigates the financial aims of organisations within the leisure and tourism industry. We are also going to look at mission statements that set out an organisation's aims and objectives, and also look at some external issues that may affect aims and objectives, such as 'green' issues.

Financial

The aims and objectives of an organisation depend on whether the organisation is private, public or voluntary. See pages 36–37 to remind yourself about these different areas. However most leisure and tourism organisations are governed by financial aims, i.e. they need to make a profit in order to survive.

If an organisation is in the private sector, its aims and objectives are usually financial. In simple terms, the financial aim of any leisure and tourism organisation is to make a **profit**. The objective is to make a profit by successfully selling products/services at a price that is attractive to the customer, but that is over and above the cost to produce/provide. If a product is sold for more than it cost to produce, this will make a profit for the organisation and will help to keep it in business.

Describe it

Profit is the difference between the income of a business and all its costs and expenses.

Mission statement

A mission statement is the way in which an organisation tells its customers and its competitors what it is trying to achieve. An effective mission statement should be:

- Brief – easy to understand and remember
- Flexible – able to accommodate change
- Distinctive – to make the business stand out.

An organisation will also set out its **aims** and **objectives** in a mission statement, in other words, how it will try to achieve its 'mission'. For instance, the mission statement of a wild animal theme park might be to provide a unique family experience, to excite visitors about the conservation of the natural environment, and provide an opportunity for visitors to get close to wild animals within a safe environment.

Other aims and objectives: 'green' issues

Leisure and tourism organisations may have other aims and objectives that are driven by external circumstances. For instance, organisations worldwide are under pressure to consider the negative impacts their business has on the environment. Many leisure and tourism organisations are considering how they can help reduce these impacts and will make a **green** commitment/promise within their mission statement.

Describe it

An **aim** states what the organisation hopes to achieve.

An **objective** describes what the organisation will do to make sure that it achieves its aim.

Green can be described as being aware of the environment, in other words, working towards reducing a range of pollution such as noise, air, water, light etc. For something to be environmentally friendly, it must help the environment, e.g. by reducing the effects of global warming.

Carbon footprint is the amount of emissions caused directly and indirectly by an individual, an organisation, an event or a product.

Case study – easyJet mission statement:

- To provide our customers with safe, good value, point-to-point air services.
- To offer a consistent and reliable product and fares appealing to leisure and business markets on a range of European routes.
- To achieve this we will develop our people and establish lasting relationships with our suppliers.

An example of an aim:

- To provide first-class customer service by all our agents and respond quickly to customer needs.

An example of the objective:

- We will do this by providing high-level training programmes for every member of staff, focussing on the needs of a wide range of customer types.

The mission statement for easyJet is very short and to the point. Mission statements for other organisations can spread over a number of pages.

1 Using the Internet, find two more mission statements from either a leisure or tourism organisation. Highlight:
a) The mission b) The aims c) The objectives.

2 Discuss how the aims and objectives are different between the two organisations. Are any of the aims and objectives closely linked to financial objectives?

Case study – David's carbon footprint

David takes, on average, five flights per year. Last year he took three short flights to London from Glasgow to visit friends and to attend concerts, one flight to North Africa due to his interest in archaeology, and one flight to the USA for a holiday at Disney World. David used a carbon footprint calculator he found on the Internet to work out how these flights had contributed to the release of emissions. He found that he had contributed 2,500 lb of gas (CO_2), which contributes to global warming.

1 In groups, discuss the alternatives available to David that might help reduce his carbon footprint.

2 As a class, discuss the ways in which airlines might be able to reduce carbon emissions.

Remember it

Britons produce more carbon emissions from air travel per head than any other country, a study reveals today, citing the country's predilection for low-cost airlines as a major factor. (Source: The Guardian, October 2007)

Hotlink

Visit the TerraPass website and use the carbon footprint calculator to work out what your carbon footprint is. A link to this website has been made available at www.heinemann.co.uk/hotlinks – just enter the express code 4110P.

Take it further

Can you think of any other aims and objectives that leisure and tourism organisations might consider? Make a list of your suggestions.

Summary

- Every leisure and tourism organisation has aims and objectives.
- These can be financial, educational, etc and some aims/objectives are dictated by external factors, such as 'green' issues.
- Most leisure and tourism organisations will have a mission statement that contains the aims and objectives for the organisation.
- A mission statement informs customers and competitors what the organisation hopes to achieve.

Assessment tip

You will need to know about mission statements and why leisure and tourism organisations have them. You will need to know about some of the aims and objectives of leisure and tourism organisations, e.g. financial.

Marketing mix

How the 4 Ps work together to make the marketing mix

Previously in this book we have looked at the functional areas of leisure and tourism organisations (pages 34–35) and saw how sales and marketing departments work closely together to help an organisation meet its objectives. The most important concept in sales and marketing is the 'marketing mix'.

The 'marketing mix' is made up of four key parts, also know as the 4 Ps. These are:

- Product
- Price
- Place
- Promotion.

Organisations within the leisure and tourism industry need to consider each of these four parts when considering the needs of their customers.

If a leisure and tourism organisation gets the marketing mix just right, it will increase its sales, which in turn increases its chances of success against its competitors. We will now look at each key part in turn.

Product

Product can be broken down into goods and services. Goods are things you can see and touch (i.e. tangible). Services are usually experienced (i.e. intangible).

Product/service features

The products and/or services offered by leisure and tourism organisations will be advertised to customers to show the 'features' and 'benefits', in an effort to persuade customers that they should choose one particular organisation over their competitor. For instance, the 'features' of a package holiday to the Caribbean would be described as:

- The flight to and from the destination
- The accommodation
- Excursions that are part of the package deal.

The 'benefits' of the package holiday would be described as:

- All year round sunshine
- Relaxation
- Room service
- No worries about paying for food and drink as these are included in the price (in resort)
- Get to see sites away from the resort at no extra cost.

A leisure or tourism organisation would advertise these key product/service features and benefits as an attempt to attract customers.

Apply it

Using travel brochures that cover different types of holiday, e.g. Winter Sun, Summer Sun, Adventure Holidays, Club 18-30, etc, choose at least three holidays and create a list of the 'features' and a list of the 'benefits' for each holiday taken from the brochure descriptions.

Branding/unique selling points (USP)

Branding is one way in which leisure and tourism organisations make their business stand out from their competitors. This is often done by designing a name and a logo that use certain colours, which are used on brochures for the organisation and any promotional material, such as advertising. The colours and the logo can even be reflected in the staff uniforms. This means that customers can easily recognise the organisation, which makes it easier for a customer to return to an organisation if they have had a positive experience with them. However, if a customer has had a negative experience, then they will also most likely avoid any advertisement with that branding on in the future.

Branding can also include what is called a 'tag line', which describes why customers should use a particular brand. For instance, the branding for David Lloyd Leisure Clubs has the tag line "LIFE. Be fit for it". Tag lines can often change depending on the advertising campaign for a particular product.

Unique Selling Points (USP) are used by leisure and tourism organisations to show how their product is different to another. It might be that the price is cheaper, or that the product is better quality, more fashionable or have more features – these are all USPs.

Price

Price is the term used to describe what a customer will pay for a service or a product.

Range of product/service prices

Leisure and tourism organisations will usually have a variety of different products and/or services which include a range of prices for each. For example, Thomas Cook offers a wide range of holidays such as beach, active (activity based holidays), faraway (to locations with a flight time of more than five hours), snow, clubbing (trips to the world's best dance spots), city breaks, etc. The prices of each will vary, according to the time of year they are being offered. For example, prices are high during peak season (school holidays) and will be considerably lower during off-peak season (term time). Many travel organisations offer a variety of fares, including more expensive first-class services, as well as economy/standard fares.

Pricing strategies

If an organisation does not get the pricing right for their product/service, they will not achieve a profit. A simple approach to pricing is to use the 'cost plus' pricing method, which is the cost of producing the product and then adding a percentage to give the organisation the profit they need. This method does rely on the organisation selling the number of products required to meet the target (profit) that has been set.

Another approach to pricing is 'competitive pricing', which is when an organisation keeps a very close eye on its competitors who are offering the same product/service at a low price. The organisation will react to this and reduce their prices also. This is quite a risky pricing strategy.

Talk about it

- Airline uniforms often reflect the colours and logo of the airline. Can you think of some examples? What other leisure and tourism organisations use their colours and logo on their staff uniforms?
- In groups, discuss how many brands you can easily recognise within the leisure and tourism industry. Make a list. Do all these organisations have logos and tag lines?

Research it

Carry out some research on a leisure organisation in your local area. What methods of branding has this organisation used to make it stand out? Do they have a tag line? If not, can you think of one for them? What USPs do they use to promote themselves?

Talk about it

Why do you think the strategy of competitive pricing is risky? As a group, discuss the risks involved with using this particular pricing strategy.

Research it

Find leisure and tourism organisations in your local area that are offering the same product/service, i.e. local bus companies or fitness centres. Do they offer the same price for the same product/service or can you see examples of competitive pricing?

Describe it

A **distribution channel** is the way that products/services are sold or distributed so that they reach the customer e.g. websites, call centres, brochures.

Place

Place is about how the product or service reaches the customer, i.e. in what location will the customer find the product/service they are in need of? How a product or service finds its way to the customer is known as the **distribution channel**.

Location

The location can be the actual physical location of the product or service, which is linked to its accessibility. For instance, a leisure centre in a city centre would want to be located in a prominent position to catch the eye of passing visitors. Having car park facilities to enable the leisure centre to be more accessible would also be an advantage.

Location can also refer to how a customer finds a product or service, i.e. how does the customer locate it? For instance, a customer trying to find out about a safari holiday could locate details in a travel agency, a holiday hypermarket, a booking office, through a call centre, on television (i.e. using Teletext), on the Internet, or through high street newsagents who sell magazines about travel.

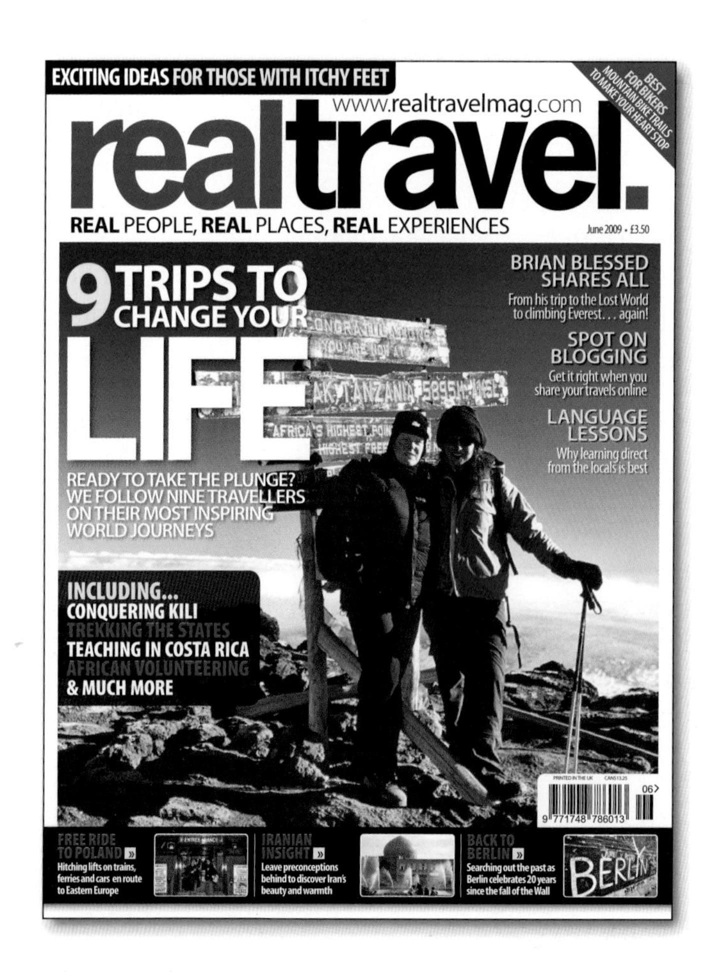

A travel magazine like Real Travel can be one way a customer is able to locate a product

Talk about it

Can you think of any specialist magazines that would help a customer locate the following:

- Cycle trips around Europe
- Trip to photograph lions in their natural habitat
- Walking tours around the UK.

What other specialist magazines can you think of?

Transport links

Leisure and tourism attractions, such as theme parks, zoos, heritage sites, etc rely on customers travelling to them in order to access their products and services. This means that these organisations have to make sure that tickets to visit them are easily obtainable, e.g. through direct booking, via the Internet, by telephone, or through tourist offices and travel agencies. Each attraction will rely on good transport links such as motorway and/or road networks, rail and bus travel to ensure that customers are encouraged to visit.

Availability of product/service

Products and services need to be available to the customers when they need them. For example, some products and services are paid for/or received at the **point of distribution**.

Describe it

Point of distribution is the place from where a customer can buy a product or service. Examples of points of distribution in leisure and tourism are: online booking, travel agency, health and fitness centre reception and a theme park entrance.

Case study – Point of distribution

Maria and Greg are going to join other school friends at the cinema. On arrival, Greg buys two tickets for himself and Maria, and they go to join their friends, who are already at the counter buying popcorn and drinks for during the film. The group then proceed to Screen 3 where their film is about to start. Maria and Greg have paid for and received the products and services at the point of distribution.

Now think of two other examples within the leisure industry when customers can receive products/services at the point of distribution.

Promotion

Promotion is the way in which leisure and tourism companies make their customers aware of the products and services that they have available.

This is through a range of techniques such as advertising, public relations and displays (e.g. posters, billboards, leaflets, etc).

We will look at promotion in greater detail on pages 90–109.

Research it

Using a range of materials, carry out research to identify ways of promoting the products and services of a number of leisure and tourism industries. You will need to collect this information and keep it in your research folder for use in Topic 2.3. Your evidence can be web page printouts, photographs that you might take, cuttings from journals and newspapers, etc.

Summary

- The marketing mix is made up of four key parts: product, price, place and promotion. These are also know as the '4 Ps'.
- Product can be broken down into goods and services.
- There are a number of pricing strategies used in relation to price, including the 'cost plus' method and competitive pricing.
- Place is about how the product/service reaches the customer. This is also known as 'the distribution channel'.
- Promotion is the way leisure and tourism organisations raise awareness of their products and services.

Assessment tip

You will need to know the 4 Ps and how they work together to make the marketing mix. You will also need to be able to give examples of each of the four elements that make up the 4 Ps.

2.2 Promotion in Leisure and Tourism Contexts

In this section we will look at the 'what, where and how' of promotion in leisure and tourism. You will gain an understanding of how leisure and tourism organisations promote their services/products through market segmentation and target marketing. We will also explore how effective different promotional materials are and you will be given the opportunity to design your own promotional material.

Market segmentation and target marketing

Not all customers want the same product or service and this is because each customer will have very different needs. However, customers will fall into groups who have very similar needs and who might be interested in the same type of product or service. **Market segmentation** is the term used for the grouping of such customers.

Market segmentation is usually determined through the marketing team conducting market research. Once this has been done, an organisation can then look at providing suitable information for the groups of customers that they want to promote their products to and these particular groups are known as the **target market**.

The following categories can be used for market segmentation and to identify target marketing:

- Age
- Gender
- Social group
- Lifestyle
- Ethnicity
- Geographical location.

Describe it

Market segmentation is when customers fall into one group or segment of people who might have similar needs or be interested in the same product/service.

Target market is a particular group of customers that organisations want to promote a product or service to.

Age can determine the target market to which a product is promoted

Age

Leisure and tourism organisations may choose to aim their products at a certain age range of customer. For example, Laterlife is an organisation aimed at providing a range of leisure and tourism activities for those over the age of 50, while Club 18-30 target a younger age range for their holidays.

Apply it

Collect a range of promotional materials. See if you can find products and services that are aimed at specific age ranges. How are these age ranges broken down? What types of products/services are offered to each group? You might want to keep copies of these promotional materials in your research folder.

Gender

Gender refers to whether a customer is male or female and some companies will market their products to a specific gender. For instance, Direct Line Holidays have **stag** packages for men and **hen** packages for women.

Describe it

A **stag party** is usually arranged by the best man for his friend who is about to get married. Traditionally, only men are allowed to attend the stag party and it was a one-night event, but in recent years this has extended to weekend breaks or up to two-week holidays in some instances.

A **hen party** is arranged by friends of the bride-to-be and works in the same way as the stag party above, but in this case it is traditionally only women who attend.

Case study – Stag parties leave Prague

By Tom Chesshyre, The Times May 5 2007.

easyJet says that fewer stag groups are visiting major cities in Central and Eastern Europe as there are now so many chances to visit less well-known spots.

The airline has tended to focus on capitals in the east of Europe such as Prague, Budapest and Warsaw, which it believes are becoming more peaceful and less dominated by noisy groups now that Ryanair, Wizz Air, SkyEurope and others are offering budget seats to so many other destinations.

'Places like Prague used to be very popular with stags and hens. Now people are going there more for traditional culture,' said a spokeswoman.

'The stag and hen bubble had to burst. Now there are some going but we're getting more families and empty-nesters who have extra cash and ask themselves: "Why don't we spend it?"' The trend looks set to continue, according to Ryanair, which is expanding from 134 aircraft carrying 42.5 million passengers in 2006 to a projected 251 planes taking 84 million in 2012: 'Eastern Europe will be a continuing big growth area for us.'

Meanwhile Wizz Air, based in Budapest, plans to increase its fleet of Airbus A320s from nine to 53 by 2012 – receiving another two aircraft in the next fortnight.

Natasa Kazmer, head of corporate communications at Wizz Air, said: 'Yes, stag parties are a phenomenon, but Budapest, for example, is still a nice city to visit.'

In 2007 easyJet carried 37.2 million passengers on its fleet of 137 planes and it has 100 aircraft on order for 2010.

1 Why do you think hen and stag parties are now not visiting major cities?

2 How are airlines preparing for the increase of visitors to less-well known locations?

3 Can you think of any other products/services that are gender specific?

Social group

Traditionally, in the UK in the 1900s, the social grouping that customers belonged to was dictated by their class. There tended to be a roughly three-tiered class structure:

- Lower class – those who were on the lowest income bracket and had a limited education
- Middle class – those who were in a middle-income bracket but who were unlikely to have had a university education
- Upper class – those who were quite often members of the aristocracy. They usually had no need to work due to inheritance of wealth and often had a university education.

Social grouping is not as clearly defined now as it was in the 1900s. Certain pastimes would have been more popular with those whose earnings were high, whilst those with lower earnings could not have afforded them. For example, going to the opera was traditionally the pastime of the wealthy and well paid, whereas going to bingo was the pastime of those on a lower income. The same would be true for certain holiday locations that would appeal and be more affordable to the middle/upper classes. Today, whilst income will still be a major consideration in terms of taking part in leisure and tourism activities, each is more likely to attract a much more varied grouping of customers as social boundaries are less defined.

Not all customers want the same product or service

Lifestyle

The lifestyle of a customer is very important as lifestyle is probably the major factor in determining the type of leisure and tourism activities that the customer is likely to participate in. The type of work, the income, the social habits and the family situation is the mix that determines a customer's lifestyle. For example a single mature male will have different needs to those of a young family.

Talk about it

For the following groups (single male, single female, parents with young children, couple over 60), think how the following could determine the lifestyle of each group:

- Type of work
- Income
- Social habits
- Family situation.

Then think of two leisure or tourism activities that each group is most likely to take part in.

Ethnicity

Customers from different ethnic backgrounds may have different needs. For example in an area where there is a large Asian community, the local cinema is more likely to show a range of Asian films that would appeal to its target audience.

Areas with a large ethnic community are likely to have products and services that appeal to those specific target groups

Research it

Find out about the different ethnic communities that you have within your local area. Identify the different leisure activities that are promoted to each target group.

Geographical location

Organisations may choose to target their marketing campaign on certain geographical locations, such as specific neighbourhoods, **rural** areas, **urban** areas and regions. Making a geographical location into a target market can be the result of something specific happening in that area, such as the hosting of the Commonwealth Games in Manchester in 2002, which led to a huge marketing campaign and promotion of products and services in that area. Country fairs, agricultural shows and camping holidays take place in rural areas, which is often part of their appeal.

Describe it

A **rural** area is one that is based in the countryside and is made up of small towns and villages.

An **urban** area is one that is built up. Often it is where one town merges into the next, or it is a large city where the boundaries are hard to define due to development and expansion.

Take it further

How would a leisure organisation promote specific products to:

a) An urban area?

b) A rural area?

What differences would there be in the approaches to these different target markets?

Summary

- Leisure and tourism organisations promote their goods/services to different segments of the consumer market.
- These segments can be broken down into target marketing, which means promoting to specific areas.
- Target marketing can be broken down into the following areas: age, gender, social group, lifestyle, ethnicity, and geographical location.

Assessment tip

You will need to know about marketing segments and target marketing, and to be able to give examples of each. You will also need to understand the specific areas that make up target markets, such as age, gender, social groups, etc and to give examples of each.

What makes promotional materials effective?

The purpose of promotion is to inform customers about a particular product or service and to persuade them that a particular organisation's products and services are the best. Organisations will use a wide range of promotional techniques, which will be covered in section 2.3, pages 98–109.

When developing a promotional campaign, marketing departments will need to consider the following:

- The design of materials
- The information that needs to be provided in the campaign
- The suitability of materials for the market being targeted.

Design

For promotional materials to be effective, the design is extremely important as the message has to be very clear whilst at the same time providing minimal information so as not to 'overload' the customer. These are some of the considerations for an effective design:

- Has an appropriate **media** been used? (e.g. online, billboard, magazines, etc)
- Is the message clear?
- Is the information appropriate for the target market?
- Is the information presented in a way to catch the attention of the customer, for example through the use of colour, a company logo and/or company tag line?

Due to the developments in technology, TV/film clips are accessible on company websites, on DVD and through the Internet on sites such as You Tube. Film as a media is very powerful as a lot of subtle information can be given without overuse of dialogue or text. Often, important information is only provided at the end of the film, so the clip has to retain the customers' interest so that they continue watching until the very end.

Information provided

Promotional materials will only be effective if the right amount of information is included. It is important not to overcrowd materials with too much information. Essential information for promotional materials would consist of:

- Company logo
- Company contact details
- Description of the product/service on offer including features and benefits
- Cost of the product/service
- How to obtain the product/service
- Where to find more details on the product/service
- How long the product/service is available for.

Describe it

Media refers to the materials and techniques used for promotion. In advertising, examples of media are TV, radio, web pages, brochures, leaflets, magazine and newspaper advertising, etc.

Hotlink

Airlines, like British Airways, create advertising for TV and film. A link to one of their adverts has been made available at www.heinemann.co.uk/hotlinks – just enter the express code 4110P.

Take it further

Using the Internet or TV, find more examples of advertising used for TV or film. For each consider the following:

- Is the message about the product/service clear?
- What is the target market for the product/service?
- Is there a company logo and tag line?
- What other media could be used to promote the product?

Leisure and tourism organisations have to make sure they provide accurate information on their promotional materials, as there are legal implications if the information is incorrect. For example, if a national hotel chain is promoting reduced room rates for a period of time, and one hotel decides to cut short the promotion and put the prices up two weeks ahead of schedule, then a customer can complain under the Consumer Protection Act 1987. Similarly, the Trade Descriptions Act of 1968 is there to protect customers from those organisations who make misleading statements about goods or services either knowingly or recklessly.

Take it further

Using the Internet, search for a good definition/summary of the following:

- The Consumer Protection Act 1987
- The Trade Descriptions Act of 1968.

Copies of this information can be included in your research folder.

Suitability for target market

When planning the type of promotional materials that need to be produced for a campaign, it is important to consider the target market at which your products and services are aimed. For example, the over 50s target market would probably not respond very well if the web pages for SAGA or LaterLife holidays pumped out loud music and had brightly coloured flashing images popping up on the screen, whereas this would probably appeal to those interested in 18-30s type holidays.

When an organisation is preparing to launch a promotional campaign, it will allocate a **budget** to cover the related costs. These budgets can be quite small for smaller organisations, but equally can run into hundreds of thousands of pounds for larger organisations, who may run a promotional campaign that involves TV and radio advertising, national newspaper coverage, national billboard posters, etc.

It is therefore very important that an organisation has carried out **market research** prior to the campaign to find out which promotional techniques work best for the target market on which the campaign is focussed.

Take it further

Using the Internet, access two or three financial reports for leisure or tourism organisations. Find out how much has been spent on marketing campaigns/ promotions over the last year. Do your findings surprise you?

Summary

- Effective promotional materials need to be well-designed, provide the right information, and be suitable for their target market.
- Market research is used to find out what promotions work best for target markets.

Remember it

Consumer Protection Act 1987 – this legislation is there to protect customers, usually in terms of the sale of faulty goods. Because many of the sales that take place in leisure and tourism are intangible (i.e. you can't touch or pick something up), there is a clause in this act to protect customers when organisations give misleading information, such as false price reductions.

Describe it

Budget – is a specific amount of money allocated to a particular task, etc.

Market research is the collection and analysis of information by an organisation in order to make decisions about its products and services.

Research it

Using a range of media, collect different promotional materials for a product/service within the leisure and tourism industry. Are the same types of information included on each piece of promotional material? Identify which of the promotional materials you find most effective and least effective. Give reasons for your choices.

Assessment tips

You will need to know what makes promotions effective. You will need to be able to explain the importance of good design, providing the right information, suitability of the promotional material for the target market and be able to give examples of each.

Designing effective promotional materials

We have looked at the importance of design and some of the considerations that make promotional materials effective, such as the type of information provided and suitability of a promotion for a target market. We are now going to look closer at how to design effective promotional materials using a formula called AIDA.

AIDA stands for:

- Attention
- Interest
- Desire
- Action.

When trying to sell and market products and services, organisations often use this formula.

Take it further

Look through some magazines at the types of advertising that appears there. How does each organisation use the headline to grab your attention? What do they do to keep you interested in their product or service? Make a list of the words and techniques used.

Attention

The first thing you need to do is grab your customers' attention with a headline. In the previous section we looked at how certain media, such as film, allows you to be subtle and sometimes only provides the important information right at the very end of the advert. However, if you are advertising in magazines, newspapers, on the web etc, the headline is extremely important. It must be clear and easy to read, and should be about your product and the needs of the customer rather than the name of the company.

For example, which of the following headlines do you think would grab the customer's attention more?

Johnsons

The Holiday Company

Great value holidays for your family!

Great value holidays for your family!

Johnsons

The Holiday Company

Interest

Once you have the customers' attention, you need them to be interested in your product/service. To do this you might supply them with some more information or a key fact.

Desire

Being interested is good, but you need the customer to really want (desire) your product/service. Often, images on promotional material help to increase desire. The customer may associate the image with themselves, so for instance if they see a happy couple on a sunny beach, they may 'desire' to be in that warm place too.

Action

If you have been successful with your formula so far, you now need to make sure that the customer knows what action to take in order to buy your product or service. In other words, you need to tell them where to find more information, or how to buy your product/service.

Benefits

Another key to getting your customers interest is by letting them know how your product/service is going to benefit them. Benefits would include products/services being cheaper, faster, better, etc. For instance an airline like British Airways might want to advertise the benefits of its fast service from London to New York by implying it is so trouble free that a customer can go to sleep in London and simply wake up in New York.

Competition

Don't follow the competition. In other words, try to make your promotional material different to that of your competitors, otherwise the customer will think that what you have to offer is just the same, and you need them to think that your products and services are better.

Talk about it

In groups, look at some different magazine advertisements. Discuss whether you 'desire' any of the products/services they are advertising and give your reasons.

Take it further

Gather a range of promotional materials covering different leisure and tourism organisations. Look at how the AIDA formula has been applied by each organisation. How effective do you think each of the promotional materials are?

Apply it

Using the AIDA formula for designing effective promotional materials, create your own billboard advertisement for a leisure and tourism organisation of your choice. Your advert will need to advertise the latest products and services available. Don't forget to mention the benefits of your product/service. And do some research into the competition!

Assessment tips

You will need to know about the key factors that help to make promotional materials effective. You will need to be able to apply this knowledge when designing your own promotional material for a leisure or tourism organisation.

Summary

- AIDA is a formula used when designing promotional materials.
- AIDA stands for attention, interest, desire, action.
- Effective promotional materials also need to show customers the benefits of the product/service.
- Leisure and tourism organisations need to be aware of their competitors so that the promotional material they produce shows that they are different.

An example of how not to advertise your business!

2.3 Promotional Techniques and Materials in Leisure and Tourism

Main promotional techniques used by leisure and tourism organisations

Promotional techniques are the different ways that organisations can market their products and services, whilst promotional materials are the actual materials used for a promotion. In this section, we are going to look at how leisure and tourism organisations use a wide range of promotional techniques to advertise their products and services. These techniques include:

- Advertising
- Direct marketing
- Public relations (PR)
- Displays
- Sponsorship
- Demonstrations
- Sales promotions.

Advertising

Advertising can be described as providing *information* about an organisation's products and services and then using *persuasion* in order to attract the customer to purchase from it.

Information

The information provided to the customer is designed to make them more aware of what is on offer and will assist them in making decisions on whether to buy or not.

Persuasion

Simply providing the information is not enough to encourage most people to buy/use a product/service as most consumers will want to know what benefits they are going to get from buying/using a particular product. Persuasion needs to be used in advertising, often in the form of a message that can range from being humorous, sophisticated, sexy or cheeky.

The image on the front of this brochure attempts to persuade the customer that buying one of these holidays will be a romantic thing to do

Advertising can appear in newspapers, magazines, on TV or radio, websites, pop-ups, DVDs, etc. It can be very expensive and needs to be planned and targeted very carefully to be sure that any sales generated from the advertisements will provide enough money to pay for the advertising costs and provide the company with a profit.

Describe it

Mailshot is the term used for a large mailing of promotional materials to specific individuals.

Direct marketing

Direct marketing is when an organisation produces promotional materials that are distributed directly to customers' homes. Examples of direct marketing include a leaflet that has been inserted into a magazine or newspaper, or a **mailshot** that has been sent directly to a customer's home. This type of promotional material is quite often referred to as 'junk mail' and is a very effective form of promotion.

Direct marketing often relies on access to or the purchase of consumer databases that include personal information such as name, address, age group, and the types of products and/or services that customers have bought previously.

An example of a mailshot

Talk about it

In groups, discuss why direct marketing is an effective form of promotion. Why do you think it is also referred to as 'junk mail'?

Case study – Direct marketing

Mr and Mrs Fleming were looking for a self-catering cottage for a week's holiday and rang six organisations they found through searching the Internet. During each phone call, the Flemings were asked their full name, address, telephone number and email address, which they gave. Mr and Mrs Fleming eventually found the cottage in the right location with all of the facilities they required and for the price that was right for them. Over the next three months, Mr and Mrs Fleming received brochures, letters and emails from all of the organisations they had contacted despite not having booked a holiday with five of them.

1. **Why do you think the organisations sent direct mail to the Flemings?**
2. **What advantages do you think there is in doing this?**
3. **Are there any disadvantages?**

Telemarketing (phone calls) is another form of direct marketing. This is when organisations telephone people at home to either sell them a product/service, or to give them the latest information on their organisation.

Direct-response advertising is carried out through the use of materials such as free scratch cards, with winning cardholders being required to ring a telephone number in order to claim their gift. This form of advertising is very popular with holiday companies, which might offer holiday vouchers as prizes encouraging 'winners' to spend more money on a holiday.

Talk about it

Why are scratch cards a form of direct response advertising? What are the advantages and disadvantages of this promotional technique?

Public relations (PR)

Larger leisure and tourism organisations will have their own **public relations team**, whereas smaller organisations with a limited marketing budget may pay for an external public relations organisation to work on their behalf. Public relations activities tend to be less costly

Describe it

A **public relations team** is a team of people that deal directly with the public and with anything that relates directly to the public. Their main job is to ensure that there is a good relationship between the organisation and the general public.

than most other forms of promotion and the activities that the public relations team would engage in are:

- Organising or taking part in events, such as conferences, exhibitions and trade fairs, as well as organising celebrity openings or visits
- Writing company newsletters for employees, shareholders and customers
- Writing press releases, for example to announce a new product or service
- Having direct contact with representatives from the media, for example with newspaper and/or TV journalists.

The main objective of any public relations team is to show the organisation they are representing in a positive way. They achieve this by publicising what the organisation has to offer to customers.

Hotlink

Sending out a press release is a good PR tool for publicising what a company has to offer. A link to an example of a press release by the travel company Thomas Cook has been made available at www.heinemann.co.uk/hotlinks – just enter the express code 4110P.

Use the Internet to find some more examples of company press releases.

Research it

PR teams may also work with celebrities who will endorse an organisations product or service. Make a list of leisure and tourism organisations that are endorsed by celebrities.

Displays

Another promotional technique used by leisure and tourism organisations is window displays. Facilities like leisure centres and shops use window displays to advertise what goods/services they have available, so that people visiting or passing can see them. Travel agencies are well known for their window displays, which advertise the latest available deals and encourage customers to enter the shop to find out more. Once inside they will be faced with further displays of brochures covering a wide range of holidays. Many companies produce point-of-sale material, which could be mobiles, stickers, book stands, etc. Point-of-sale materials help to make displays more interesting and are another promotional opportunity for an organisation as they often display the company logo or colours.

Describe it

Trade fairs are exhibitions and shows which focus on a particular industry.

Point-of-sale materials are additional advertising materials such as leaflets.

Trade fairs and exhibitions are good places for organisations to have displays to promote their products/services. These displays may be simple brochure and poster/leaflet displays, or may be more elaborate and include 'hands-on' activities, for example a ski simulator or an interactive touch screen.

Research it

Visit your local leisure facilities or travel agencies and see what **point-of-sale materials** they are using in the displays for their products/services.

Travel agencies often use their window displays for promotion

Sponsorship

Quite often, a company may decide to sponsor an event or product as a promotional technique to promote their own product/service. For instance, a company may make a financial contribution to a particular sport or an event in return for their logo and tag line being included in any literature or advertising for that sport or event. For instance, United Emirates sponsor Arsenal Football club, so their logo appears on the players' kit, on any promotional literature, and even the stadium is named after them! Many TV programmes, such as soaps and reality shows, now have company sponsorship. This is a good promotional technique for a company as it means that adverts containing the company logo and details often appear before, after and in the breaks.

Demonstrations

Leisure and tourism organisations may demonstrate their products/services so that customers can see more clearly what is on offer. Some leisure facilities may have a demonstration of sports coaching in order to promote the service they provide. Many organisations, particularly those who offer accommodation now provide **virtual tours**, so that a customer knows what to expect when they arrive at their destination.

Sales promotions

Because the leisure and tourism industry is so competitive, organisations have to work very hard to attract new customers to their products and services. They do this by trying to persuade non-customers to try their products, usually by offering an incentive. There are a variety of sales promotions that organisations might use such as:

- Offering free gifts or discounts with certain products
- Giving away free samples of products – an example of this is a BOGOF (Buy one, get one free) offer
- Competitions that can only be entered after you have bought the product/service
- 'Buy now – pay later' schemes (so customers don't have to have the money to pay for their goods immediately)
- Celebrity endorsement – for example having a famous sports person at the opening of a new health and fitness club.

Summary

The main promotional techniques used by leisure and tourism organisations are: advertising, direct marketing, public relations (PR), displays, sponsorship, demonstrations, and sales promotions.

Talk about it

In groups, make a list of some of the TV programmes that are sponsored. Why do you think companies have chosen to sponsor those particular programmes?

Describe it

A **virtual tour** is when an organisation has filmed the facilities they have available and this footage is then available through their website or a DVD.

Apply it

Using the Internet, find examples of virtual tours for the following leisure and tourism organisations:

- Hotel chains
- Health & fitness centres
- Tour operators (e.g. for package holidays and cruises).

Assessment tip

You will need to know the main promotion techniques used by leisure and tourism organisations and be able to provide an example of each.

Promotional materials used by leisure and tourism organisations

Promotional materials are the actual materials leisure and tourism organisations design and use to promote their goods and services. Promotional materials include:

- Leaflets/brochures
- Advertisements
- Websites/pop-ups
- Promotional DVDs
- Merchandising
- Direct mailshots
- Press releases
- Special offers.

Hotlink

Have a look at the leaflet created by Staffordshire Moorlands Council advising on places to stay in the Peak District. A link has been made available at www.heinemann.co.uk/hotlinks – just enter the express code 4110P.

1 What useful information does the leaflet contain? Is it easy to use?

2 In groups, discuss whether you think this is a successful form of promotion.

Leaflets/brochures

Leisure and tourism organisations will use leaflets and brochures as a major form of promotional material in order to attract customers to their products/services. For instance, when taking a journey on any motorway or major road network, if you stop at a service station for refreshments you will find a stand with a wide variety of leaflets advertising the many visitor attractions and leisure activities on offer in that locality and region.

The most widely known brochures within the leisure and tourism industry are those advertising package holidays. However, other organisations such as Visit Britain will provide brochures which advertise the leisure and tourism activities and facilities available within a particular region.

Remember it

Money spent on UK television adverts fell in 2008 for the first time since 2001, according to new research. TV advertising spend declined 4.7% from 2005 levels to £4.59 billion, but still accounted for the second-largest advertising medium after the press.

Advertisements

TV

Television is an extremely expensive but equally successful form of advertising as it manages to reach a mass audience. Also, as some TV channels such as ITV are regionalised, it means that advertising can be targeted to a specific region and audience. For example, if Chester Zoo wanted to promote a particular campaign, they might advertise on Granada Television to encourage people from the local area to visit.

Radio

In recent years there has been an increase in the number of independent radio stations each with their own target market. For these radio stations to be able to sustain their business, they rely heavily on the money they earn from allowing organisations to advertise on air.

For example, Classic FM offers regular competitions with holiday prizes of a cultural nature. A particular travel company would provide the holiday in return for advertising space on the radio. If the holiday was for a cruise of the Norwegian Fjords, the radio station may link the promotion by playing music by Grieg, a Norwegian composer.

Billboards

Billboards are very large advertising displays that are found strategically placed by the side of the road and/or on the sides of buildings. Traditional billboards showed one advertisement for a number of months, however more modern billboards consist of vertical strips which when static will display an advert. After a few seconds each strip will turn to display a different advert altogether. Rather than just being located on sides of roads/building, these new billboards can be found on the sides of bus shelters, free standing on pavements, or on local transport, such as the London Underground.

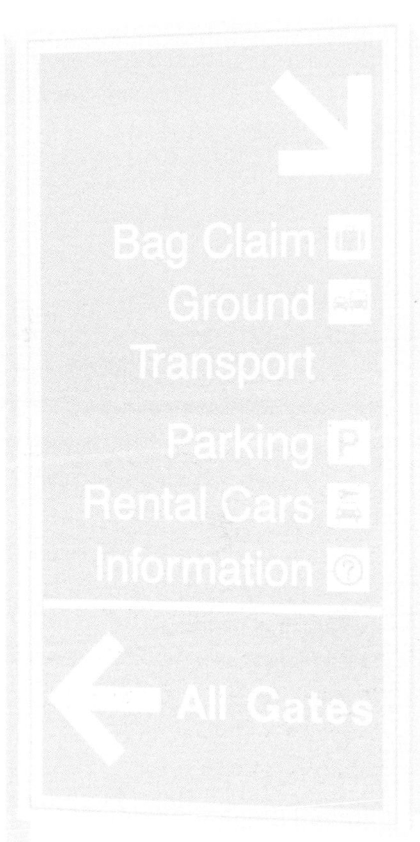

Billboards are very large advertising displays

Magazine/newspaper

There are two types of magazine:

- Consumer magazines
- Business/professional journals.

Consumer magazines are frequently used to advertise the products and services of leisure and tourism organisations. There are a large number of consumer magazines in the UK, covering a very broad range of interests, so organisations can target the market they need through the most appropriate magazine. Business/professional journals are a perfect way to target key markets.

There are three types of newspaper:

- National press
- Local press.
- Regional press

Statistics show that over 60% of the adult population in the UK read a daily newspaper, which makes newspapers a very effective promotional aid. Due to the localised and/or regionalised focus of some newspapers, organisations are able to target specific markets. Newspapers can be very expensive for advertising, with full-page advertisements in national newspapers costing thousands of pounds, whereas local papers will cost much less.

Remember it

In 2007, over 28,817,000 'red top' newspapers were sold. Examples of 'red top' newspapers are the *Sun*, *The People*, and the *News of the World*. (Source: The *Guardian*, 6 December 2007)

Research it

Look through a local newspaper and make a list of the leisure and tourism organisations that are advertising in it. Do you think this is good promotional material for these organisations?

Hotlink

The Dealchecker website is for customers to find and compare prices of holidays. A link to the website has been made available at www.heinemann.co.uk/hotlinks – just enter the express code 4110P.

1 Which holiday company have paid the site to include their banner to advertise their holidays?

2 Discuss whether you think this is a successful form of promotion.

Research it

How many homes in the UK have access to the Internet? How important does this make websites/pop-ups as a promotional material?

Websites/pop-ups

Most leisure and tourism organisations have a website. It is important for organisations to encourage people to visit their website to find out about their products and services. Search engines on the Internet, such as Google or Ask Jeeves, are a method for promoting products and services. For example if you were to carry out a Google search on holidays to the Costa Brava in Spain, you will get about 376,000 'hits'. Hits are the number of websites/links that come up as a result of a search for a particular product/service.

Search engines often display a list of 'sponsored links' on the right of the screen. Sponsored links have been paid for by an organisation in order to bring their website to the immediate attention of the viewer.

Display advertising on the Internet includes pop-ups and banner advertising. A pop-up is an advert that appears in a separate window on top of another window/site that is already open.

Banners usually appear across the top of the screen or down the side of the screen and will have been paid for by a particular organisation to promote their goods or services.

Promotional DVDs

Promotional DVDs are created so that customers can see more clearly what it is they are buying. For example, hotels, cruise ships and some tour operators will provide DVDs to show what is available.

Case study – P&O DVD give-away

A DVD introducing cruise holidays was incorporated in P&O Cruises' first edition 2007 brochure. The half-hour DVD was designed as a sales aid for agents to help attract customers who have not considered cruising as a holiday option, according to the commercial director Nigel Esdale.

The 'Introduction to P&O Cruises' DVD explores the company's five ships as well as destinations visited.

Esdale said: 'P&O Cruises is committed to working with its travel agent partners to attract and convert newcomers to cruising, and this introductory DVD is one way we are doing this. We also offer a number of taster cruises, two-night party cruises, four-night city breaks and seven-night short holidays. These options provide an excellent entry point for agents to tempt customers to test the water, and are featured in a dedicated section of the brochure.

It is important people understand the different experiences we offer across the fleet. This DVD is a visually inspiring tool to help agents and customers identify the right cruise holiday for their needs, whether they are groups of friends, young couples, families or seasoned cruisers.

The brochure includes 2008 spring Caribbean itineraries on board *Arcadia* and *Oceana*, as well as itineraries for all ships in the fleet from April to December next year.'

1 What other promotional techniques are P&O using in this case study?

Research it

Use the Internet to find UK football clubs and see what merchandising is available. How much money do you think an organisation can make from this type of promotional material?

Merchandising

Another way for an organisation to promotes itself and its products and services is to provide products that advertise the company. For example, most visitor attractions will have gift shops attached, where many of the products will display the company logo and name. Products would include items of clothing, cups, pens, bags and so on.

Direct mailshots

Direct mailshots are leaflets that are sent out direct to customers' homes which advertise the latest offers. Mailshots can either be sent through the post using personal data obtained by a consumer database organisation, or will be added as inserts into a daily paper or magazine. An example of a mailshot would be a theme park sending out a mailshot just before the half-term holidays to encourage families to book tickets.

Press releases

A press release is usually issued just before a new product or service is about to be launched. For instance, prior to a new cruise destination being launched or a ride at a theme park being opened, the organisation will prepare customers and generate a level of excitement in the run up to the opening, which will in turn boost ticket sales.

Case study – Alton Towers press release

Where else can you come face to face with sharks, swashbuckle your way through Mutiny Bay and get your first driving licence, all in one day? With over two-thirds of rides and attractions available for children under ten, Alton Towers Resort is proud to announce the opening of two brand new attractions that are guaranteed to entertain families for hours on end!

Alton Towers Resort opens its gates for the new season on March 28th to welcome the brand new Sharkbait Reef by SEA LIFE! Also in Mutiny Bay, experience the brand new pirate-themed show: The Pirate of Sharkbait Reef show. Watch the swashbuckling adventure of an innocent heroine called Emily, who is held hostage by an evil pirate! Will loveable deck-washer Billy come to her rescue? Or will Emily become Shark Bait?

Apply it

A theme park is about to open a new and exciting ride. Not for the faint-hearted, this ride is faster than any other in the country. The ride involves being shot up into the air one minute and then disappearing into subterranean depths the next.

1 **Practise writing a press release similar to the one in the Alton Towers case study above. The press release should encourage customers to book tickets either for the opening or to visit the park very soon after the opening.**

Assessment tip

You will need to understand the range of promotional materials that leisure and tourism organisations use, and be able to provide an example for each.

Special offers

Special offers are an effective way of attracting customers to an organisation's products and services. For instance, travel agencies may advertise late availability or special offers in the last week or so before the departure date. Visitor attractions and other leisure facilities will advertise special offers to encourage customers to visit during off-peak periods i.e. out of school holidays.

Summary

Leisure and tourism organisations use the following promotional materials to promote their products/services: leaflets/brochures, advertisements, websites/pop-ups, promotional DVDs, merchandising, direct mailshots, press releases, special offers.

Advantages and disadvantages of promotional techniques and materials

Now that we have looked at the range of promotional techniques and materials that leisure and tourism organisations use, we are now going to explore some of the advantages and disadvantages of these techniques and materials.

Advertising

Advantages

Advertising can be targeted to reach a specific market. It can also reach a wide market through various materials such as leaflets, brochures, TV and billboards.

Disadvantages

Advertising can be expensive. Smaller organisations may not have the budgets for many types of advertising campaigns. Also advertising needs to be planned and targeted to reach the right audience, so time needs to be taken when planning a campaign.

Direct marketing

Advantages

Promotional material goes straight to a potential customer's home, i.e. by mailshot, so direct marketing can reach a wide market. Telesales also mean that organisations can speak to potential customers directly by telephone.

Disadvantages

Customer details are purchased through consumer databases, which are expensive and often inaccurate. Many people dislike being called at home and will be put off by this approach.

Talk about it

What impact do promotional techniques such as direct marketing have on the environment?

Public relations (PR)

Advantages

PR can be an inexpensive form of promotion and can target specific markets. It is also important for organisations to present themselves in a positive way to encourage customers to use their products/services.

Disadvantages

Often the target market can be too broad for PR to deal with. Also, any negative PR will have a bad effect on an organisation and may discourage consumers from using their product/service in future.

Displays

Advantages

Displays can be an inexpensive promotional technique and can target a specific market.

Disadvantages

One disadvantage is that displays are limited, i.e. they are not often available to a wider market. For instance, a display in a travel shop or leisure facility will only be seen by people passing the shop or using the facility already, which does not increase the potential of new customers.

Sponsorship

Advantages

The advantages of this promotional technique are that sponsorship can reach a wide market, especially if an organisation sponsors a popular TV programme or event, for instance. Sponsorship can also be tailored to reach a specific market, such as sponsoring merchandise that will be popular to those customers that support a particular sports team.

Disadvantages

Disadvantages of sponsorship are that when programmes, celebrities, teams and events are no longer popular, it can have a negative effect on the organisation that is offering the sponsorship as potential customers will be focussed elsewhere.

Sponsorship can raise an organisation's profile

Demonstrations

Advantages

Some demonstrations can be an inexpensive promotional technique, particularly if an organisation uses staff to demonstrate what is on offer, i.e. staff from a leisure centre demonstrating new equipment. Demonstrations can also target a specific audience.

Disadvantages

One disadvantage of demonstrations is that they can be expensive, for instance, videos and DVDs are expensive to produce and have to be good quality to show the product/service off to its full advantage or people may be put off buying/using it. For instance, if a virtual tour of a hotel shows it to be dated or unclean, customers would be put off visiting.

Sales promotions

Advantages

Incentives/special offers can be targeted to specific markets and can reach a wide audience.

Disadvantages

One disadvantage of sales promotions is that they can be expensive for the organisations that are offering the free gift or BOGOF offer. 'Buy now, pay later' schemes have also run into difficulties in times like an economic recession as customers have received their goods and then find they are unable to pay for them. At the end of the day, organisations need to make money.

Summary

- Advantages of some promotional techniques and materials may include price (i.e. inexpensive as a method of promotion), being able to reach a specific target market, and also reaching a wide market.
- Disadvantages of some promotional techniques and materials can be expense, the fact that they only reach a limited market or a target market that is too broad.

Talk about it

Make a list of organisations that sponsor sporting events. How important is it that these events are successful for the organisation that is sponsoring them?

Apply it

Look at the list of possible sales promotions that organisations can use on page 101. Think of disadvantages and advantages for each sales promotion and give reasons for your answers.

Assessment tips

You will need to be aware of the different types of promotional techniques and materials, and the advantages and disadvantages of each. You will need to be able to provide examples of advantages and disadvantages for the different promotional techniques and the materials used by leisure and tourism organisations.

Factors that affect the choice of promotional techniques and materials used

Due to the costs involved in promoting an organisation's products and services, organisations have to be sure that they are using the most effective promotional techniques and in order to make the necessary decisions, they need to weigh up both the advantages and disadvantages of using certain methods (see pages 106–107), and also take into account other factors that will affect the choice of promotional techniques and materials.

These factors can include:

- Placement
- Cost/budget
- Target markets.

Placement

When planning a promotional campaign, the following needs to be considered:

- How?
- When?
- Where?

How refers to the promotional techniques to be used, i.e. advertising, sponsorship, sales promotion, etc.

When refers to the timing of a promotion. An organisation needs to assess if the customer is ready to consider purchasing its product/service. For example, tour operators will advertise summer packages in the winter before the packages are available, or health clubs often have special offers on membership after Christmas, when people feel they need to do some exercise after the Christmas break.

Where refers to the place that the advertisement/promotion is to appear/take place. Package holidays are usually advertised in brochures in travel agencies, visitor attractions are advertised in tourist information centres, libraries, leisure facilities and so on. The place needs to be appropriate for the target audience.

Talk about it

Why do you think holiday companies advertise summer packages in the winter? Can you think of any other leisure and tourism organisations that may promote their products/services out-of-seasons?

Apply it

Look at the following products/services and decide in groups where would be the best place to advertise to reach the target audience:

- Cheap flights to Spain
- Pony-trekking holiday for all the family
- A new exercise machine that helps you lose weight
- A new adventure theme park ride.

Cost/budget

The amount of money to spend on promotional activities will largely depend on the size of the organisation. Large organisations such as Thomas Cook, British Airways, and Holiday Inn Hotels and Resorts, will tend to have large budgets which will enable them to use the more expensive forms of promotional techniques, whereas small local organisations such as Stockley Farm in Cheshire or the Fitness Factory in Taunton, will be much more restricted.

Target markets

Organisations will need to know the types of media most popular with the target market they are trying to attract, otherwise they will not be making the most cost-effective use of their budget and may end up losing money as they have failed to attract enough customers to cover the costs of the promotional campaign.

An example of not promoting to the right target market would be to advertise 18-30-type holidays on a radio station such Radio 4, as this particular radio station attracts the more mature listener.

Talk about it

In groups, make a list of promotional techniques and then put them in order, with the most expensive first and least expensive last. Now imagine you are a leisure or tourism organisation with a limited budget to promote a new product/service. Which three promotional techniques from your list would you consider as the most important and why?

Take it further

As a group, discuss recent advertisements for holidays that you have seen either on the TV or in the newspaper.

Discuss the following:

- Timing
- Placement – the how, when and where
- Cost/budget – how much you think each type of advert might cost?
- Who do you think the advert is aimed at? (i.e. who is the target market?)

Assessment tips

You will need to be aware of the different factors that affect the choice of promotional techniques and materials used by leisure and tourism organisations. You will need to be able to give examples for each factor.

Summary

- Factors that affect the choice of the promotional technique or material used by leisure and tourism organisations include: placement, cost/budget and target markets.
- Placement means the 'how, when and where' of the promotional campaign.

2.4 Operations Used in Leisure and Tourism Organisations

In this section we will look at the impact of new technologies on the operations used by leisure and tourism organisations. But first, we will explore how leisure and tourism organisations have changed due to advances in technology and the use of up-to-date business systems.

Impacts of changes on operations include:

- Overseas call centres and administration
- Home working
- Online reservation systems
- Online check-in
- E-brochures/virtual tours.

Impacts of changes on operations

Over the years, consumers have developed the need to invest more in their leisure and holiday time. For example, people are earning more money, which means that overseas holidays are more affordable, and increased stress from working long hours means that people are keen to spend more on activities that help them to relax. Leisure and tourism organisations have had to adapt and improve in order to meet customers' needs.

New and developing technology impacts on the leisure and tourism business on a daily basis and it is important for organisations to react quickly, as failure to respond could have drastic consequences for the organisation. For example, an organisation that does not have a website will lose out to their competitors who do.

Developments in technology have also affected advertising and the way adverts are designed. Previously a single artist would draw the advert, whereas now all the design is done on computer, and photographs and illustrations can be included.

Due to the improvements in technology and the introduction of more flexible ways of working, there have been many changes in the operations of leisure and tourism organisations.

The Internet has had a major impact on the structure of the leisure and tourism industries, as people have increased access to the Internet through home computers. Organisations are now able to advertise their products and services on the web and customers can also purchase products/services online. This development has had the greatest impact on travel agencies as you will see from the case study below.

Research it

Find some examples of adverts from the 1920s–1950s for leisure and tourism organisations. What differences can you see between these and modern adverts?

Case study – Changing times

Back in the early 1980s, Barbara took a job working for Pendle Travel, a small family run business consisting of a number of travel agencies around the Pendle area in Lancashire. Barbara worked for a couple of years in the shop, but then was asked to move to the offices above the shop to work in the small and newly formed tour operators known as Pendle Airtours. Barbara got involved in the writing and issuing of flight tickets to customers, booking holidays for customers over the telephone by completing paper forms, booking customers' hotel rooms overseas, and their flights from airports around the country. The most modern forms of communication at this time were the telephone, fax and the telex machine. Invoices were still sent out to customers after being typed on an electric typewriter by the typist. Over the years, there were many changes to the organisation – it grew to become one of the major tour operators in the UK – Airtours Holidays (which was more recently known as MyTravel). In terms of the operations, tasks were divided between specific departments and much of the work became computerised. For example tickets were all generated by computer, and holiday bookings were handled by the computerised reservations system.

1 **What changes in operations can you identify in this case study? Make a list.**

Case study – The effect of the Internet on operations

MyTravel chief executive Peter McHugh reportedly said customers were increasingly booking holidays online and refused to rule out further closures among the 500 outlets that remain. The move follows German-owned Tui UK's recent closure of 100 Lunn Poly shops and will save £10 million a year.

'Ten years ago, the vast majority of us booked a holiday by simply going into our local high street travel agent and choosing a destination, which was booked there and then,' said Peter Rothwell, managing director of Thomson. 'Today we are a nation of self-made travel agents who derive great pleasure from seeking out cheap deals, hand-picking destinations that match our individual tastes and planning every detail of our trip, from accommodation to flights to arranging local transport.'

1 **In groups, discuss how becoming a 'nation of self-made travel agents' will affect how travel agencies operate.**

Overseas call centres and administration

Many leisure and tourism organisations use call centres based overseas, such as those in India. The reason for this move is the low cost of employing staff, the low cost of office space and the fact that communications technology is now extremely effective. With improvements in communication technology, a call made to India from the UK will sound as clear as if the caller and receiver were both within the UK. Many organisations are also moving their administration operations overseas due to the improvements in Internet connections and email. Administration can now be done from anywhere.

However, many customers do not like using overseas call centres as quite often they feel that the operative they are speaking to does not have enough knowledge, so many organisations are now moving their call centres back to the UK.

Overseas call centres are cheaper to run, but many customers do not like them

Case study – Coming home

The North's fastest-growing tour operator, Jet2holidays.com, has announced that its overseas call centre, previously located in Gurgaon, Delhi, has returned to Yorkshire creating 30 new jobs. Katriona White, Call Centre Sales Manager, said: 'We have been successfully running the overseas call centre for more than a year now, but feedback from our customers showed that they wanted an enhanced service where they can book a holiday with people who have first-hand experience of our destinations.'

'Jet2.com has a strong established relationship with its outsourced call centre provider in Delhi and is actually in the process of extending that particular contract. However, there are significant differences between booking or amending a flight and booking a Jet2holiday for customers.'

1 **Make a list of the advantages and disadvantages of a leisure or tourism organisation using a call centre overseas.**

Home working

Advances in technology have made it possible for people to carry out work from home rather than in an office. This reduces costs for an organisation as they no longer have to pay for office space and it may be more convenient for staff to work from home. The increased use of personal computers (PCs) with Internet access, phones, scanners and fax machines means that work that can be carried out at home. Travel Counsellors is an example of a home-based travel agency that employs staff who work from home booking travel packages for customers using the Internet.

Hotlink

Adventure Engine is an example of a reservations systems specialist company. A link to their website has been made available at www.heinemann.co.uk/hotlinks – just enter the express code 4110P. You can watch some demonstration video clips on how the online reservation system works. What advantages are there to using this type of system?

Home working is now an option in many leisure and travel jobs

Talk about it

In groups, discuss the advantages an online reservation system and online check-in have for the customer.

Online reservation systems

Internet technology enables customers to book their leisure and travel requirements (e.g. entry tickets to an attraction or flights/travel tickets) online, with the online reservation system being directly linked to the organisation's central reservation system (CRS). For small tour operators and travel agencies that cannot afford their own CRS, a 'host' reservation system can be used. This means that the company pays for a reservations systems specialist company to hold, update and maintain their information for them.

Online check-in

Online check-in is a facility whereby a customer can go on to the website of the organisation with which they are travelling and check themselves in for a flight or journey. This would normally have to have been done in person at the airport/ferry terminal, etc. Customers are also able to request specific seats using the online check-in. Online check-in also means that customers will spend less time queuing at the airport/ferry terminal prior to travelling.

E-brochures/virtual tours

Another impact of changes in how leisure and tourism organisations operate is the replacement of printed brochures with e-brochures and virtual tours. An e-brochure is where you access a holiday company's website and through browsing the different holidays on offer, you can save the information you are interested in as an e-brochure which can be sent to you by email. A virtual tour means that you can see your accommodation, mode of transport, facilities at a leisure centre, etc, either online or on a DVD before you even get there. For instance, some travel companies provide virtual tours through their websites of the accommodation available at some resorts. This can allow the viewer to see 360° angles of a property/location.

Hotlink

The Titan HiTours website allows you to create e-brochures. You can also watch a video itinerary of a wide range of holiday destinations. A link to their website has been made available at www.heinemann.co.uk/hotlinks – just enter the express code 4110P. Have a go at creating your own e-brochure. You should be able to see it straight away on your screen rather than have to wait for an email.

Talk about it

Why might an e-brochure have a positive impact on the environment? How would a virtual tour on a leisure or tourism website help the following people:

- A family with young children
- People with limited mobility
- Someone who has never travelled overseas before.

Assessment tips

You will need to know how the operations within leisure and tourism organisations have changed as a result of advances in technology and the use of up-to-date business systems. You will need to give examples to support these changes.

Summary

- The impact of advances in technology and the use of up-to-date business systems have affected how leisure and tourism organisations operate.
- Examples of how leisure and tourism organisations have changed include: overseas call centres and administration, home working, online reservation systems, online check-in and e-brochures/virtual tours.

Impacts of new technology on organisations

Leisure and tourism organisations have made use of new technology to increase and improve the products and services they offer to the customer. However new technology can have an economic impact on organisations affecting profits and costs. It can also have an impact on employment, leading to changes in the following:

- Employee numbers
- Location of staff
- Staff training.

Economic impacts

Technology can have both a negative and a positive impact on an organisation, therefore it is important that very careful consideration is given as to the benefits of introducing new technology to an organisation.

Profits

Every organisation needs to make money, but if they are going to remain in business and be a serious competitor, they have to make a profit in order for them to develop more and better products and services. If a company spends too much money investing in new technology, this could affect an organisation economically.

Costs

Technology is expensive and organisations need to be confident that any new technology they purchase will increase sales and so cover the cost of the technology, as well as make profit for the company. Some organisations will use technologies developed, managed and owned by other companies which cost less. Adventure Engine is a specialist reservation systems company who offer such a service.

Employment impacts

Change in employee numbers

Advances in technology have led to a reduction in the number of staff required to do certain tasks within the leisure and tourism industries. For example, the number of people employed in travel agencies has decreased as customers have become much more independent, the number of car hire and tour booking operators have been reduced as most bookings can now be done electronically online rather than using 'front-line staff', i.e. staff that come face-to-face with a customer.

Location of staff

Due to the high cost of office space in or close to large towns and cities, many services such as call centres and administration services are located in areas of the country where office space is much better value and where there is a history of high unemployment levels. For example, towns in the North-East of England had high unemployment levels due to decline in the ship-building industry. Service centres were set up in the North-East to address unemployment.

Assessment tips

You will need to know about the economic impact new technology has had on leisure and tourism organisations. You will also need to have an understanding about how new technology has had an impact on employment within the leisure and tourism industry.

Talk about it

In groups, make a list of ways in which new technology has had an impact on the location of staff and the number of staff employed within the leisure and tourism industry.

Fewer staff required overall

With so many automated systems such as online check-in, online reservations systems, etc, it means that companies require less staff. For example, back in the 1980s airline tickets had to be handwritten. Today, tickets are mass-produced by computer technology which takes just one person to press the button and that person can be the customer themselves.

Training staff to use new technology

Whilst technology is a wonderful thing, it can only produce great results if the person who is using the technology has had the right level of training on how to use it. A successful organisation is one that invests time and money, not only in the development of technology, but also in its workforce. Organisations need to provide the training the workforce needs to use the new technology, however costs for this training can have an economic impact.

An interesting promotional technique that does not require modern technology

Summary

- New technology has had an economic impact on leisure and tourism organisations affecting cost and profit.
- New technology has also had an impact on employment, creating a change in employee numbers, location of staff, the increase of more front-line staff, and the need to increase training of staff.

Research it

Research some key jobs within the leisure and tourism industry, and find out what specialist and technological knowledge is needed by someone wanting to apply for one of these jobs. What training is offered by the different organisations involved?

Case study – Staff training

Training and development is important from their first day at Knock Travel and all new starters receive a comprehensive induction. This is designed to introduce the staff member to the company, its different departments and their colleagues.

Each staff member has a personalised Training Development Plan, which includes core training and specialist training based on their own skill needs. In business travel, for example, all staff complete the basic training modules shown in the table below and specialist and sales/marketing training modules as required:

Basic training	Specialist training	Sales/marketing training
ISO 9000 Awareness Training	Computer Skills	Staff Meetings
ABTA Awareness and Training	Presentation Skills	Customer Care
IATA Awareness and Training	Excel Spreadsheets	Procurement Handling
	Travel Law	Telephone Techniques
	Dealing with Disability	Handling Complaints
		Researching Itineraries
		Galileo Focalpoint
		Internet Usage

1 What advantages are there for leisure and tourism organisations to have staff trained to use new technology?

Unit 2 Make the Grade

Once you have completed your studies for Unit 2 and compiled your research folder, you are ready for the **controlled assessment task**. This is set by Edexcel and will involve carrying out research on leisure and tourism organisations that you will then use to answer questions. There is no need to panic about the controlled assessment as this Make the Grade section will help to guide and prepare you so that you are aware of what is required.

Remember it

A **controlled assessment task** is where your coursework is monitored by your teacher and you carry out your written work at school or college, not at home.

Your research folder

Throughout this unit (and Unit 4, which is also assessed by a controlled assessment task) you will need to compile a research folder which you can then refer to during the assessment task. You will be given research tasks to carry out during the study of each topic in Units 2 and 4, which in some instances you will develop further into your own independently produced end product. This might be a presentation, a report or a diagram.

Whilst the Internet is an excellent resource for research activities, it is not the only resource and failure to acknowledge other sources will be reflected in the marking of the assessment. There are many leisure-, travel- and tourism-specific journals which your school or college will subscribe to and these can usually be found in your Learning Resource Centre (or library). It is also a good idea to do your own research (primary research), where you go out and ask questions of people actually working in the industry. Your teacher will most likely have invited visiting speakers from industry sectors to come in and talk to your group, but find out where your local travel agencies, tour operators, leisure centres and so on are and go and see them when you need help.

- You should aim to have a wide variety of evidence collected within your research folder using a wide range of research methods and sources.
- Make sure your research folder is well organised and easy to use. Separate your folder into sections and create a contents page or index so that you can find the information you need quickly.
- You cannot add information to your folder once the controlled assessment task has started so make sure you collect lots of relevant information during the research and investigating time.
- Manage your time well whilst researching. Create a plan and detail everything you need to find out and where you are to find it from.
- Look through the evidence you have collected for each topic and check: Is anything missing? Is the information organised and in order?

The controlled assessment task

Before you start to answer the questions, read through the task thoroughly and work out how much time you think you will need to answer each part and form a time plan. Then stick to it! If you finish one part early, move on to the next. If one part is taking longer than you planned, leave it and come back to it later. You might find that you can focus better after doing another section and coming back to it.

Make sure your work is set out neatly and logically. Even your time plan needs to be clear as the assessor will want to see how you approached the task, whether your plan was realistic and whether you kept to your planned targets.

How does the controlled assessment task work?

- Through a range of tasks, both within your centre and outside of it, you will research and produce evidence which will help you with your assessment task.

- Your teacher will check the evidence you collect to ensure that it is all your own work.
- You will be allocated a set amount of time to carry out your research and your teacher will keep a record.
- Research can be a mix of independent or group work, depending on the evidence you need.
- When it comes to answering the assessment task questions, your teacher will supervise your responses. This must be done in sessions that have been specifically allocated for this purpose to ensure that the work you submit is entirely your own.

Assessment tip

It is important that you carry out research on your local area early on in this unit to assess what leisure and tourism organisations are accessible and whether they can help you by providing information. They may even consider coming to talk to your class as a whole.

Planning ahead

Your teacher may have arranged for some speakers from leisure and tourism organisations to help you with certain topics within this unit. Similarly, you may go on visits to organisations both locally or further afield. It is important that before you take part in any of these activities you work together as a group and on your own to come up with questions to ask. This will ensure you get the most from the speaker's visit and get answers that will help you with your assessment tasks.

Assessment tip

You may choose to make some of your own independent visits to local organisations. It is very important that you are clear on what information you need from those you will be speaking to. Remember that these are busy people with important jobs to do. Make sure that you use the time you have with them to your advantage.

Before visiting organisations or having speakers in, check to see if some of the information you need is readily available from other means such as a website. You may be able to find the information you need from there first. Visiting the website may generate more questions, which will demonstrate to your visiting speaker that you have taken an interest and prepared in advance.

Apply it

Don't forget to read newspapers for relevant articles, as well as leisure and tourism journals. These can be great sources of up-to-date information.

- If you are working in a group, organise yourselves and allocate clear tasks to each member, making sure the work is evenly spread. Create a group plan of action so that everyone is clear on which task they are responsible for and what they have to actually do.
- When carrying out research, make sure you keep copies of all the relevant pages you print out or photocopy. However, don't keep bits of paper that you don't need. They will clutter up your folder and make finding information much more difficult.
- When you are issued with your assessment task, make sure you read it then read it again. It is very important that you fully understand what you are being asked to do and that you understand the language being used. Understanding the command words can make the difference between an average mark and a high mark. Look at the table on page 118 which shows some of the command words that may appear in the assignment task along with what they mean.

Command word	What it means
Analyse	Identify the facts and how they relate to each other. You also need to explain the importance of each fact.
Compare and contrast	What are the similarities and differences? For example, you might be asked to compare and contrast the products and services offered by two leisure and tourism organisations, as well as how they market them.
Describe	Provide a detailed picture in words so that the reader can formulate an idea of what you mean.
Evaluate	Draw conclusions from information you have been given or from an investigation you have carried out, with an explanation of how you reached your conclusion.
Explain or Justify	Provide clear reasons for your views and ideas.
Suggest or Recommend	This is where you are encouraged to put forward your own ideas, for example, you may be asked to recommend ways to improve an organisation's promotional leaflet.
List	Create a list but don't use sentences. For example, if you were asked to write a shopping list you would write: 5lb potatoes not 5lb of potatoes for making mash.
Outline	Identify the main points in brief, but don't give too much detail.

The words in the above table will be used in both your internal and external assessments, so are useful for all the units you will be studying.

Remember it

Don't forget your spelling and grammar when answering the assessment task questions.

Take it further

In small groups, identify the ways in which you can ensure that your work is presented well. For example, might a bullet list or graph present certain types of information better than a paragraph of text?

Practice questions

We will now look at an assessment task question and see how two students started their answer to it, along with the comments they received.

Q1 Investigate the sales and marketing mix of one of your chosen organisations.

Sarah's answer:

For this task, I have chosen to investigate the sales and marketing mix for Alton Towers. In order to find out all the information I need for this task my class visited Alton Towers where we received a talk on the marketing activities of the organisation. We also got the chance to ask further questions. Before we made the visit, we discussed as a group what questions we might need to ask, and in addition I thought of some questions myself.

I have also looked at the Alton Towers website to help me as it tells me what products and services the attraction offers to customers, as well as the prices. I also looked for newspaper articles to see if there were any new products due in the future.

In order to discuss my findings, I am going to talk about each of the four Ps in the marketing mix in turn and the approach that Alton Towers has to each of them.

The four Ps are:

- Product
- Price
- Place
- Promotion.

Comments on Sarah's answer:

Sarah has made a good start to this task, choosing to use an organisation that is able to provide a good range of information both through its promotional activities and through face-to-face provision of information. Sarah has also shown that she understands the task by talking about her knowledge of the four components that make up the marketing mix. Sarah has taken a very organised approach to the question.

Sarah could improve her marks if she were to provide some examples of the types of questions the group came up with, as well as the question she came up with herself. In addition, if Sarah had given further information about the specific web pages she found useful and given further explanation about how she searched for newspaper articles this would also have improved her marks.

Boran's answer:

We went to Alton Towers for a talk and a trip round the theme park and the rides were great. We had a talk about how Alton Towers sells itself to customers and about its marketing mix. We asked the lady lots of questions and she gave us some handouts at the end. When we got back we also looked at the website to see what else we could find out.

Comments on Boran's answer:

Boran has been too brief and has not really shown his understanding of the task. In order to improve his chances of higher marks, Boran would need to write in much more detail to show the assessor that an organised and independent approach had been taken.

Assessment tips

Whenever you are responding to questions, you need to ask yourself a few questions to make sure that you respond in the depth necessary for higher marks. The following examples taken from Sarah's answer will illustrate this for you.

'For this task, I have chosen to investigate the marketing mix for Alton Towers.'

- **Why?** What were Sarah's reasons for choosing Alton Towers? Sarah could have added: 'Alton Towers is a theme park in the Midlands which is very well known and appears quite often in the newspapers for its developments. We were able to visit the park and receive firsthand information from an employee on how they approach the marketing mix. Also, because Alton Towers relies heavily on Internet sales it has a very good website that provides further information.'

- **How?** How did Sarah find the website for Alton Towers? Did she use a search engine? Did she find the web address through promotional leaflets? By explaining how she found the website Sarah would be demonstrating her independent learning skills and showing that she is confident using technology to carry out her research.

Use the following open questions to help you be more descriptive in your responses to the controlled assessment questions. For example:

- **How?** How did Sarah find out the prices for Alton Towers?
- **Why?** Why did Sarah add her own questions to the ones the whole class put together?
- **What?** What reasons does the organisation have for using specific promotional techniques?
- **Where?** Where did Sarah find specific information? She says she looked at newspapers. Which ones? On what dates? Did she find any articles?
- **When?** When did Sarah carry out specific research? She needs to show that she has taken an organised approach to her research and that each research task has been planned out in advance.

Planning and organisation

The table below is an example of how you might want to plan and organise your work. Using a system like this one can help you ensure you have enough information for your responses and that you carry out your research in an organised way. Sarah used this table to collect information relating to the products component of the four Ps.

Organisation: Alton Towers			
Researching: Four Ps – products			
What do I need to know?	**Where will I find the information?**	**What have I found?**	**Collected and stored in research folder?**
What products and services does Alton Towers offer?	Through visit to Alton Towers in April Search engine to find website address Newspapers and journals	Rides for young children, teenagers and adults Merchandise – cups, bags, pens etc. First Aid centre Ticket office Education Centre Bag store Ride assistance for those with disabilities Café Takeaway food and drinks	Have printed out some sheets from website showing different rides and the price list for entry to the park Found article about new ride and other attractions in newspaper (Daily Mail, 12 March)

By taking this approach for each of the four Ps, Sarah is increasing her chances of achieving a higher mark. This is because she will have lots of organised information to refer to when writing her response to the questions. She has not only been very clear about what information she needs and where she is going to find it, but she has also made notes about what she found and where this information is in her research folder.

Creating a separate table for each of the four Ps will help Sarah focus on them one at a time when carrying out research. It will also save her time during the controlled assessment task and ensure that she is able to write responses in the depth required to gain high marks.

Assessment tip

Make sure that when you collect information for your research folder you don't copy large pieces of information word for word. Don't cut and paste huge chunks of information from websites either. You must be able to demonstrate your own understanding, which means writing in your own words. Small passages can be copied as long as you acknowledge where you got the information from and give an explanation of why you have used this passage.

Unit 3: The Leisure and Tourism Environment

This unit looks at how the leisure and tourism industry changes, as well as the factors that cause these changes and how the industry responds. You will need to be able to explain and analyse how these factors create change and lead to new products and services. The factors that influence change are:

- Technology
- Consumer trends
- Unforeseen and uncontrollable events.

We will also look at some popular tourist destinations in the UK and why people choose to visit them. There are 50 destinations that you need to know about, divided into six destination types. You will need to focus on some of these destinations, locate them on a map, describe them, and identify the features and appeal that make them fit into their category.

Not everyone wants a lazy beach holiday

The types of tourist destination are:

- Seaside resorts
- Countryside areas
- Tourist towns and cities
- Business and conference destinations
- Purpose-built destinations
- Historical and cultural destinations.

We will also look at what tourist boards do to promote the destinations and which tourist board region covers each destination.

Finally, we will explore the positive and negative effects of tourism and the importance of **sustainability** to the leisure and tourism industry. Leisure and tourism can affect the environment, as well as communities, for better and for worse because whenever people travel, they have an impact on their destination. We will look at the impacts of tourism and ecotourism, and you will need to be able to analyse and evaluate the effects by considering the advantages and disadvantages. We will also look at the ways these impacts can be controlled and you will need to evaluate them. Ecotourism is a key issue in this topic and we will look at the associated products and services.

Describe it

Sustainability is about being able to maintain things as they are despite change. In leisure and tourism this relates to keeping destinations and locations unspoiled despite the increasing demands of tourists.

We will explore the issues relating to sustainability and its importance, both in the UK and overseas. We will also investigate sustainable transport issues. We will look at the ways in which sustainability is introduced to the leisure and tourism industry and the trend for 'going green'. You will then be able to evaluate different types of sustainable projects, transport, award schemes and initiatives.

This unit covers the following topics:

3.1 A Dynamic Industry
3.2 UK Tourist Destinations
3.3 The Impacts of Tourism
3.4 The Issue of Sustainability

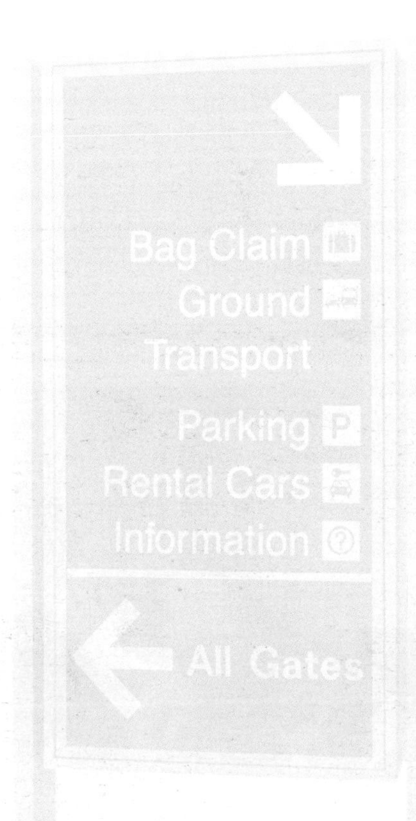

How you will be assessed

This unit is compulsory for the GCSE (Double Award) qualification. This unit should not be studied by students working towards the Single GCSE award. Assessment of this unit is via an exam, which is set and marked by the examination board Edexcel. The exam is one hour long and there are questions on all four topic areas. Each topic area is clearly indicated on the examination paper so you can't get mixed up! There are three types of question within the exam: multiple choice, short-answer questions and extended-answer questions. You will find examples of these question types in the Make the Grade section, along with examiners' tips on how to go about answering them and some revision tips (see pages 176–181).

3.1 A Dynamic Industry

You will need to understand and explain what drives change in the leisure and tourism industry, and question how change leads to new products and services.

Technological developments

Advances in technology often influence the leisure and tourism industry. In this section we will look at the following examples of products and services that have affected the industry:

- Social networking sites
- Virtual reality games
- Digital TV
- Home cinemas
- DVD writers
- MP3 players and audio trails
- Podcasts
- GPS and geocaching
- Ticketless travel/e-tickets
- Automated check-in
- Online booking.

Describe it

Social networking sites are online 'communities' of people who often have shared interests or activities. Members exchange emails, leave messages, set up profiles and make 'friends' with other users. The first social networking site was set up in 1997 and popular sites today include MySpace, Facebook and Bebo.

Technological change in home-based leisure

Not too long ago, families used to gather around their one and only TV in the living room, and read or play board games to amuse themselves. Today, many homes have more than one TV and a computer, which allows families to spend time apart but within the same house, to be entertained and educated, to socialise with friends in cyber space, play games and book travel online. **Social networking sites** are becoming an increasingly popular way for people to spend their leisure time, enabling people to communicate and share information with each other.

However did they manage with just one TV?!

Take it further

Research the history of social networking sites on the Internet. What do you think are good aspects of such sites and their communities? What do you think is not so good about them?

Research it

Create a short questionnaire to find out how people spend their leisure time. Ask members of your class, your friends and family to complete it. Give your questionnaire to some older people you know and ask them to complete it by telling you how they spent their leisure time when they were young. Compare your results from the different age groups.

Technological change in sport and physical recreation

The first computer game was invented in 1952 and was based on 'noughts and crosses'. Today, games technology has progressed so that the physical actions of the player can be fed into the computer, which reacts by 'playing' with the participant. The Nintendo Wii, which is a very popular example of a virtual-reality games console, can make it easier for people to participate in some activities that they may otherwise find it difficult to do due to transport or cost.

Technology has enabled gaming to be a very physical activity

Technological change in arts and entertainment

There have been many technological advances in arts and home entertainment:

- Digital TV provides perfect pictures in high definition on multiple channels, making it more likely that people enjoy home-based arts and entertainment.
- Home cinemas developed from televisions but include extra features such as high-definition picture quality and surround sound. Decreases in price have meant that more people can afford them and watch movies together as a family.
- DVD (Digital Versatile Disc) writers and TV hard drives, which record programmes, enable people to choose when they watch their favourite programmes.
- Audio technology has seen many innovations. Digital Audio Technology development makes your MP3 player work and gives you the chance to listen to music while you do other activities such as running or dancing. Podcasts, which can be downloaded on to an MP3 player, allow you to listen to audio broadcasts whenever you want. MP3 players enable people in art galleries or on city trails to listen to an audio commentary, replacing the need for a personal guide.

Technological change in the countryside

You may have heard of instances where people get lost in remote places and contact their friends by mobile phone for help. You may also have seen **GPS** technology in a car or taxi. Advances in satellite technology have made an impact on countryside recreation by making it safer to be in remote areas, giving travellers more confidence. This in turn has led to the emergence of new activities such as 'geocaching', whereby people hide a 'treasure' and then post the treasure's location co-ordinates on the Internet. They invite people to find it and offer a prize to the winner.

Describe it

GPS stands for Global Positioning System. A series of satellites orbiting the Earth are able to tell people with GPS receivers their location.

Apply it

Your local swimming pool is not as popular as it used to be and is facing closure. A consultant suggests that the manager employs some new technologies to attract people to the pool.

1. **Suggest how one new technological development you know about could be adapted to offer a new product at the swimming pool and who it might attract.**
2. **Make a poster, leaflet or flyer aimed clearly at the target market of this new product telling them all about it.**

Research it

Conduct some research to try and find out when the following technological changes were introduced and how their introduction affected people's leisure time:

- Passenger train
- Cinema
- Car
- Television.

Technological change in booking and information

Tour operators work with holiday providers to create packages of holidays. In the past, these met a few simple needs for people who went on a two-week summer holiday. The tour operators sold their products to travel agents, who produced brochures detailing the holidays available. There were few options and single people had to pay a premium because tour operators catered for the 'average' family.

The introduction of the Internet and home computers have meant that:

- People can search for, customise and book their own holidays online, bypassing traditional tour operators and travel agents. They can also book transport and other kinds of services, all from the comfort of their own home.
- The smallest tourist destinations and providers are able to have websites and can now take online bookings without depending on travel companies.
- As travel companies lost business they were stimulated to provide more flexible products to meet the needs of the increasingly segmenting market (i.e. demand for short, weekend and occasional breaks).

Automated check-in has made air travel quicker and easier

Technological change in accommodation

What would you like in your hotel room? You want at least the comforts of home, so probably a comfortable bed, a warm room and access to a bathroom. Travellers' expectations of their accommodation have been increasing in the last 20 years or so, with hotels eager to keep up with their guests' needs as well as new technology. Many hotels offer virtual tours on their websites as well as facilities to book and pay online. Some motels offer automated check-in, whereby travellers are given a code to access their room, allowing them to arrive and depart with complete flexibility. This is particularly useful for airport hotels where a 24-hour checking in and out service is essential.

Research it

Travelodge is a low-cost hotel chain, whilst De Vere is a high-end chain of hotels. Visit the websites of both, and compare and contrast the technology available at each.

1 **Which hotel would best attract business travellers? Which would best attract a couple on a relaxing break? Justify your answers.**

Remember it

Ticketless travel can mean two things: travelling without a ticket or travelling with a pay-as-you-go electronic card.

Ticketless travel, e-tickets and automated check-in air travel

Technological change in the airline industry has been very rapid in the last few years. Computer technology and the Internet have led to **ticketless travel**, e-tickets and automated check-in/bag drop. These changes have helped reduce airport waiting times, which had increased because of security measures introduced after a number of terrorist attacks involving air travel.

Travellers can now check flight availability, choose an airline and book their flight online, after which a boarding pass is printed off or a code given. At the airport there are computer points where the traveller either scans the barcode from their boarding pass or enters their code. Bag labels can be printed off and bags taken to the drop-off. The process is relatively quick and the traveller then simply presents their boarding pass at the gate.

Oyster card

An Oyster card is a plastic, credit card-sized smart card that can be used on public transport services in London. It is topped up like a mobile phone card and swiped past terminals on buses and at Underground and train stations. The terminals read the chip inside the card and remove the correct fare from the balance on it. Both Sydney and Hong Kong have similar systems in operation. An Oyster card is a type of ticketless travel because travellers don't have to queue for a ticket or carry cash for fares.

Oyster cards cut queues

The future: mobile phones and the ticketless traveller

Travellers will soon be able to pay for train journeys using their mobile phones. The London Underground is working with mobile phone manufacturer Nokia and phone network O2 to launch a handset with a built-in Oyster card. It is thought that the phones will be swiped across the terminals just as Oyster cards currently are. This type of payment method could also be used on London buses, trams and some overland train journeys.

Apply it

A family of four (two parents and two teenagers) are taking a short weekend break in the Lake District. They are packing their bags and decide that they should make a list of the technology they are taking with them to ensure they have all the correct cables, connections and software.

1. **Make a list of the types of technology they might possibly take with them.**
2. **Explain when and why they might use each piece of technology.**

Take it further

If you were stranded on a desert island, which piece of technology would you miss most while you were waiting to be rescued and why?

Summary

The products and services of the leisure and tourism industry change to meet the demands of customers who are increasingly able to access sophisticated technology.

Consumer trends

In this section we will look at how consumer trends can influence the development of new products and services in the leisure and tourism industry. We will explore the following factors that can make people change their behaviour:

- Changing tastes
- Changing lifestyles
- Changes to holiday patterns
- Growth of 'silver surfers'
- Changes to family patterns
- Changing appeal of cruising.

Changing tastes

Over time, people have become more environmentally aware and how they spend their leisure time has reflected this. Travel companies have been quick to offer products to environmentally conscious travellers, with the introduction of a new concept in travelling: **ecotourism**.

Describe it

Ecotourism means visiting destinations whilst also reducing the impact of tourism on the environment. It sometimes involves directly helping the environment and its community by volunteering to take part in conservation activities taking place there.

As standards in our homes have developed and become more comfortable, so we want similar or higher standards in our holidays. For example, if we have a dishwasher in our home, we might want them too in our holiday cottage. Many people would expect Wi-Fi in their hotel so that they could use their laptops. Five-star accommodation is very luxurious and offers a number of facilities and services that are additional to lower-rated accommodation. As tastes become more sophisticated, 5-star accommodation is becoming more popular, with guests making use of facilities such as gyms, swimming pools, saunas and hot tubs, and hair and beauty salons. The table below describes typical 5-star accommodation.

★★★★★	Luxurious accommodation and public areas, with a range of extra facilities and a multilingual service available. Guests are greeted at the hotel entrance. High quality menu and wine list.	Awareness of each guest's needs with nothing being too much trouble. All bedrooms are ensuite or have a private bathroom (from 1 January 2008). Excellent quality beds and furnishings. Breakfast includes specials/home-made items, high-quality ingredients, and fresh local produce.

Source: AA Hotel Recognition Scheme – summary of standards for 5-star accommodation

New experiences are changing peoples' tastes as they go on holiday more frequently and want to do something different with their increasing disposable income. The development of multi-media advertising and multi-channel television has led to an increased

awareness of 'alternative' holiday activities. Adventure holidays and those that include participation in extreme sports are becoming more and more popular. Healthy living and an increase in cooking for leisure have lead to an increase in holidays and breaks where people learn to cook. Likewise, the popularity of wine drinking in the UK has led to a growth in holidays that feature vineyard visits and wine tours. Many people are also interested in spending their holiday learning about different cultures and experiencing a different way of living by visiting less economically developed countries.

Zorbing – your perfect break?

Changing lifestyles

Most of the products and services of the leisure industry are luxuries that people pay for with their disposable income. Sometimes the UK has good or 'boom' times when most people are in work, wages are high and costs are low, so that there is money left over for trips and treats.

At other times, there is an economic downturn or 'slump', like that at the end of 2008, when people have less money to spend on travel and leisure pursuits. This usually causes an increase in home-based leisure and holidays in the UK. People often take part in more outdoor home-based leisure activities when finances are tough, enjoying gardening, eating outside and barbequing.

In 2008, the beginnings of economic problems and concerns about global warming led to an increase in the number of people camping. Campsites, which had been suffering because of people taking foreign holidays, saw an up-turn in trade, particularly if they were imaginative with their marketing. 'Glamping', with its high standards and luxury equipment, became a glamorous and fun alternative to the 'roughing it' idea of camping many people have. Campsites also offered accommodation alternatives such as yurts (a circular tent originating from Central Asia) and wigwams (a tent used by Native Americans).

Changes to holiday patterns

The last 50 years or so have seen great changes in the way people can take holidays from work. In the 1950s, most people worked in industry and had two weeks' paid holiday a year. Many worked Saturday mornings, so weekend holidays were rare, with many going to football matches and the cinema for their weekend recreation.

In the 1980s, work started to become more flexible and holiday entitlements increased. People began taking time off throughout the year, not just in the summer, and increased incomes together with more flexible working meant that more people could take long weekend breaks, short breaks and even long-haul (flying for more than four hours) city breaks. More people chose to marry abroad, taking their families and friends with them, and the number of older people travelling increased because of their better pensions and savings.

Research it

Many people are keen to do something different on their holiday and not just stretch out on a beach for two weeks. Perform an Internet search to find out more about some of the different kinds of activity holidays available.

Apply it

Make a list of the things you think sometimes put people off camping. Which three things from your list do you think people dislike most? Now create three products or services to offer campers which would overcome these dislikes and make the experience more 'glam'.

Growth of 'silver surfers'

'Silver surfer' is a term that is used to describe older people who use the Internet (silver describing their grey or white hair!). Many older people now have good pensions and savings, and use them to travel and enjoy different kinds of leisure activity, including surfing the Internet. Although they were born before computers were common, many will have used them at work before retiring and are likely to have the time to browse the Internet for good holiday deals and book online.

Many older people are fit and active nowadays and because they no longer have the usual family responsibilities, they can seek adventure and visit unusual and challenging destinations, such as Everest base camp or Mongolia, as well as taking long cruises.

Research it

Explore the Saga Zone website by clicking on 'Things to do' and following the various links. Compare and contrast the site with some of the social networking sites you use or know of. How is it the same? How does it differ? Do you think you might use a site like this when you are older?

Silver surfers can use their computer skills on home-based leisure activities too. Where social networking sites such as Facebook and Bebo cater for the young, so Saga Zone meets the socialising needs of the over 50s. Gyms and leisure centres are also becoming popular with older people as their better health enables them to keep fit and lead a healthy lifestyle. Many regularly take part in activities such as swimming, aerobics, yoga and Pilates, with some choosing to simply work out in the gym.

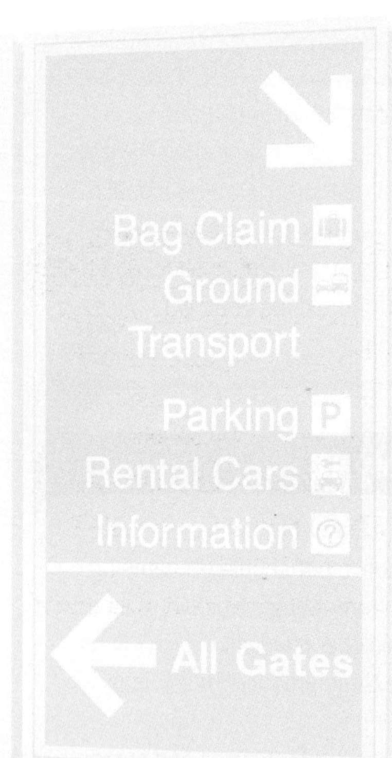

Changes to family patterns

Following World War II a 'baby boom' happened, with a huge increase in the number of babies being born. This was because, during the war, many men were away from home helping with the war effort. When the war was over, families started having babies again. In 2007, the population of the UK was almost 61 million. One in five people were under 16 and a similar proportion were of retirement age. Family patterns have been changing over recent years, with a decline in the number of babies being born.

Recent years have seen a decrease in the number of young people as a percentage of the total population. Families have become smaller with fewer children and more disposable income as a result. Leisure and tourism products have been changing to meet the needs of the new type of family. Lots of parents are now choosing to take their children on adventure or educational holidays, instead of the usual lazy two weeks in the sun. The growth in popularity of these types of holiday reflect many modern parents' desire to make sure their children are healthy, fit and given the best start in life.

Leisure activities for young people have been developing too. Ceramic cafés have been springing up all over the country, where families can go and enjoy producing clay objects, and have something to eat and drink. Even the smallest of children are catered for with soft-play areas and 'parent and toddler discos'.

Changing appeal of cruising

Once, cruising was an exclusive pastime. Only the most affluent people had the time and money to cruise. Others aspired to cruise. They saved up for years, booked years in advance and spent lots of money on all the right clothes to look the part. Cruises were expensive because there were few cruise liners. There are now more cruise ships and they can carry vast numbers of people. As supply has increased, costs have gone down and cruising has become low cost.

Attractions on board the new cruise ships include open air parks, shopping malls, swimming pools, activity areas with zip wires, and climbing walls, and ice skating rinks. These changes have helped the industry move away from the smaller wealthy and older market and find a more general appeal.

Some cruises are still very exclusive and expensive. They tend to be adventure cruises costing several thousand pounds per person, usual advertised as the 'cruise of a lifetime'. A typical adventure cruise migl include the following types of attraction:

- A first-class flight to join the liner
- A visit inland from the port, such as a safari
- A small boat cruise to swim with dolphins
- Meals cooked by a celebrity chef
- Wine-tasting sessions
- Lectures by well-known broadcasters and academics
- Very high standard of accommodation.

Apply it

A recent survey by Eurostat, the EU's statistical office, found that people in Britain spend about 45% of their free time watching television, 24% socializing, 22–23% on sport and hobbies, and 10% on other activities. Use Eurostats' website to investigate the patterns in more depth.

1 Make a diary of your week's leisure activities. Ask a parent or teacher to keep a diary too. Answer the following questions:

a) How closely does your leisure time match the national averages?

b) Does the leisure time diary of the parent or teacher differ from yours?

c) Has gender affected how leisure time is spent?

d) Do you think some people have different perceptions of what 'leisure' is? Justify your answer.

Summary

- Over time, customers have wanted new leisure and tourism products and services as work patterns and the economy have changed.
- Changes in leisure participation happen as circumstances affecting the population alter.

Unforeseen and uncontrollable events

In this section we are going to look at how 'outside' events can influence the leisure and tourism industry. We will cover:

- Global credit crunch/recession
- Increases in the cost of fuel/inflation
- Acts of terrorism
- Natural disasters
- Changes in exchange rates
- Accidents/injury to customers
- Cancellations and compensation.

Tourism is both a fragile and a resilient business. People travel because they seek enjoyment; they do not want to take risks unless it is the 'managed' risk of extreme holidays. Even quite small events can attract people to a place or discourage them from visiting it. Weather can prevent or encourage travel; you might look out of the window and decide not to visit your friend that day because it is raining. On the other hand, a beautiful sunny day brings people outside to sunbathe in the park, buy an ice cream or set off for the beach.

Global credit crunch/recession

Banks make money by charging interest on the money they lend to individuals and businesses, as well as other banks. When borrowed money can't be paid back the banks stop lending. This is known as a 'credit crunch'. If people cannot borrow money or have to pay a lot of interest on loans they do have, they may not be able to move house and may also have to reduce their spending. Businesses suffer because they can't afford to pay their suppliers when customers aren't spending money. They may have to reduce the number of employees, which means that people lose their jobs and have less money. This is called a 'recession'. By the end of 2008, there was a global credit crunch.

With many people having to reduce their spending during a recession, businesses face heavy competition in the fight to stay successful. Leisure and tourism businesses often offer discounts or take part in 'price wars' in order to win customers, but these tactics usually increase in periods of financial hardship. In August 2008, when the UK weather was very poor, many travel companies significantly reduced their prices in order to cash in on Britons making last-minute holiday bookings to escape the rain.

Holiday companies can cash in on a poor British summer

When times are tough, many businesses suffer. Leisure and tourism businesses can be especially vulnerable as the products and services they offer are often considered luxuries and not necessities. Companies can and do go out of business for this reason and because:

- Their product no longer appeals to people, e.g. British beach holidays
- Rival products attract people away, e.g. cheap flights to better destinations
- Prices rise above what people are willing to pay.

When businesses are in trouble they sometimes close and cease to exist or they can be taken over by other companies.

Increases in the cost of fuel/inflation

The cost of fuel is increasing and some airlines have gone out of business because they could no longer afford to fly their planes. Other airlines increased their prices in order to cover the cost of fuel but then lost out to other companies with cheaper prices.

High fuel costs cause rising prices throughout the whole of the economy. Nearly all of the things we buy are transported using fuel and the increasing price of fuel is adding to the cost of all products – this is called inflation. Inflation causes the prices of necessities to rise and so disposable income is reduced. Leisure and tourism businesses suffer because of this and face closure or takeover by more successful firms.

Acts of terrorism

Acts that are intended to create fear amongst people are called terrorism. The acts are often carried out by groups of people with political or religious motives and are intended to be harmful or violent. Probably the most well-known acts of terrorism are the attacks on the United States on 11 September 2001, otherwise known as 9/11.

The number of travellers fell after the 9/11 terrorist attacks. Transatlantic travel reduced, Americans stayed in the US for holidays and fewer people went to the US on holiday. Worldwide, tourists were quite resilient and continued to travel despite terrorist threats, but they were less happy when increased security measures made check-in times lengthy and there were restrictions on taking liquids in hand luggage. Tourist numbers fell as a result.

After the Madrid train bombings in 2004, European train services began to use airport-like bag checks, but far from putting off passengers, people have been reassured and passenger numbers have increased.

One major change in products and services has been caused by the restrictions on liquids being taken through security at airports. Beyond security, airports have encouraged the development of a thriving shopping area where cosmetics and drinks can be bought for the flight.

Talk about it

The place where the twin towers of the World Trade Center fell after the 9/11 attacks was called Ground Zero. This is now a tourist attraction. Some famous war cemeteries and ex-prisoner of war camps are also popular tourist attractions, sometimes referred to as 'tourism of grief'. In small groups, discuss your thoughts about people visiting such places. What do you feel about the businesses that make money selling trips and holidays to see them? Would you visit Ground Zero?

Research it

What are the current restrictions on what you can take on an aeroplane in your hand luggage?

The Asian Tsunami in December 2004 caused widespread devastation

Natural disasters

On 26 December 2004, an enormous under-sea earthquake triggered a tsunami (a giant wave) in the Indian Ocean known as the Asian Tsunami. Like many natural disasters, it could not have been predicted and no one was prepared. Many countries suffered devastation, loss of life and damage to their tourism industry. The infrastructure (roads, power and water supplies, recreational facilities and public buildings etc) of many coastal areas was destroyed and it has been difficult for these poorer nations to rebuild and bring back the tourism they relied on. Images of the disaster were seen all across the world and they did not encourage tourists to visit. Now, several years on, these areas are starting to recover as a result of aid from abroad and investment by the countries affected. But still the image remains negative and the industry is only able to encourage people back by cutting prices.

Changes in exchange rates

The value of the pound varies against other currencies. If lots of traders want to buy the pound, the price goes up. If lots of traders want to sell the pound, the price goes down. When the pound is weak in value, it is good for companies in the UK offering holidays to tourists from abroad as foreign tourists get more pounds for their money. The UK is also more affordable to many tourists and so they want to visit because of the good value for money. However, this means that it is expensive for British people to travel abroad as they don't get as much foreign currency for their money.

When the pound is 'strong' and it costs a lot in another currency to buy it, foreign visitors are put off and the UK economy suffers. However, this means that British people can travel cheaply as they get more foreign currency for their money. Visits abroad by the British often increase when the pound is strong.

Accidents/injury to customers

Deciding where to go on holiday depends on many factors, and we can certainly be influenced by the things we hear about a destination or travel/leisure company by people we know or by the media, especially if it is bad news. We might be put off using a certain product or service or visiting a town or city, at home or abroad, if we hear that someone we know had an accident there. If an accident or injury was very serious, involved a lot of people or resulted in a death it can become very newsworthy, which may greatly affect the business and/or destination involved. A sudden fall in business can put companies in serious trouble, which is why they try hard to prevent them happening in the first place or being publicised when they do occur.

However, people are resilient. In 2008, after an air collision killed 20 people near the Grand Canyon in the USA, there were queues of people waiting to fly the next day. In ski resorts where avalanches

Research it

Hurricane Katrina, which devastated the US city of New Orleans in 2005, is another example of a natural disaster that has not only ruined lives but seriously damaged a tourism industry.

1. **Use the Internet to find some more examples of natural disasters that have affected the leisure and tourism industry.**
2. **Would you visit a place that had recently been affected by a natural disaster? Give reasons for your answer.**

Apply it

You are travelling to Florida on business, but it is the hurricane season. Visit the Federal Emergency Management Agency website to find out what precautions you should take.

disrupt travel and deter tourists, deaths and accidents rarely do! One of the biggest problems some ski resorts face is deterring tourists even when the avalanche risk is high.

What is more likely than accidents and injury to cause falls in visitor numbers is bad publicity, especially if it is about poor facilities, dirty accommodation, food poisoning or pest infestations, such as rats or cockroaches. General inconveniences such as long queues and bad service are also just as likely to cause negative publicity and be bad for business.

Case study – Walking in a 'Winter Wonderland'?

In December 2008, a new attraction opened on the Dorset-Hampshire border just in time for Christmas. It boasted a 'winter wonderland', Lapland-style theme park, where children could see huskies and reindeer, touch lifelike snow and skate on an ice rink. Adults were invited to visit the 'bustling' Christmas market and view the log cabins and Nativity scene. As you may have heard, visitors were very upset by their visit to the park, complaining that the animals looked sad and uncared for, the ice rink was broken, the snowy decorations were poor, the Christmas market was small and disappointing, and the Nativity scene was a joke.

1. **How do you think the bad publicity affected the theme park?**
2. **If you were the manager of the theme park, what would you do to try and make the customers who visited the park happy again?**
3. **What could you do to 'undo' the bad publicity and bring people back?**

Cancellations and compensation

When many people are put off visiting an attraction or destination by unforeseen or uncontrollable events, travel decreases and companies have to cancel flights and accommodation. In extreme situations, travel companies can go out of business, leaving people stranded on their holiday. Travellers whose holidays are cancelled usually get compensation if they have taken out insurance. This is good for the traveller but puts pressure on the travel industry and can lead to closures and further cancellations. It also adds further to the cost of travelling for the tourist.

The Association of British Travel Agents (ABTA) represents travel agents and tour operators if the company has paid for accreditation (approval). ABTA accreditation suggests to customers that there is safety in booking with these companies, giving the company a competitive advantage. However, the cost of paying for accreditation is passed on to the customer in higher prices.

As more travellers use the Internet to package their own holidays, there is an increasing range of insurance products to protect against cancellation and provide compensation.

Research it

The euro was launched in 2002 as a brand new currency for 320 million people in the European Union.

1. What currencies did the euro replace?
2. Over the next few weeks, find out and make a note of the exchange rate for pound sterling against the US dollar. When would have been the best time to visit the US? Justify your answer.

Assessment tip

It is a good idea to keep an eye on news stories about leisure and tourism. Cut out clippings from newspapers and magazines, and make notes on things you read on the Internet or see on television. Your work will benefit greatly from being up-to-date and informed!

Summary

- Even the smallest of events can alter patterns of travel very significantly.
- Very serious events such as acts of terrorism, natural disasters, wars and civil unrest, accidents and disease outbreaks can have a global impact on the patterns of travel, leisure and tourism. But people soon forget – what prevented tourism one year may well lead to lower prices the next, which in turn encourages people to visit again.

3.2 UK Tourist Destinations

In this section we will look at the location of some UK tourist destinations. You will need to be able to locate these destinations for your assessment and describe their location using your geographical knowledge of the UK. You will also need to be able to recognise which regional tourist board is responsible for promoting each of the destinations.

Popular UK tourist destinations

Below is a list of some popular UK tourist destinations and their locations. They are grouped according to the type of destination they are. You will need to understand the specific features and appeal of each of the destinations in **bold** text.

Seaside resorts: Oban, Portrush, Llandudno, **Blackpool,** Whitby, Great Yarmouth, **Newquay**, Eastbourne.

Countryside areas: Loch Lomond and the Trossachs, Antrim Coast and Glens, **Snowdonia**, Lake District, Yorkshire Dales, Cotswolds, Dartmoor, the **New Forest**.

Tourist towns and cities: **Glasgow,** Bangor, Conwy, Liverpool, **York,** Warwick, Oxford, Cambridge.

Business and conference destinations: Edinburgh, **Belfast,** Cardiff, Manchester, Leeds, London, **Birmingham**, Brighton.

Purpose-built destinations: **Aviemore,** Galgorm Resort (NI), Celtic Manor Resort (Wales), Keldy Forest Holidays/Hoseasons, Center Parcs – Sherwood Forest and Longleat Forest, **Alton Towers Resort**, Butlins – Bognor Regis.

Historical and cultural destinations: St Andrews, Derry, St Davids, **Chester,** Lindisfarne, **Bath,** Stratford-upon- Avon, Canterbury.

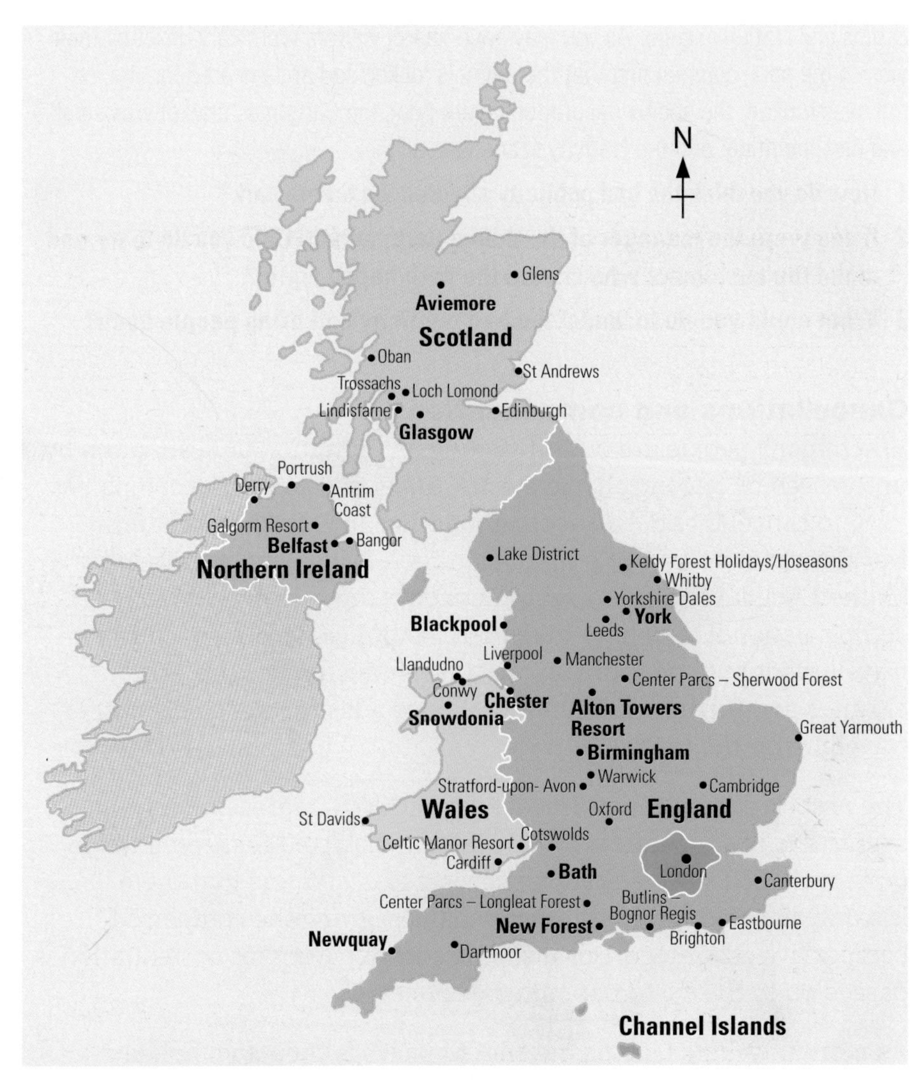

Locations of popular UK tourist destinations

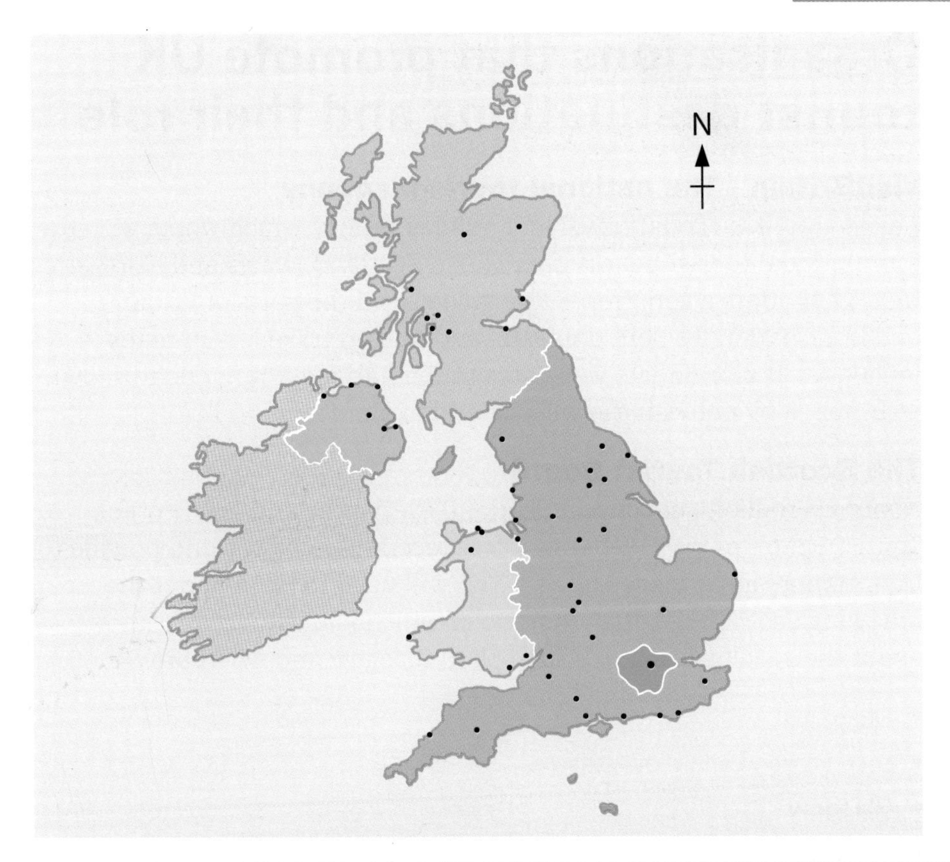

Cover the map on the opposite page and add the tourist destination names to this map from memory

Apply it

Copy and complete the table below using the map on this page.

Destination name	Type of destination

Apply it

Using an atlas or maps from the Internet, as well as this unit, describe the location of each destination on the list on page 136. Use the writing frame below to help you.

__________ is a __________ (add destination type) in __________ (location). It can be reached by the __________ (road name), and it is __________ (add direction from another place on the list) and __________ (add another place on the list).

For example: Oban is a small seaside town on the west coast of Scotland. It can be reached by the A85, and it is north-west of Loch Lomond and the Trossachs and Glasgow.

Take it further

For each destination in **bold** in the list on page 136, add another column to the table above giving one extra detail about its features or appeal.

Assessment tip

You will need to be able to locate UK tourist destinations on a map for the exam. Don't panic! If you make an effort to learn their locations before the exam, you can identify all the ones you know straight away and add the others as they come back to you.

Organisations that promote UK tourist destinations and their role

VisitBritain –The national tourism agency

This is the UK's official travel and holiday agency which works with the four national tourist boards of England, Scotland, Wales and Northern Ireland. It offers a comprehensive guide to all the parts of Britain and information for both domestic and foreign travellers in many languages. It also directs web users to the national tourist boards' own websites. Why not visit the website and explore it?

The Scottish Tourist Board

About 2¼ million people visit Scotland every year and The Scottish Tourist Board (or VisitScotland) offers recommendations and provides information about places to visit. You will need to learn about the following Scottish destinations, two of which you will need to know about the specific features and appeal: Glasgow and Aviemore.

- Oban
- Loch Lomond and the Trossachs
- **Glasgow**
- Edinburgh
- **Aviemore**
- St Andrews.

A 4 star hotel award

Like many tourist boards, The Scottish Tourist Board has a quality assurance scheme. This means that visitor attractions, accommodation and places to eat are visited and assessed for things like comfort, cleanliness, service and food. They are then awarded a star rating which corresponds with the standard of the product or service. The more stars, the better! You can find out more about the scheme and tourist attractions in Scotland by visiting the VisitScotland website.

Assessment tip

You may be asked to plan a trip for a particular type of person to do with a particular theme.

Case study – Aviemore

Aviemore is a small town in the Scottish Highlands, which was transformed by a private initiative during the 1960s. A £50-million makeover updated the facilities in 1998 to make the purpose-built leisure and tourism destination it is today.

Getting there – By road (A9), by plane (only one and a half hours from London) and by rail (there are direct links to Edinburgh, Glasgow and London).

Features and appeal – Located between Perth and Inverness, Aviemore was intended as a ski resort but it has unreliable snowfall. Activities include climbing and mountaineering, walking at different levels and skiing. There are also water sports, fishing on the nearby River Spey and local lochs, shooting, archery and golf.

1. **Visit the official Aviemore website. Identify activities that might attract people of different ages, family types and ability groups.**

Case study – **Glasgow**

Glasgow is a tourist city in the Strathclyde region of Scotland. It is the largest city in Scotland and lies on the River Clyde. As the third-largest British city, it can be reached by all major means of transport.

Glasgow was an industrial city but with the decline of heavy industry it has had to redefine itself. There are three main museums, of which the Burrell and the Charles Rennie Mackintosh are the most famous. The Burrell is based on the collection of William Burrell and has a wide range of exhibits, appealing to a broad range of people. The Charles Rennie Mackintosh Museum is very 'niche' (appealing to a very particular group of people). It celebrates the work of one man and his design. What might increase its appeal is that his designs are widely used today.

1 Using the Internet and other resources, find out more about the city of Glasgow, its appeal and some of the features mentioned in this case study.

The Welsh Tourist Board

Visit Wales is the tourism arm of the Welsh Assembly Government and it offers recommendations and information on visiting Wales. You will need to know about the following destinations in Wales, as well as the specific features and appeal of Snowdonia.

- Llandudno
- **Snowdonia**
- Bangor
- Conwy
- Cardiff
- Celtic Manor Resort (Wales)
- St Davids.

You can find out more by visiting the website.

Case study – **Belfast**

At first glance it may be difficult to see why Belfast is a business and conference centre. Geographically remote from mainland UK, it has only 3% of the UK population. However, there has been a £300 million investment in the city, which includes four major conference centres: Creative Events, Mount Conference Centre, Northern Ireland Conference Bureau and the Kings Hall Exhibition and Conference Centre. These offer access to quiet, beautiful countryside, modern facilities and a city with an attractive cultural evening life.

Northern Ireland Tourist Board

Northern Ireland shares a border with the Irish Republic and lies on the island of Ireland. Northern Ireland is part of the United Kingdom. The Northern Ireland Tourist Board offers information and recommendations on places to go to in Northern Ireland. You will need to learn about the following destinations in Northern Ireland as well as the specific features and appeal of Belfast:

- Portrush
- Antrim Coast and Glens
- **Belfast**
- Galgorm Resort (NI)
- Derry.

Northern Ireland has an historic appeal, and the tourist board actively promotes the heritage and family history features of the region (mass migration in the past means that there are many people who want to visit Northern Ireland to retrace their family histories). You can find out more by visiting the website.

Research it

Visit the Belfast Visitor & Convention Bureau website and find out more about Belfast as a business travel destination.

Summary

Tourist boards work together to promote the British Isles

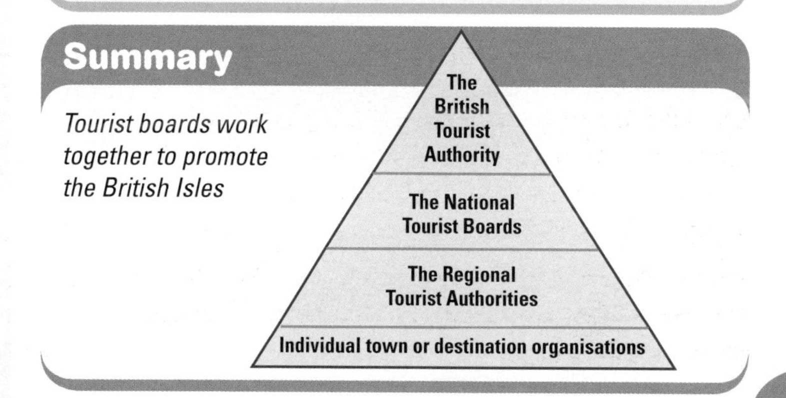

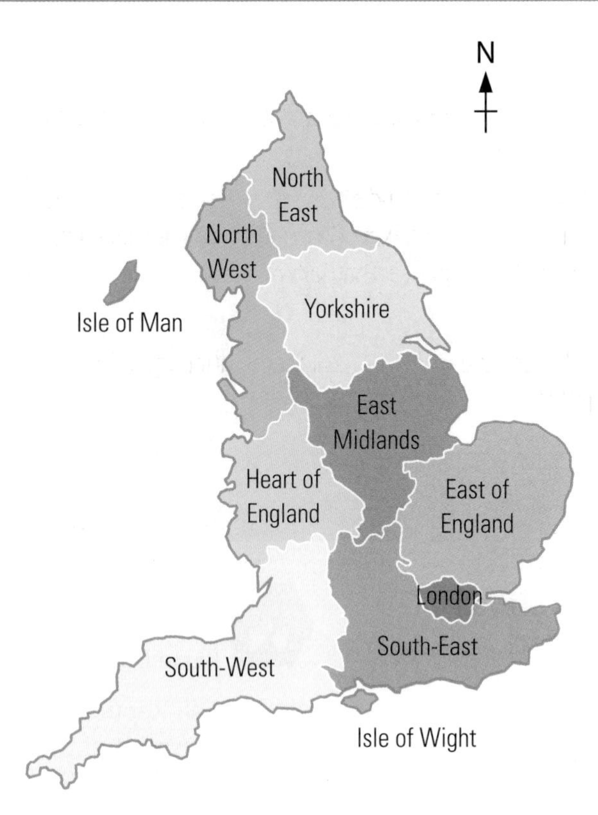

The regions of the English Tourist Board

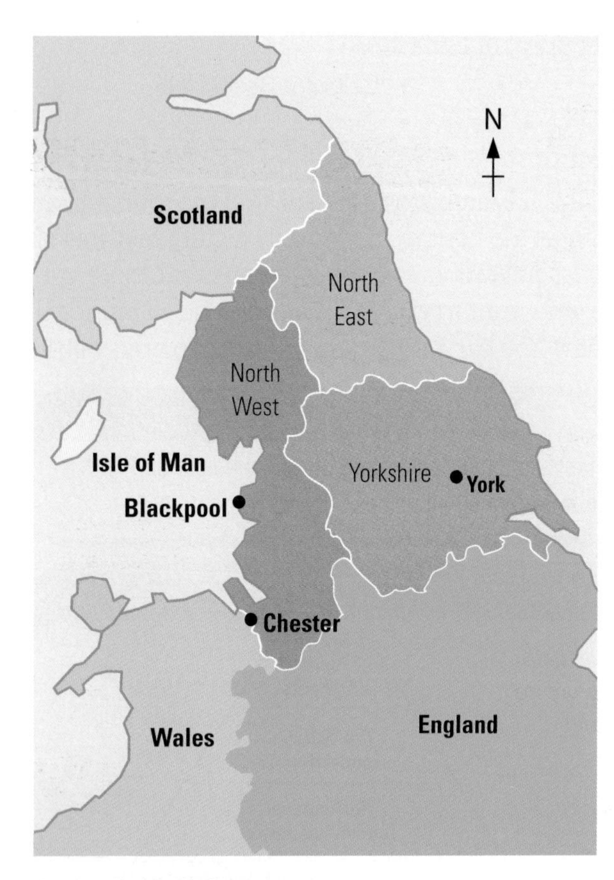

England's North Country

English Tourist Board and its regions

We are now going to look at the following English Tourist Board regions, together with some popular destinations in each. Remember that you will need to learn about the destinations in **bold** in greater detail.

- England's North Country
- Heart of England
- East Midlands and East England
- London and South-East
- South-West.

The English Tourist Board

VisitEngland is the official tourist board for England. Its purpose is to promote tourism throughout the English regions, both domestically and internationally throughout the year, in order to increase tourist income for England. Enjoy England is VisitEngland's public-facing brand, which is used in marketing and advertising campaigns throughout the UK. VisitEngland often provides information which is themed. For example, in 2009 it was the 200th anniversary of the birth of Charles Darwin. VisitEngland promoted events and destinations associated with Darwin under the Enjoy England brand on its website enabling people to research the Darwin theme easily.

England's North Country

England's North Country is made up of the North-East, the North-West and Yorkshire. There are 11 destinations you need to know about, three of which you will need to know about the specific features and appeal: Blackpool, Chester and York.

- **Blackpool**
- Whitby
- Lake District
- Yorkshire Dales
- Liverpool
- **York**
- Manchester
- Leeds
- Keldy Forest Holidays/ Hoseasons
- **Chester**
- Lindisfarne.

Case studies – Blackpool, Chester and York

These locations are grouped together for the purposes of comparing features and the appeal of different destinations.

Locations

- Blackpool is in Lancashire, North-West England. It is a seaside resort that serves the Manchester/Liverpool areas. It is reached on the M55 spur, west from the M6.
- Chester is in North-West England. It is an historical and cultural destination which serves the Manchester/Liverpool area. It is reached by the M56 spur, west from the M6.
- York is in Yorkshire, located on the East Coast Mainline rail link.

Features

- Blackpool has its Pleasure Beach, which has 125 rides including the Pepsi Max. It has a tower, which was intended to be like the Eiffel Tower in Paris, as well as the famous illuminations.
- Chester boasts Chester Zoo, Chester Cathedral and shopping in its historic core.
- York has many museums and places of historical interest such as York Dungeon, Jorvik Viking Centre, The Castle Museum, The Yorkshire Museum and The Railway Museum.

Appeal

- Blackpool: mass tourism, short-stay destination for family fun and nightlife.
- Chester: an upmarket location; does not expect huge visitor numbers; a short-stay destination.
- York: appeals to a very wide range of occasional and short-stay tourists; family destination but for more educational purposes.

The Heart of England

The 'Heart of England' is the West Midlands region. There are five destinations you need to know about, two of which you will need to know about the specific features and appeal: Birmingham and Alton Towers Resort.

- Cotswolds
- Warwick
- **Birmingham**
- **Alton Towers Resort**
- Stratford-upon-Avon.

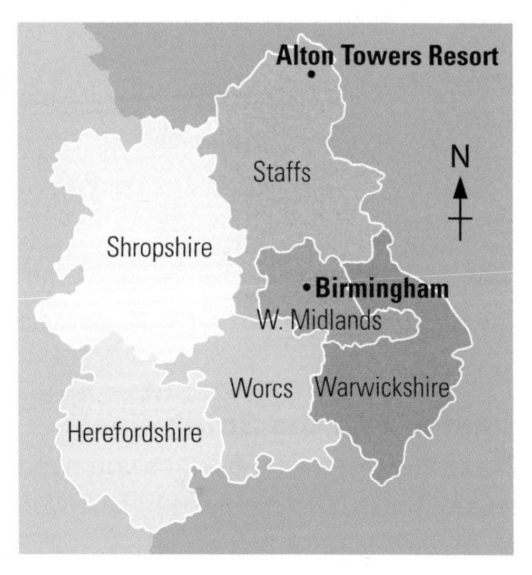

Assessment tip

If you need to describe a destination's location think: north, south, east, west, inland, coastal etc.

Case studies – Birmingham and Alton Towers Resort

Locations

- Birmingham is the principal city of the West Midlands and is a major conference and business centre.
- Alton Towers is a purpose-built destination east of the M6, reached by the A50.

Features

- Birmingham is one of the world's major conference cities – there are 177 venues in and around the city which cover all sorts of needs. The International Convention Centre (ICC) and National Exhibition Centre (NEC) are two of the most well known.
- Alton Towers is advertised as 'fantastic family fun' with the Oblivion and Nemesis rides. It is a theme park which aims to thrill people with fear.

Appeal

- Birmingham: very good business destination as it has good transport links to the rest of the world.
- Alton Towers: mass market, short-stay destination for families and school groups.

East Midlands and East England

There are three destinations you need to know about in the East Midlands and East England. You don't need to cover any of these in great detail.

- Great Yarmouth
- Cambridge
- Center Parcs – Sherwood Forest.

visiteastofengland.com

The Peak District is in the East Midlands region

VISIT LONDON

VISITLONDON.COM

TOURISM SOUTH EAST

London and the South-East

There are seven destinations you need to know about in this English region. None of these need to be covered in great detail.

- Eastbourne
- The New Forest
- Oxford
- London
- Brighton
- Butlins – Bognor Regis
- Canterbury.

The South-East and London have their own tourist boards.

South-West

There are four destinations in the South-West you need to know about, two of which you will need to learn about their specific features and appeal: Bath and Newquay.

PROUDLY SUPPORTING
South West
England

- **Newquay**
- Dartmoor
- Center Parcs – Longleat Forest
- **Bath**.

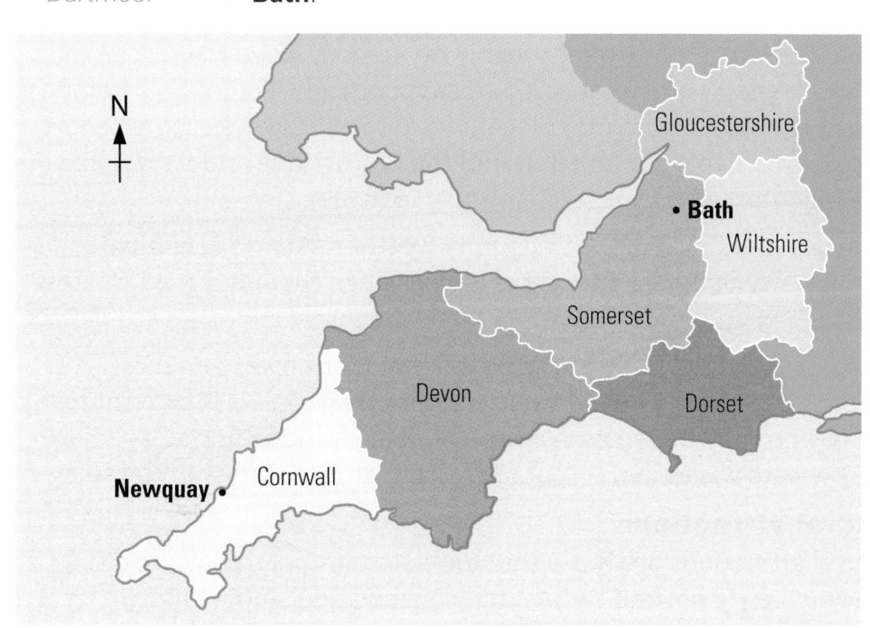

The ancient Roman baths in Bath are a popular attraction

Case studies – Newquay and Bath

Locations

- Newquay is in Cornwall, west of Dartmoor and is a seaside resort. It can be reached via the M5.
- Bath is close to Bristol, south of the M4, and can be reached by the A46.

Features

- Newquay is the surfing capital of Britain.
- Bath is an historical and cultural destination. It is a world heritage site known for its Roman Baths and the Royal Crescent. The novelist Jane Austen lived in Bath but found it impossible to write there. Nevertheless, tourists want to visit Bath because her books are full of references to it and places that still exist.

Appeal

- Newquay: the sea, the surf and youthful activities.
- Bath: a compact town that is easy to walk around; short-break destination; educational and literary bias.

Talk about it

In pairs or small groups, visit the websites of the UK tourist boards and English regions, and look at the logos of each. Some of them appear on pages 138–143. Which do you think are good? Which do you think are not so good? Why? Choose one of the logos your pair/group thought was not so good and say how you would improve on it, or suggest a new one.

Summary

Tourist boards promote and recommend tourist destinations, products and services in their own areas or regions.

The features and appeal of UK destinations

In this section we will look at the sorts of thing that make a place a good tourist destination.

Climate

The climate of a country or region is the typical weather and refers to things like rainfall, hours of sunshine and prevailing winds. UK tourism destinations can rarely offer reliably dry periods. Even the resorts of the South and South-West can be disappointingly wet in the summer, so many people choose dryer locations abroad. However, some people do look for reliable winter snow and the Cairngorms and Snowdonia have high rainfall which turns to snow in winter.

Some destinations like to offer sunny weather, such as Brighton for example, which appeals for short breaks when there is a good weather forecast.

A prevailing wind is the wind direction that is strongest and most frequent in an area. Finding a reliable prevailing wind is important for people who want activities such as kite flying, windsurfing and gliding. Winds create waves in the South-West and attract surfers to Newquay.

Research it

Perform a search on the Internet to find out what the wind is like today in different areas of the UK. Where do you think would be a good place to go for a day of kite flying?

Natural attractions

Natural attractions are those that are not manmade. They are often areas or sites of natural beauty and conservation, and include coastlines, moorlands, waterfalls, lakes (or lochs in Scotland), rivers, forests, fens and mountains.

UK coastlines are varied so there are different reasons why people are attracted to them. Oban and Whitby are fishing towns that appeal to sightseers; Portrush and Great Yarmouth offer traditional sandy beaches; Llandudno is warmed by the Gulf Stream and offers good bathing; Eastbourne, with its chalk cliffs, appeals to walkers.

Dartmoor is a rugged moorland area remote from centres of population, which appeals to people who want a wilderness 'get-away-from-it-all' experience.

High Force is a waterfall in County Durham. At 21 metres, it is the highest unbroken waterfall in England.

Running through many of the cities of the UK are rivers. Boat trips appeal to many city visitors because they are able to see key sites whilst relaxing. Boats can also be set up as night clubs, attracting young people.

Fens are areas of land that were marshy. Drained fenland is flat, so it is ideal for cycling and riding. The canals that drain the land are good for boating, and the grasslands are rich in wildlife and natural vegetation, making good walking country with plenty to see.

Snowdon is the highest mountain in Wales. It is sometimes also described as the busiest since it appeals to serious walkers and to visitors who use the mountain railway.

Case studies – National parks

Loch Lomond and the Trossachs

Loch Lomond and the Trossachs is a national park in Scotland. North of Glasgow, the highland boundary fault runs through this park so that the north is in the Highlands and the south is in the lowlands. This area boasts many natural attractions: moors, mountain, lake, rivers, forest and a waterfall. The lake and rivers Fruin and Leven bring people who want to sail and fish, whilst the mountain (Ben Lomond) and forest (Argyll Forest) attracts those who like to walk and climb. The famous Inversnaid waterfall provides a romantic setting in this otherwise rugged destination. It is an area that attracts people from nearby Glasgow and Edinburgh who want to get away from urban areas to walk and pursue countryside activities, as well as those from further afield.

The New Forest

The New Forest is a national park located near Southampton in Hampshire. It can be reached by the M3/M27 and overlooks the Isle of Wight. Within easy reach of London for a short break, the New Forest attracts people who want a gentle time rather than a rugged and challenging break.

1 A couple you know are planning their honeymoon but can't decide whether to choose Loch Lomond or the New Forest. Using the official website of Loch Lomond and the Trossachs, stirling.co.uk and thenewforest.co.uk, plan a five-day honeymoon at each location to help them to decide, detailing where they could stay and what they could do.

Built attractions

Ancient monuments are a type of built attraction, and Stonehenge in Wiltshire is probably the UK's most famous. Built over 3,000 years ago, it is visited by about 18,000 people each year and is a UNESCO World Heritage Site. Stonehenge appeals to all sorts of people, including those who are interested in history and those who belong to what some might call 'counter cultures' and 'alternative groups'.

Built attractions also refer to themes parks. People have always enjoyed gathering together to enjoy themselves and have fun, whether it be at a festival, fair, carnival or circus. As it became easier for people to move around regions and areas of the country, these types of attraction began to settle in certain locations, attracting people to visit them. Popular theme parks today include **Alton Towers** and **Blackpool** Pleasure Beach, which appeal to adults with young children and teenagers because they offer a 'one stop' reliable day out or short break.

Stonehenge is a set of huge standing stones arranged in a circular formation, which some believe were used as a burial ground

Indoor arenas are another type of built attraction. Rather like ancient Roman amphitheatres, they enable people to gather together to see events. The National Indoor Arena in Birmingham is a multi-purpose arena that stages sports events, concerts, business conferences and exhibitions. Glasgow has the Scottish National Indoor Arena, whilst the M.E.N in Manchester is the largest indoor arena in the UK. Indoor arenas are often sponsored by companies, such as the Metro Radio Arena in Newcastle, or can be themed, like the Edinburgh International Climbing Arena and Belfast Indoor Tennis Arena. These destinations appeal to people who are happy to travel distances to see events that match their interests.

Summary

Climate, natural attractions and built attractions can make a destination an appealing and attractive place to visit.

Events

Research it

Find out what local events are happening in your area soon.

1. **Make a list of events that would appeal to people of different age groups and with different interests.**
2. **Do the local events you have found out about tell you anything about your area?**

Agricultural shows draw people from the surrounding counties

Events can be local, regional or national. Local events are things like school fêtes, country fairs and agricultural shows, art exhibitions, firework displays and fun runs. Regional events include things like county shows, such as the Northumberland Country Show. These types of event attract people who live in the county or neighbouring counties, which is what makes it regional.

The Great North Run is an example of a national event, so called because it attracts people from all over the country. It is the world's biggest half marathon and people travel from other countries just to take part. Sports events are good examples of national events as people from all countries of the UK will travel to watch their team participate. The Millennium Stadium in Cardiff hosts rugby internationals and boxing, Celtic Manor hosts the Welsh Golf Open Championships, and St Andrews is home to The Open Championship, the Alfred Dunhill Links Championship, and the Links Trophy.

The Last Night of the Proms, an annual music and concert event held in London, is another example of a national event.

The appeal of some destinations is the chance to take part in a national event, like the Great North Run

Apply it

Interview your friends and family about the local, regional and national events they attend. Which ones do they like to go to? Do some of them like to go to particular types of event – music, sport, animal shows? How far would they travel to watch or take part in an event?

Food, drink and entertainment

Eating and drinking are necessary parts of life, but sometimes we make a point of visiting somewhere just to have a meal or a drink. It could be the type of food, the quality of the service, the entertainment on offer or an occasion such as a birthday or funeral that takes us away from our own kitchen. The destination may be a restaurant, a bar, a café, a pub or a club.

Pubs, clubs and bars

The ages of those visiting a pub, club or bar is likely to be 18 plus because of restrictions on drinking age. They are typically adult places where drinking, smoking and sometimes cultural activities (such as music or entertainment) have enabled friendship groups to gather. Of course, smoking is now illegal in public places such as these.

In many tourist towns, such as **Whitby**, tourism has diluted the community appeal of many pubs and bars since many people only visit them for the short period of time they are on holiday. The smoking ban has also reduced numbers of customers. In non-tourist bars, where local communities gather without 'intruders', pubs and bars have survived as important parts of the community.

Talk about it

1. In pairs or small groups, talk about when you last went to a restaurant. Why did you go? What sort of restaurant was it? Was it cheap and cheerful or posh and expensive? Would you go back?
2. In pairs or as a group, make a list of the different types of restaurant you know of. Why do you think there are so many different types? Who do you think would typically go to each type?

Research it

Talk to an older person you know about how they think pubs and bars have changed during their lifetime. Gather these opinions together as a class and discuss the outcomes.

Case study – Derry, NI

Derry is located on Loch Foyle in the north of Northern Ireland. Desperately troubled by the violence of the last century, it has become a tourist destination where good food and fine bars and cafés are a city attraction. Derry is one of the places you need to be able to locate on a map and describe. As a destination that cannot rely on its weather to draw in tourists (as with many areas of the UK, mild with rain all year), no beaches and few well-known historic sites, Derry has had to make use of its main resource: its reputation for good food and drink, namely seafood and Guinness!

1. **Visit the Derry Visitor website and explore the various places offering food, drink and entertainment.**
2. **Make a list of five of the venues you have seen. Who do you think is the target market for each? Justify your answers.**

Assessment tip

You will need to know the features and appeal of some UK tourist destinations. Just remember that you are simply telling the examiner why people should go somewhere and what they can do whilst they're there!

The world's biggest cruise ship, The Royal Caribbean's Project Genesis, *will have an outdoor park on board!*

Transport services and links

In this section we are going to look at:

- Water transport
- Rail transport
- Buses, coaches and airports.

Water transport

Ferries and cruise ships, which are forms of water transport, can be destinations in themselves. Some offer a whole raft of facilities to keep travellers happy and entertain them, including cinemas, cafés, bars and restaurants. Accommodation ranges from 'couchettes' (basic sleeping facilities) to luxurious cabins for the more affluent. There are also usually shops, play rooms for children and even swimming pools. Cruise ships usually also offer activities such as games, dancing, sports and competitions, which vary depending on the size of the ship and its destination.

Ferry ports offer a much smaller range of facilities because people will spend much less time there. Often arriving at all hours of the day and night with tired families, the main types of facility on offer are 24-hour toilets and refreshments. Freight drivers are offered lounges where the food might be more substantial.

Portsmouth is a ferry port and offers more than basic facilities, aiming to 'capture' the traveller before they depart. The Historic Dockyard, the remains of the ship *Mary Rose* and the birthplace of Charles Dickens are only three of a huge range of attractions.

Rail transport

Whilst London is the major railway hub of the UK, York is home to the National Railway Museum. With easy, rapid and regular train services for the east of the UK, York attracts visitors and tourists because it is a transport hub.

Buses, coaches and airports

Often seen as the 'poor relation' to the train, buses and coaches appeal to people because they are inexpensive. The facilities available on coaches rarely amount to more than toilets and drinks, either on board or at the bus station, whilst buses usually offer no such facilities.

Contrasting these basic services with those common at airports might suggest that airports draw people with their huge range of attractions, but this is not the case. Airport services are there, in part, to keep passengers tranquil and occupied in a place where they are often anxious, unhappy and having to wait, subject to checks, queues and security. What appeals to people about airports is the ability to get to the destination of their choice in the most efficient way.

Remember it

When Thomas Cook first introduced his package holiday trip from Leicester to Loughborough in 1841, he used the new railway system. Since then, transport hubs have become major tourism destinations.

Accommodation

Accommodation can be the reason people visit a destination and we will now look at some different types.

Serviced accommodation

Hotels provide for those who wish to have a complete service. They attract by offering a completely carefree environment. Their main disadvantages are that guests have to conform to set times for meals and they can be expensive, depending on the type of hotel. Hotels appeal to a whole range of tourists and business travellers because they are very varied in nature.

Lack of flexibility is also a part of staying in cheaper B&B accommodation where residents live in the owner's accommodation. B&Bs appeal to singles and couples on short breaks rather than families, where being flexible is usually a necessity. Guesthouses are family houses that have been made over to the exclusive use of visitors so, unlike B&Bs, visitors are unrestricted by rules and times, although they may have to cater for themselves. Guesthouses often appeal to families because of the increased flexibility.

B&Bs and guesthouses can be found in most areas, such as cities, towns and villages, but they can have an increased appeal when they are in the country on a farm. By offering spare rooms for B&B, farmers can make additional income from their land. Inns and pubs sometimes offer rooms too, allowing guests a central location and flexibility regarding where they choose to eat. A disadvantage for families might be the noise from these accommodation types, so pubs and inns usually appeal to singles and couples.

Youth hostels are another type of serviced accommodation. They offer cheap, communal (shared) accommodation to young people, often walkers or cyclists. Owned by the Youth Hostel Association (YHA), they are now in competition with privately run bunk barns (budget communal accommodation and catering facilities).

Self-catering accommodation

Cottages and converted barns in the country are popular choices for self-catering accommodation. Idyllic settings and having a home from home are all part of their appeal. A group of purpose-built self-catering cottages can develop into a holiday centre with some refreshment facilities or a shop, entertainment, trekking and trails, and play areas.

Caravans, tents and motorhomes can also be fun and cheap ways to travel or spend leisure time. There are numerous camping and touring sites all over the country offering anything from the most basic of facilities to bars, shops, activities and entertainment. Some people enjoy nothing more than the sense of freedom they get from packing up their caravan or tent and travelling around a region or area, booking a campsite as and when they need it.

Research it

Visit the YHA website and find out more about youth hostelling and the facilities available at some of the locations.

1 **Why do you think youth hostelling appeals to some people?**
2 **Why do you think some people don't stay in youth hostels when they travel?**

Summary

The features and appeal of a destination might include: its climate, its natural and built attractions, events, food, drink and entertainment, transport services and links, and accommodation.

Center Parcs resorts in the UK

How features of destinations appeal to different types of visitors

In this section we will look at some different types of visitors, sometimes referred to as 'markets', and match them to some destinations you need to know about.

Families

Center Parcs resorts are great family holiday destinations. This is because researching and booking all the elements that go to make a family holiday can be time-consuming and expensive. Most families are busy, with one or more parents working and children may be at different schools. Families are also usually restricted by budget, making a holiday in the UK with lots of facilities and activities on site an attractive option. A holiday at a resort like Center Parcs can also be appealing to families due to the safe and organised environment. Unfortunately, the British weather is not so dependable, which is obviously a drawback.

Talk about it

Families may gather together for all sorts of reasons, not just for holidays. In small groups or as a class, think of some other reasons why families may travel to a destination to be together. To get you started: weddings, birthdays, Bar Mitzvahs, anniversaries...

Groups

Some destinations cater to groups of people such as students, young people and those with a shared special interest. The Field Studies Council is an environmental educational charity that has a network of 17 centres across the UK offering day and residential fieldwork and environmental activities to groups of students. Special interest groups, such as the Girl Guides, visit destinations to take part in group activities or holidays. Music festivals like Glastonbury and Leeds Music Festival are another type of destination that attracts groups of people with a common interest.

The YHA (see page 149) is the UK's leading group accommodation provider due its numerous locations, low cost and opportunities to mix with other people from all over the world.

Couples

Honeymoons, romantic breaks, shared activities/interests and meals out are just some of the reasons a couple may travel to a destination. Couples are just as likely to be mature and have children as those who are young with no children, but honeymooners are typically young people with considerable disposable income. As so many people live in busy urban areas, it is not surprising that countryside areas are the top honeymoon destinations for those who stay in the UK, with the Lake District being the most popular. The Lake District offers peace and tranquillity after a hectic few weeks preparing for the wedding.

It is important to remember that couples also include people in same-sex relationships and civil partnerships. Manchester has a well-known gay scene, with a gay pride march and a gay village. It is a cosmopolitan destination where openly gay couples can feel safe and are less likely to be discriminated against. For many destinations such as Brighton, Liverpool and London, this is an increasingly important market.

Music festivals attract groups of people who all share a love of music

Senior citizens/empty nesters

There are 20 million people aged 50 or over living in the UK. Some of these are senior citizens and they can be couples or singles. They often travel in groups, particularly as coach parties. Others are sometimes referred to as 'empty nesters', which are a parent or parents with grown-up children who have left home, leaving them with an empty nest. This group of people often feel that their leisure and travel time is their 'me time' – their chance to enjoy themselves again now that their childrearing and financial responsibilities have decreased.

Senior citizens can have special needs due to poor health or fragility, whilst others are perfectly fit and healthy and don't require any kind of extra care. Coach travel to destinations with good scenery and places to visit are popular among senior citizens and empty nesters. Countryside areas such as the **Yorkshire Dales** and the **Cotswolds**, and tourist towns and cities with historical appeal such as **York** and Warwick are particularly appealing to these groups.

SAGA is an organisation that provides holidays for older people. SAGA Volunteer Travel enables older people to travel to places where they can offer help to charitable projects, particularly in less economically developed countries.

Individuals

Whilst many individuals join groups to enable them to enjoy travel and tourism, there are people who choose to travel alone and genuinely enjoy it. They might see it as an opportunity to get away from it all, meet new people, find out more about themselves, learn new skills or increase their confidence. Trekking and adventure holidays are popular choices.

Business travellers

Business travellers often don't have much choice about their destination – they may simply have to go there to carry out business. They usually have very specific needs, wanting somewhere to sleep and get refreshments. Arriving late at a hotel in a strange town or city, perhaps with work to do, means it is also important that there are good technology facilities, room service and reliable information. Business travellers may also need things like conference facilities or meeting rooms.

Visitors with specific needs

There are 8.6 million people with disabilities in the UK, and whilst all destinations need to comply with the law (it is unlawful for service providers, landlords and other persons to discriminate against disabled people), some destinations cater specifically for people with disabilities.

The Leeds Wall is a climbing wall that has good disabled climbing access and is part of The National Indoor Climbing Achievement Scheme. Other organisations offer holiday packages to people with disabilities, organising accommodation, activities and visits to attractions tailored to their needs.

Apply it

A recently retired couple in their early 60s have asked you for advice on planning a short city break in the UK. Where would you recommend? How would you advise they travel? Where should they stay? What could they do whilst there? Remember to explain your choices.

Talk about it

Which destinations might be appropriate for those who truly wish to travel alone?

Research it

The Sheraton Hotel chain was voted the best business hotel chain in the world. Find out what they offer business people which makes them so good.

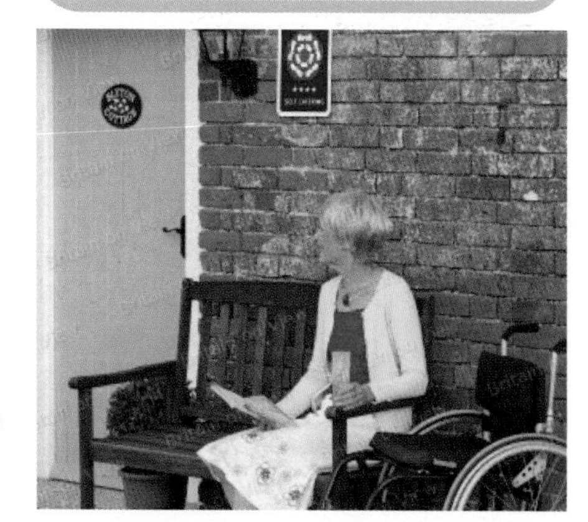

Some destinations cater specifically for people with disabilities

Research it

Use the Internet to find out more about organisations that offer information and holiday packages to disabled people. What destinations and activities are on offer?

Summary

Some destinations have features that appeal to different visitor types.

3.3 The Impacts of Tourism

This topic looks at how tourism affects destinations, both in positive and negative ways. We will look at the effects on local communities as well as the local environment. Then we will look at the methods that are used to reduce the negative impacts of tourism and how effective they are. Finally we will learn what ecotourism is, the products and services associated with it, and its advantages and disadvantages.

Positive impacts on local communities

Some less economically developed countries have poor infrastructures (roads and transport, water and electricity supplies, schools and hospitals) and high levels of unemployment, resulting in little money to pay taxes and a government that has little money to provide these facilities and services.

When tourism spreads to such areas there are usually some positive impacts on the local communities. The infrastructure and employment levels improve, improving the quality of life for people who live in the area. Tourism can also increase awareness of the cultures of the local communities.

We are going to explore the positive impacts tourism has had on Nkhata Bay in Malawi. You should then be able to use the information and ideas in the case study to apply them to other destinations you have learned about.

Research it

Visit the Lonely Planet website and explore the destination pages. By attracting tourists to areas that are 'lonely', are guides such as Lonely Planet destroying the very things that make a destination appealing? Do you think the benefits to the local people outweigh the 'untouched' nature the destination had before tourism began?

Talk about it

When two different cultures meet, it is always the hope that there will be a greater understanding and appreciation of each other. But serving rich Western tourists, used to 'the customer always being right', may lead to resentment. Talk about this idea in groups or as a class. Do you think tourists really connect with the local communities they are visiting?

Apply it

Identify an area which is in need of redevelopment. Come up with a small leisure facility project that would improve the quality of life for local people in the area. How would it improve their lives? How might it have negative effects on local people?

Case study – **Nkhata Bay, Malawi**

Malawi is a small, landlocked country (i.e. it has no coastline) located in the south-east of Africa. Nkhata Bay is a large village, located on the shore of Lake Malawi. This is now an adventure holiday destination where tourists can fish, dive and sail, visit the historic Livingstone Mission and see plantations of rubber, coffee and tea. Most visiting people stay in lodges.

Improved infrastructure

To attract visitors, accommodation had to meet Western standards and transport links have had to be improved to enable visitors to explore the area and get to and from their accommodation. Water supplies and treatment works were also improved, as well as medical facilities and the number of available doctors.

Increased employment

Many of the lodges in Nkhata Bay employ local people, which along with the increased demand by tourists for other products and services, has led to a rise in employment levels in the local community. Employees are paid in money, which is not usual in Malawi, where many people live by growing or making the food and other items they need. Having cash enables members of the local community to buy electricity, which in turn means they can refrigerate their food, reducing illness and disease. Lodge owners also often pay their employees' medical and school fees, as well as those of their families. Members of the local community also make money by selling souvenirs to tourists. Local woodcarvers make carvings, while women sew dolls and handbags, and gather honey to sell. Local musicians play in the lodge restaurants and some people act as tour guides. There are also all the other usual tourism-related jobs such as waiting, cooking, cleaning and making beds.

Improved quality of life

As you can imagine, all the changes to Nkhata Bay brought about by tourism have improved the quality of life for many of the people who live there. They can make use of the improved infrastructure and facilities, they have better access to medical care, as well as recreational facilities – Nkhata Bay now has its own pizza restaurant that can be enjoyed by both tourists and locals, as well as swimming pools and children's play areas. Many local people have found jobs or even started their own businesses as a result of the increase in visitor numbers. The Foundation for International Community Assistance (FINCA), offers small loans to local people, helping them get started with new business ideas, which in turn feeds back into the local community by encouraging the tourism industry.

Improved awareness of other cultures

Nkhata Bay is home to the Tonga people. The increase in tourism to their communities has lead to an increased awareness, understanding and interest in their cultures and customs.

Summary

- Tourism can have positive impacts on local communities, both on small and grand scales. Improvements can include: better infrastructure, better access to leisure facilities, increased employment opportunities, an improved quality of life and an increased awareness of other cultures.
- For many less economically developed countries, tourism can help people break free from the cycle of poverty.

Assessment tip

In this section we have been looking at the positive impacts of tourism on local communities. In the next section we will be looking at the negative impacts. This is an 'analysis'. You may be asked to analyse a leisure and tourism topic in the exam.

Negative impacts on local communities

Tourism can have just as many negative effects on local communities as positive ones, and we will look at some of these now.

Disruption to everyday life

Have you ever been in a traffic queue with lots of tourist buses? Ever had to wait to use leisure facilities because of large numbers of tourists using them? What about not being able to get on your bus because it is full of tourists? Increased visitor numbers to destinations can make everyday life for the local community difficult.

Case study – Oban

Oban is located in Western Scotland, about three hours' drive from Glasgow on the A83. The summer is when most tourists visit and also when most locals notice increased noise, litter, congestion and pollution. Tourism has a big effect on the town because it is so small.

Tour buses arrive suddenly and often, with tourists all wanting the same things within a very short time: toilets, food and souvenirs. If several buses arrive at the same time, ordinary life in the town can come to a standstill.

1 Create a leaflet to distribute to the residents of Oban, reminding them how tourism can bring benefits as well as irritation.

Crime and prostitution

Crime and prostitution inevitably go where tourists go because tourists usually carry lots of money, may be more reckless or not as careful with their possessions as they would be when at home, and may take part in practices that they normally wouldn't.

Italy's capital Rome is a big and busy tourist destination, with an unfortunate reputation for wallet and handbag theft. Criminals called *scippatori* drive around the streets of Rome on scooters snatching tourists' belongings, even ripping off watches and jewellery as they pass by.

Crime in tourist destinations has many negative impacts on the community, including the fact that the rich pickings from tourists attracts more criminals. Also, when the tourism season ends or slows down, the criminals turn to the local people as targets.

Cultural exploitation happens when people who find it difficult to access activities that are illegal or frowned upon in their own country go to other countries in order to practise them. Some may excuse activities such as prostitution by saying that the practice is culturally acceptable in the tourism destination or that they are benefiting the people by giving them money. In Thailand, poverty, war and corruption has led to the perception or idea that Thai society accepts prostitution and paedophilia, but this is not the case. Instead, extreme poverty forces many people to cities, where they fall prey to tourist demand for their services.

Loss of culture/Westernisation

Areas that want to promote tourism often use their distinct cultures as a unique selling point. Tourists only visit places briefly and usually want to experience and capture a small piece of an alternative culture. Local people can be forced by circumstance to sell their cultural artefacts. Culture can also be affected by lack of participation on the part of locals. In some parts of Australian Aboriginal society, traditional 'dream paintings' are created for tourists to buy. It has been argued that whilst the native Australians make money from these, they no longer involve themselves in the normal activities of their culture as a result.

Some women of Padaung in Myanmar (formerly Burma) traditionally made their necks longer by adding metal rings to their necklaces. This phenomenon has become a tourist curiosity and women who would not normally practise this are under pressure to show themselves for the tourist trade.

Tourist destinations can also suffer losses to their cultural practices due to the influence of Western ways. This is known as 'Westernisation'.

Hostility and resentment/increased cost of living

In the Lake District, there are 22,930 homes, 15% of which are holiday or second homes (Cumbria County Council). The high demand for houses in some of these 'honey pot' areas like the Lake District makes house prices rise so that they are often outside the reach of the people who live and work in the area. Holiday homes are also left empty for considerable parts of the week or year, which means that a lot of the time there are too few people to use local shops and facilities. They sometimes have to shut down, forcing local people to travel further. Increased travel costs increase their cost of living and the cost of their food. These impacts can cause hostility and resentment towards tourists.

Summary

Not all aspects of the leisure and tourism industry are positive for local people. Negative impacts can be due to disruption of everyday life, crime, prostitution, loss of culture, Westernisation, hostility and resentment, and increased costs of living.

Apply it

Misperception and misconception of people and their cultures mean that we may do things as tourists that we should not do. Arrogance about our own way of life in the West means that tourists sometimes do things that are offensive to others.

1 **Write two short paragraphs: one giving an example of something that you have seen or heard about that has caused offence in a tourist destination; and one that discusses whether this might be a decreasing problem as the world becomes more globalised, and media and technology (especially the Internet) enables people to get a better idea of other ways of living.**

Research it

1 Find out the meanings of 'Westernisation' and 'globalisation' using the Internet.

2 What are the positive and negative impacts of each on the tourism industry?

Positive impacts on the local environment

We will now look at the positive impacts on local environments at tourist destinations, such as regeneration, conservation, creation of more open spaces and improved 'street furniture'.

Regeneration

'Regeneration' means to create again or to improve something. In some tourist destinations, housing and facilities can be old and in need of repair. Land and buildings may be derelict. 'Urban renewal' is where rundown and underused areas are revamped and given a new lease of life. Tourism can offer the opportunity to start again and improve destinations via regeneration and urban renewal.

Case study – London 2012 Olympics

Some leisure and tourism projects are designed to make an area better, whilst others do so as a knock-on effect. The 2012 Olympics site was a 'brownfield' site, which is where land that has been previously used and built on is left abandoned and disused. Some of this area had been contaminated with heavy metals, which can be harmful to humans, animals and plant life. The idea was to put the games in a place where regeneration and urban renewal were necessary and this has had a positive impact on the environment. For example, the site will be home to the biggest park in London.

1 Find out more about the Olympic park in London, as well as other areas around the UK where sporting events will be taking place. You could start by visiting the official website.

2 Do you think the Olympic park and the Olympic Games in 2012 will benefit the environment or cause negative impacts? Justify your answer.

This old barn has been given a different purpose

Throughout the UK there is reuse of traditional buildings, for instance a derelict railway station may become a children's play facility or restaurant. When traditional buildings lose their economic value they fall into disrepair and become derelict, dangerous and unsightly. By giving them new functions, there is a positive visual impact on the environment.

Conservation

Conservation means safeguarding and managing the environment in order to protect it. Human activity, including tourism, can have both positive and negative impacts on the environment. People sometimes find ways to combine tourism with conservation. For example, after the Second World War, Sir Peter Scott (son of the great polar explorer Robert Scott) decided that he wanted to help protect his local environment and its wildlife. He established the Slimbridge wildlife conservation area in Gloucestershire. He needed visitors to help to keep the park open so it became a tourist venue, which still attracts tourists today.

National parks, both in the UK and abroad, exist to help protect the environment from human development. For instance, timber can be gathered and sold and farming continues, but these activities must be 'sustainable', meaning that trees must be replanted and farming must not spoil or damage the environment.

National Nature Reserves were set up to protect important wildlife habitats. Their goal is to protect scarce and threatened areas, plants and wildlife. Tourists are welcomed but at the same time regulated and educated to be aware of the need to protect some parts of the countryside. World Heritage sites are a United Nations initiative. Vast areas of land and sea are protected. Tourists visit World Heritage sites, such as Hadrian's Wall in the UK, to learn more about their history. A benefit of this tourism is that the income can be used to help further maintain and protect the sites.

Creation of more open spaces

When more open spaces are created to attract tourists there can be positive impacts on the environment. For example, if a derelict railway line is redesigned to be a countryside walk, the vegetation will be managed and the litter cleared.

Improved street furniture

'Street furniture' refers to things such as:

- Lighting
- Seating
- Floral displays.

Many town centres can be frightening, dark and empty places at night, with few people staying once commuters have left work for home. Tourist towns have been keen to improve their street furniture in order to attract tourists and enliven the urban environment. Lighting makes places safer and more attractive at night. Seating encourages people to sit outside at pavement cafés. With more people using clubs, bars and restaurants, many towns have developed as vibrant and attractive tourist destinations.

Floral displays make a place more attractive and also encourage wildlife. Competitions like the Royal Horticultural Society Britain in Bloom, where individuals, groups or local authorities create floral displays and landscaped areas in their local region in order to compete with other regions, can bring good publicity to a destination. This in turn can inspire visiting tourists to go home and make an effort to improve their own environment, to try to win next time.

Research it

Find out more about Britain's national parks by visiting the National Parks website.

Apply it

There are probably some unused or wasteland areas near where you live. Do you think they should remain like this? Would they be better if they were built on or turned into conservation areas, parks or children's play areas? Think of a place you know and write a short letter to your local newspaper saying what should be done with it and why.

Summary

Regeneration, conservation, the creation of open spaces and improved 'street furniture' can have a positive impact on local environments.

Negative impacts on the local environment

We are now going to look at some of the negative impacts of tourism on local environments.

Loss of habitats and wildlife

A habitat is a unique environment that supports particular forms of life. When tourists visit a habitat they usually change it. Their presence and the changes they make may drive away the animals and plants that depend on the habitat.

Pollution

You may immediately think of air pollution when you hear the word pollution, and this does result from tourism largely due to transport. Aeroplanes, cars, buses, coaches and motorbikes all release fumes that pollute the air, although their impact is felt more on a global scale rather than local. However, in some destinations buildings can become dirty because of air pollution, which may require them to be cleaned or repaired. Air pollution in built-up areas can also affect people with respiratory conditions such as asthma. Some tourist destinations make use of more environmentally friendly forms of transport, such as Delhi in India where cycle rickshaws are a common way to get around. There are frequent threats to ban the rickshaws because of accidents, but it is argued that air pollution would increase as a result due to increased use of cars.

Water pollution can be another consequence of tourism. Human waste may overwhelm sewage systems in some destinations and be discharged straight into rivers or the sea. Pleasure boats discharge waste into the water if laws are not in place to control their activities.

Pollution can also be caused by noise and light from things like transport, buildings and people. Both can lead to lack of sleep and disruption, and in severe cases mental health problems.

Visual pollution may be something you have never thought of before, but think about some of the big tourist resorts and how 'unsightly' some people think they are. Hotels, holiday parks, visitor attractions and the construction work that must happen in order to create them can be very unappealing to look at. Their contribution to pollution is increased if they also create noise, light, air or water pollution as well as being an eyesore!

Overcrowding

Tourists sometimes choose to visit destinations with small populations. Such locations often have an infrastructure that matches the needs of the resident population. Narrow streets and pavements become congested by visiting cars and tourists. Beaches become overcrowded because they are backed by high-rise hotels which have a greater capacity than the beach.

Talk about it

Think of some places you have visited as a tourist. Were they heavily built on or were they more rural? What did you think about how they looked? Do you think that tourism affected the appearance of the places? Do you think you would feel differently about the appearance of the places if you lived there?

Traffic congestion

Increased visitor numbers to a place almost certainly bring increased numbers of vehicles, which can lead to congestion. This means slower speeds, queues, longer travel times and ultimately irritation! Some destinations have introduced methods to overcome traffic congestion, including congestion charges whereby drivers are charged to enter certain areas. Durham was the first city in the UK to introduce charges, with London following and Manchester considering a similar scheme.

Take it further

Throughout this unit there are examples of negative impacts on the environment caused by leisure and tourism activities. Scan the pages and identify the examples. Share these with the class and see if you can come up with any of your own.

Case study – Goa

Goa is an Indian seaside destination located south of Mumbai, on the Arabian Sea. In 2004 there were 2 million tourist visits to Goa, which has a population of 1.4 million. There can be times when the area has over 1,000 people per km^2! Unsurprisingly, this has a huge impact on local habitats, the wildlife and environment, as we will see.

In attempts to try to increase the land area on which to build new hotels to house increasing numbers of visitors, mangrove forests are being destroyed. As the mangroves go, so do the fish. With their habitat gone, wildlife that relies on the fish for food starts to disappear too.

The sea water in Goa has become polluted too. Water sports are popular and power boats sometimes leak pollution into the sea. In addition, plastics dropped by tourists pollute the water and make it look unsightly. Fresh water in Goa is becoming salty because of tourist demands – as fresh water is pumped from underground for pools and showers, salty water has the opportunity to seep in to its place. As freshwater becomes polluted by salt, it threatens the habitat of freshwater species of animals and those that rely on them for food.

The sand in sand dunes along the beaches in Goa is used to make cement for the construction of hotels and roads. This destroys the plants that live on the dunes and also removes the barriers created by the dunes, which protect the roads and houses from being covered in sand. The more hotels built, the more people visit, and the more people are employed. They bring their families and need more homes to live in, and the area becomes congested and overcrowded.

Research it

Use your school VLE to ask parents and students to list what they think are the five worst environmental impacts of tourism. Write an article about what you have found for your school website.

Summary

Tourism can have negative impacts on local environments due to loss of habitats, loss of wildlife, pollution, overcrowding and traffic congestion.

Reducing negative impacts of tourism

We are going to explore how the negative impacts of tourism can be reduced by focusing on the Lake District National Park. You should then be able to use the information and ideas in the case study to apply them to other destinations you have learned about.

Case study – **Lake District National Park**

The Lake District National Park is a good example of the conflict many tourist destinations face. On the one hand, there is the desire to encourage people to visit and experience the area for themselves; on the other there is the need to preserve the area and keep it unspoilt, after all, that is what the 12 million or so visitors each year are coming to see.

Planning and legislation

All building work in the Lake District has to be planned and strictly regulated. It also has to go before a hearing and given the 'green light' before it can take place in order to restrict the amount of development and the impact on the area. Footpaths in the Lake District National Park can become eroded (worn down) due to visitor use. The Lake District Park Authority regularly looks at footpath use, as well as road use, and makes plans to build new ones before excessive erosion occurs. The Park Authority also regularly looks at information provision at the park. Signs and maps can not only be informative but also ensure that visitors use the correct paths and facilities. Road signs can also help prevent traffic congestion at busy times.

Some laws have been introduced in order to keep the Lake District environment safe. The Environment Protection Act 1990 allows the Park Authority to impose Traffic Regulation Orders. This means that a path or bridleway can be closed for a period of time to allow for repairs or to let it recover from overuse. Anglers have to obtain a licence in order to fish. This restricts the number of people who can fish at the Lake District National Park and encourages good practice such as fishing responsibly and respecting the environment. Licences are also only issued at certain times of the year, allowing the fish and other wildlife to be undisturbed during their breeding seasons.

Vehicles such as four-wheel drives and motorbikes can damage countryside areas and also cause problems related to pollution and noise. As a result, The Natural Environment and Rural Communities Act 2006 prevents open access to off-road vehicles. Traffic on Lake Windermere is also regulated. Many leisure activities take place on or near the lake, such as cruises, boating, rowing, sailing and swimming as well as cycling, golf, horse riding and walking. Because visitors want to use the lake and its surrounding areas in so many different ways, a speed limit of ten nautical miles per hour was introduced on the lake in order to reduce noise and make the lake safer.

Some activities are regulated in order to reduce their impact on the environment. We have already read that anglers need to obtain a licence before they fish. The RSPB (Royal Society for the Protection of Birds) has set up special places where people can bird watch at locations in the Lake District. This is important as it means that people can still enjoy the activity but are less likely to disturb the birds, particularly during their breeding seasons.

Managing traffic

We have already seen that traffic is managed in the Lake District by planning and legislation. Certain vehicles have restricted access, roads can be closed to allow for repair or recovery, signs can help reduce congestion, and speed limits can reduce noise and increase safety. In addition, one-way systems and off-street parking can stop cars cluttering paths and verges, which increases congestion in small towns and can create resentment amongst local people.

Managing visitors

It is the job of a park ranger to protect the park and the people who visit it. An important part of their job is to provide information to visitors and advise them on where they can go and what they can do. They therefore have a very important role to play in reducing the negative impacts of tourism in the Lake District.

Education

The park rangers are a good source of information whilst visiting the Lake District and educating visitors is one of their most important tasks. Information is also available from various visitor centres, which provide education about the environment and its wildlife. By educating tourists, they can learn more about the natural ways of the area and how it can be affected by human activity, including their own. This can increase understanding and respect, and hopefully help reduce the negative impact of tourism.

The success of all the strategies we have looked at follow a pattern. To begin with, they may only have a small effect on reducing the impact of tourism. However, as the strategy matures and people gain more understanding, it will often have a greater impact. A well-managed strategy is regularly reviewed and maintained by the national park team. Meanwhile, other negative impacts will arise and require attention.

Research it

Find out more about national park rangers by carrying out some research on the Internet.

Apply it

The Countryside Code aims to help people respect, protect and enjoy the countryside. Here is the code:

- Be safe, plan ahead and follow any signs.
- Leave gates and property as you find them.
- Protect plants and animals, and take your litter home.
- Keep dogs under close control.
- Consider other people.

1. **For each of the five parts of the code, identify how it can reduce the negative impacts of tourism at a countryside destination.**
2. **You are planning a field trip to the countryside, taking with you people not used to such an area. Use the Countryside Access website to research the five parts of the Countryside Code and then create a short movie or PowerPoint presentation to raise awareness of the code in your group.**
3. **Come up with a code similar to the one above for another type of tourist destination (i.e. seaside resort, tourist town or city, business travel destination, purpose-built destination, or historical or cultural destination).**

Summary

Planning and legislation, managing traffic and visitors, and education all help to reduce the impact of tourism.

Ecotourism

We will now find out what ecotourism is, how it has grown, the products and services associated with it, and its advantages and disadvantages.

What is ecotourism?

Ecotourism is short for 'ecological tourism' and it means to visit a place and help preserve or maintain the local environment, its wildlife and plant life. It is seen as a responsible way of travelling and usually involves volunteering time to take part in projects that benefit the local environment and its people.

The growth of ecotourism

Ecotourism began in the late 1980s and has experienced the fastest growth of all other areas of the tourism industry. This is because there has been an increasing awareness of environmental issues, with some people realising that their holidays don't just have to be about self-indulgence, luxury and negative impacts on the destination they visit. Companies catering to these needs have grown with the increased demand.

Remember it

A product is a thing that is produced and is usually something you can touch and hold, like a souvenir, or it can be something like a package holiday. A service is something you either can't touch and hold or something you don't actually own, like a tennis lesson or a ride on a jet ski.

Take it further

An ecotourist guide has a very special role. What knowledge and training do you think they need? Do you think they might need any particular personal qualities?

Products and services of ecotourism

Products

Products related to ecotourism aren't really tangible (i.e. items that are able to be held) but rather are things like package holidays. These are put together by tour operators and sold either direct by the operator or by another company. Many people are keen to buy package holidays as they make life easier and can be cheaper. This can be especially true of ecotourism holiday packages where travellers may not feel they can put together such a specialised holiday themselves.

Services

An example of an ecotourism service is a guide. Guides are usually local people who help protect and maintain an area by educating visitors about it and showing them around.

The advantages and disadvantages of ecotourism

Advantages	Disadvantages
45% of the income of ecotourism stays in the UK. (Source: UNESCO)	55% of the income goes abroad.
Endangered species are protected by conservation projects.	Endangered species come into contact with humans, leaving them less wary of humans and more vulnerable to activities such as poaching.
Greater knowledge and involvement in endangered ecologies, such as rain forests, can help put pressure on governments to protect them.	The presence of tourists can put stresses on the environment they are visiting. Accommodation, heating, water supplies, access routes, transport and rubbish can all have negative impacts.
Ecotourism income can bring material comforts and medical care to people who otherwise could not afford them.	Ecotourism can disrupt the social and cultural structures of people.
Regulations introduced to protect the environment for ecotourists can benefit local people by protecting their local area from people who might exploit it.	These same regulations can stop local people from using their own resources in order that the 'untouched' nature of the environment is maintained.

Case study – **Goyo**

The chief guide of ecotourism company Panoramic Journeys, Goyotsetseg Radnaabazar or Goyo, was honoured with a Royal Geographical Society travel guide award in 2007. Born in 1979 in a small town in the Gobi Desert, Goyo worked hard at her studies and was rewarded with places at the Mongolian-Turkish secondary school and the University of Humanities in Ulaanbaatar. She was subsequently awarded a scholarship from the British Council to study tourism at the University of Surrey in the UK where she gained her Masters degree. During this time she met the directors of Panoramic Journeys who were setting up a travel business specialising in Mongolia. For the past three years she has worked for the company as the head guide and operations manager. She has also set up a fund supporting her mother's tree-planting conservation project.

The small group holidays provided by Panoramic Journeys allow people to visit countries such as Mongolia and Bhutan, enjoying the landscape, wildlife and culture whilst, at the same time, travelling responsibly and respectfully. Guides such as Goyo enable visitors to learn more about the country they are visiting from someone who has lived there and understands it.

Apply it

Using the information you have read in the table and the case studies, create a presentation to give to your class arguing either for or against ecotourism.

Case study – **Advantages of ecotourism**

Tourism is largely responsible for saving the gorillas of Rwanda from extinction. The gorillas were threatened by both poachers and local farmers, whose land-clearing practices were destroying the gorillas' natural habitat. Rwanda's Parc des Volcans has become an international attraction and the third-largest source of foreign exchange for Rwanda. Visitors pay to enter the park, and that money has allowed the creation of anti-poaching patrols and the employment of local farmers as guides and guards.

Case study – **Disadvantages of ecotourism**

When Chitwan in Nepal became a tourist area, foreign companies bought land to build hotels. This increased the cost of land and many local people took advantage by selling their land. The income was misused by some to buy alcohol and by others to build Western-style homes, which destroyed the traditional extended-family structure. Likewise, traditional dress has become unpopular. Even the age-old tradition of tattooing women has been abandoned.

Summary

Ecotourism is a growing part of the leisure and tourism industry. Although it has its disadvantages, it has also been very helpful in protecting and conserving some threatened or endangered areas and their inhabitants.

Assessment tip

Ecotourism is a key theme in the leisure and tourism industry. It is very important that you have a good understanding of ecotourism and sustainability.

3.4 The Issue of Sustainability

Sustainable leisure and tourism means enjoying activities associated with them in a way that does not damage the environment. This can be as simple as taking litter home after a day out or mending something we have broken, or as complex as **carbon offsetting** or staying in accommodation that relies on renewable energy such as solar power. You probably know that 'green' issues such as sustainability are very hot topics and they will affect the leisure and tourism industry more and more.

In this section we will be looking at:

- Sustainable development projects both in the UK and abroad
- Transport issues
- 'Going green'.

Describe it

Carbon offsetting is the practice of working out the volume of greenhouse gases that has been created by an activity and then doing something to make up for it, like paying for a tree to be planted.

Sustainable development projects

Sustainable development projects are initiatives that address issues such as climate change, the use of energy and resources, and ecosystems. Some of these projects are happening at tourist destinations and we will be looking at some of them now.

National parks

We have already looked at what a national park is (see page 65) but how are they sustainable development projects? The National Parks Sustainable Development Fund was set up by the government to give grants to people and organisations with good ideas that help protect the environment whilst still enabling people to visit national parks. Examples of these projects include:

- Buildings with living roofs (a roof covered with soil and vegetation)
- Shelters built only from local wood
- Farmers' markets, where the buying and selling of local produce reduces the carbon footprint caused by transporting goods
- Micro-hydro power generation, where the energy needs of tourism in the area does not increase carbon output.

Research it

National Parks Sustainable Development Fund information appears on each national park website. Why not visit the site of your nearest national park and find out about the sustainable projects going on there.

1. **Focus on one project that interests you and explain what is 'sustainable' about it and why it could be called 'development'.**
2. **Write an article for a local newspaper that describes this development and encourages people to visit.**

Ecotourism villages

Ecovillages are small communities that have been created by people who aim to live by making as little impact as possible on the environment. They do this by growing their own food or buying it locally and using renewable energy, amongst other things. Ecovillages also provide an alternative way of holidaying for like-minded people. There are three well-known ecovillages in the UK: Findhorn in Scotland, BedZED in England and Brithdir Mawr in Wales. They are all rather different, and their designs reflect their locations and the type of people who have built them. However, they all have in common a

Take it further

Use the application form on the National Parks Sustainable Development Fund website to apply for a grant for a project you have designed yourself (but don't send it without talking to your teacher first).

Case study – The Cairn Gorm funicular

Cairn Gorm, a mountain in the Scottish Highlands, got its own funicular in 2001. A funicular, in case you're wondering, is a kind of train that goes up the side of a mountain. The Cairn Gorm funicular increased the number of people who could get up the mountain and enjoy the scenery. However, it was soon realised that the numbers would be unsustainable and damage would occur to the fragile environment. The National Park Authority identified two distinct visitor needs: in winter, skiers needed access to snow, and in the summer people came to bird watch. To minimise the impact of tourism to the environment, summer visitors are not allowed to leave the Ptarmigan building and viewing terrace, facilities that have been built for tourism. In the winter, skiers are not allowed to ski on the area near the tourist buildings to conserve the vegetation there.

1 Some visitors to Cairn Gorm are taking short cuts across fragile land and walking on the ski areas, which are supposed to be people-free zones in the summer. The visitor areas could be fenced it in, but this would be unsightly. In groups:

- **Work out a strategy to keep visitors from roaming areas they shouldn't.**
- **Design a method of communicating this strategy to visitors.**
- **Design a way of monitoring visitor compliance to your strategy.**

shared vision for sustainable living. Once considered very 'alternative', such developments are becoming more mainstream and interesting options for tourists looking for something a little different.

Red Sea resorts

The Red Sea is an inlet between Africa and Asia, and is well known for its diving sites. There are 17 resorts on the Red Sea Riviera (a long stretch of coastline on the Red Sea), the most famous of which is the Egyptian resort of Sharm el Sheikh. Egypt is a poor country that needs tourism to help employ its people and obtain income, but it also needs to protect its very special ecosystems and the wildlife and plants that live in them.

Most of the Red Sea Riviera is a national park and desert, and is protected by law. Below is a summary of the environmental regulations tourists must follow.

- Don't touch, for any reason, any kind of marine life, for the protection of the environment and your own safety.
- Don't pick up from the sea or the beaches anything apart from rubbish. Even a piece of dead coral or an empty shell needs to be left in place for the environment's balance.
- Sports fishing is strictly forbidden.
- Hunting is strictly forbidden.
- Walking on the reefs is strictly forbidden.
- The area is home to the northernmost mangroves on the globe and they live in a delicate balance with their environment. Do not touch them.
- Plants in the desert are untouchable. They belong to the Bedouins who know exactly when to cut them for fire or to use them for any of their tasks.

(Source: goredsea.com)

Research it

Visit the Findhorn Bay Holiday Park website and explore its pages. How does the site compare to other holiday pages you have seen on the Internet?

Summary

National parks, ecovillages and the Red Sea Riviera are examples of sustainable development projects.

Advantages and disadvantages of sustainable development projects

Sustainable development projects, like the ones we looked at on pages 164–165, can have both positive and negative impacts on local communities and the environment.

Case study – The Galapagos Islands

The Galapagos Islands are a collection of volcanic islands that lie west of Ecuador in South America. They are very remote. The flight time to Quito, the capital of Ecuador, from London is 17 hours, with a further two hours flying time before reaching the Galapagos Islands. Travel costs were so high until recently that the islands were rarely visited by tourists. Because of their remoteness, the islands are home to some very unique wildlife and plant life, and this is a big selling point to tourists. One of the most famous inhabitants is the giant Galapagos tortoise, which along with many of the other animals that live on the islands, helped Charles Darwin develop his theory of evolution after he visited in 1835.

The Galapagos Islands have a population of about 40,000 and were visited by 108,436 people in 2004. Ecuador, of which the Galapagos Islands are a part of, is a poor country. Tourism is a very important way of bringing money into the country. The money enables the people who live on the islands to have a better way of life and also helps protect the valuable environment. However, the fragile Galapagos ecosystems are very vulnerable to the ever-increasing numbers of visitors. Cruise liners stopping off at the islands can drop off up to 500 people, which means that the infrastructure and facilities have to be able to cope with them. This has led to an increase in building work which, of course, can disturb the animals and destroy their homes. There can also be unintentional environmental consequences, such as when rats and mice found their way on to the islands via boats. They not only introduced new infections and diseases to the islands, but also began to destroy the eggs and young of some of the endangered animals.

Tourism has also affected the way of life for people on the islands. Their culture has been negatively affected by the presence of tourists, as well as the influence of migrants who moved to the islands due to a sudden growth in employment caused by the tourism industry there. The increased population has put more stresses on the environment because of the need for homes, facilities and infrastructure. There are now strict limitations on immigration. Some of the other regulations and initiatives that have been imposed include: only one visiting cruise ship per month; visitors are not allowed on some of the islands; visitors must not leave any waste or litter; educating visitors about how they can minimise the impact they make. Regulating visitor numbers may decrease the amount of income that can be made by tourists, but it will also mean that the islands are better protected and are around longer for people to enjoy.

Summary

Advantages for the local community of the sustainable development project:

- Jobs
- Income
- More frequent contact with the rest of the world
- Tourism is not seasonal so income is all year round.

Disadvantages for the local community:

- Population pressure
- Interruption to cultural life
- No 'off season' in which to relax.

Advantages for the environment:

- Income enables research and conservation projects.

Disadvantages for the environment:

- New buildings and infrastructure spoil the untouched nature of the islands
- Threat of incoming pests and diseases.

Local/regional and national organisations that promote sustainable tourism development in the UK

There are a growing number of organisations that promote sustainable development in tourism, including charities, non-governmental organisations (NGOs) and private companies, as well as government-led initiatives. Below are some examples:

- Local organisations
  - o Local councils like Tynedale
- Regional organisations
  - o The Regional Development Agency
  - o Regional tourist boards, such as Tourism South-East
  - o The national parks
- National organisations
  - o VisitBritain
  - o The National Parks Authority
  - o Department of Culture, Media and Sport.

We will now look at examples of a local, a regional and a national organisation.

Tyndale Council

Individual destinations have clear plans to safeguard them. For example, Tynedale Council, the local council for Hadrian's Wall World Heritage Site states the following:

- Provision of the Hadrian's Wall Bus aims to promote public transport and reduce carbon emissions.
- The Housesteads' Limits of Acceptable Change Conference aims to provide guidelines to maintain a balance between the use of the area for tourists and the need to conserve a World Heritage Site.

Tourism South-East

Advice posted on the 'Green' part of the Tourism South-East website tells visitors to:

- Use public transport
- Eat local food, drink and buy local products
- Switch off lights
- Follow the Countryside Code
- Use venues endorsed by the Green Tourism Business scheme.

Department of Culture, Media and Sport

This government department has a Sustainable Development Action Plan and its aims, amongst other things, is to champion tourism.

> 'We promote the sustainable development of tourism through working closely with VisitBritain, the Regional Development Agencies and other government departments on planning, countryside and rural development. We are currently developing a new framework for sustainable tourism in England in conjunction with our partners in regional and local government, academia and business.'

Talk about it

In small groups, choose one of the following viewpoints and talk about it. Come up with a convincing argument to put to a group with the opposite viewpoint.

View 1: Tourists bring money to the Galapagos Islands, improving the quality of life for the people who live there and enabling conservationists to help protect the animals and plants.

View 2: Tourists are damaging the environment of the Galapagos Islands and should not be allowed to visit anymore.

Now join up with a group with the opposite viewpoint and debate the issues. Can you change the other group's mind? Can you come up with a solution that makes both groups happy?

Assessment tip

We have looked at advantages and disadvantages in this section. In the exam, you may be asked to 'analyse' or 'evaluate' something, which should include looking at the advantages and disadvantages.

Summary

- There are some projects and developments that aim to increase the positive impacts and decrease the negative impacts of tourism. These are called sustainable development projects.
- They exist so that people can enjoy a destination with the minimum of community and environmental disruption.

Transport issues

Current issues

Transport and tourism always go together because otherwise people wouldn't be able to get to the destinations they want to visit and tour them. There are many different varieties of transport available and they all have an impact on the environment at some level. Most forms of transport with a motor use oil-based fuels, usually petrol or diesel. Electric vehicles, such as trams and some trains, may appear cleaner as they don't release fumes themselves, but the electricity that powers them is made mainly by burning fossil fuels such as coal or gas. Therefore the environmental impact is simply happening at the power station rather than in the engine.

All fossil fuels release carbon dioxide gas when they are burned. This is one of the main causes of global warming. Transport for tourism is a significant contributor to the problem. Two very important issues currently relating to transport are fuel prices and carbon footprints. We will look at each of these issues, how they affect the leisure and tourism industry, and what is happening to help make them sustainable.

Fuel prices

As we have already read, many forms of transport rely on oil-based fuels such as petrol and diesel. The price of oil varies depending on the demand for it. When demand is high, the price is high. Fossil fuels like coal, natural gas and oil take millions of years to form and we are using them up much faster than they can be replaced. Eventually oil will become very scarce and then the price is likely to be extremely high, unless we have found a good alternative by then.

A large part of the cost of most holidays is the cost of travel, which is usually related to the price of oil. As oil prices rise, companies either have to try to absorb the increase in price or pass it on to the customer. Transport providers such as airlines can be badly hit when oil prices are high, especially if it is during a recession when the demand for holidays decreases and companies want to cut holiday prices in order to be competitive. For some travel providers, this can mean bankruptcy.

Carbon footprints

A carbon footprint is a measure of the environmental impact an activity has by its release of greenhouse gases into the atmosphere, particularly carbon. There is very little agreement on the impact of tourism on total carbon emissions across the globe. If you exclude the carbon emission of travel, it is possible that some tourism has a positive effect because typically tourists go from cooler places where energy consumption is high to warmer places where energy consumption is low. Tourism at ski destinations may have a large carbon footprint because people need to keep warm in cold places. Equally, very hot places like the Red Sea resorts may use a lot of energy keeping hotels cool, which creates a large carbon footprint.

It is always the case that if air transport is used, the carbon footprint of the holidaymaker is large. Here are a few things you can do to help keep your holiday carbon footprint low:

- If travelling abroad, use a train and a ferry to get to your destination and walk, take a bus or a coach when you are there.
- Long-haul flights are more fuel efficient than short-haul flights. It is better to take one long holiday than several short ones.
- Urban destinations are likely to be a lower carbon choice because you can walk to places or take public transport rather than use the car.

The impact of these issues on customer choice

As we have seen, transport is one of the main contributors to our holiday carbon footprint and it is making many people think carefully about the decision they make when they travel.

Case study – Planes, trains or automobiles?

Say a family wanted to travel from the east coast of the USA to the west coast. They might think that travelling by aeroplane is bad because of the huge release of carbon directly into the atmosphere. By plane, the family can do their journey in about six hours, but in a car the same journey would take about two days. The car journey would not only be longer, but it would probably also involve lots of rest stops where the family would need to be cooled down or warmed up and entertained etc. These kinds of activities would also contribute to their carbon footprint.

If they made their journey by train, their carbon footprint would be less than the plane but, again, the journey time would be greater. Unless going on a long sight-seeing trip, most holiday makers do not see the journey as part of the holiday and want to maximise their time at the destination. Likewise, if the traveller taking this journey was on a business trip, their company would probably want them to get there and back as quickly (and as cheaply) as possible.

Most tourists and businesses are not, as yet, making decisions about travel based on environmental factors. Cost, journey time, convenience and good old preference are usually the deciding factors.

Local, regional and national transport initiatives

Local initiatives

Case study – Antrim Coast

Antrim Coast is a picturesque tourist destination in Northern Ireland surrounded by forests, glens and sleepy villages, with a beautiful rugged coastline too. Initiatives have been introduced to increase the opportunities for people to explore the area using carbon-low methods of transport, such as cycling, including:

- The creation of cycle routes, including the Ecos Trail and coastal routes
- The distribution of free leaflets advertising the cycle routes
- downloadable maps from Cycle Northern Ireland
- The inclusion of cycle information in The National Trust guides
- The advertising of cycling companies by The Northern Ireland Tourist Board
- Encouraging companies to offer both specialist and non-specialist holidays.

1 **Why do you think cycling is referred to as a 'carbon-low' activity rather than a carbon-free activity?**

2 **Can you think of another carbon-low form of transport that could be encouraged in a tourist destination? What ways can you think of to encourage people to use it?**

3 **What barriers might there be to people using cycling and walking as methods of transport while visiting a destination?**

Providing people with information can help them plan their journey and encourage people of all abilities to participate

Research it

Find out more about carbon-low activities such as cycling and rambling by visiting the Cycle NI and Ramblers Association websites.

Take it further

Make a short PowerPoint presentation to show to a member of your local council making a case for the council to introduce some walking routes to the area. Make your case based on sustainable low-carbon leisure and tourism even though there are clear healthy living benefits too. Keep the message simple and remember your target audience.

Regional initiatives

The Department for Transport (DfT) Regional Section provides advice to encourage good transport practice. Here are some examples:

- **'Give the Car a Holiday'** – Perthshire in Scotland ran a campaign to encourage tourists to use public transport by saying that the driver could get a fair share of the sightseeing if they travelled by bus instead.
- **'My other car is a bus'** – In 2004, a £2 million three-month advertising campaign aimed to attract Londoners and visitors on to buses.
- **'In Town Without My Car'** – This campaign has been ongoing since 2002. A recent re-launch was aimed not at the public but at Local Government

A regional transport initiative

National initiatives

The government tries to influence us to travel in a sustainable way through the tax system. When governments increase fuel taxes it is very unpopular, but such decisions can reduce the number of journeys we make and therefore the environmental impact of travel.

Aviation (aeroplane) fuel is not taxed very much. Cheap flights are dependent on cheap fuel. The government could reduce flight numbers by increasing aviation fuel tax, but it would be unpopular and damage the economy.

Carbon offset programmes

Some people may feel they have no choice but to travel using carbon-releasing aeroplanes but also don't want to damage the environment. Carbon offset programmes are now very popular and involve offsetting or 'making up' for the carbon you release. This usually involves working out how much carbon you have released by doing something and then doing something that doesn't release as much carbon as an alternative activity (such as walking to work instead of driving), or doing something that absorbs carbon (like planting a tree). Tree-planting schemes are very popular, with one tree absorbing half a tonne of carbon dioxide over its life.

Some travel companies buy **carbon credits** to offset your travel footprint. Governments are given a certain amount of carbon that their country can produce which they allocate to industries. If the industry produces more carbon than it is allowed to, it is required to buy into carbon reduction schemes like tree planting projects.

AIRMILES is a travel loyalty scheme that works like lots of other loyalty schemes. When members of the scheme spend money on products and services with certain companies, they collect miles that can be exchanged for free flights.

The bad thing about AIRMILES is that they often encourage frequent short-haul trips, which are carbon inefficient. AIRMILES have therefore introduced a carbon offsetting system. Instead of redeeming your miles on flights, you can use them to offset your carbon and AIRMILES will put your money into sustainable energy projects. AIRMILES schemes are also now letting people redeem their air miles against travel by the Eurostar train.

Research it

Visit the Department for Transport website and find out about the regional transport initiative 'In Town Without My Car'.

Research it

Using a website like the Energy Saving Trust, find out what you can do to offset your own carbon emissions.

Describe it

Carbon credits are used in emissions trading schemes and allow businesses to buy carbon credits if they exceed their emissions quota. The credits are then used by carbon reduction schemes.

Summary

- Current transport issues include oil prices and carbon footprints.
- These issues are starting people thinking about the way they travel, but most people still travel by whatever method is cheapest and fastest.
- There are local, regional and national sustainable transport initiatives, as well as carbon-offsetting schemes.

Apply it

Imagine you are going to turn your house into bed-and-breakfast accommodation.

1 **Make a list of possible 'green' issues you might face during the day-to-day running of your business.**

2 **Now come up with some strategies for making your business more sustainable and green.**

3 **Do you think advertising your business as sustainable would help attract customers? Why?**

Assessment tip

Addressing green issues can be a marketing opportunity for many businesses in the leisure and tourism industry. You will need to know about real life examples of how businesses you have studied are tackling green issues.

Green Start initiative

The Green Tourism Business Scheme

Going green

In this section, we are going to look at the trend for 'going green', and its influence on the leisure and tourism industry. If you have stayed in a hotel recently, you have probably noticed that the industry has been reacting to an increased global concern for the environment. You were probably asked by a sign or pamphlet in your room to think about the amount of water and washing powder used every day by hotels just for washing towels. Many hotels now don't automatically wash all towels and ask guests to think about whether they really need clean towels for each day of their stay. This is reducing costs, water usage, energy usage and the impact of waste and chemicals on the environment. Just by not washing as many towels!

'Green' tourism is all about organisations, businesses and individuals improving their practices in order to be more environmentally friendly and conscious. We will be focusing on:

- Reduce, Reuse, Recycle campaigns
- The Green Tourism Business Scheme.

Reduce, Reuse, Recycle

This is an initiative designed to encourage a reduction in the use of new materials and resources by carrying out the three Rs instead: Reduce, Reuse, Recycle. The leisure and tourism industry has been influenced by this campaign, with the tourism organisations VisitBritain and VisitScotland providing awards and accreditation to organisations that meet their green criteria.

Green Start is the name of the sustainable tourism initiative started by VisitBritain in 2008. The scheme is closed at the time of writing as it was initially a pilot to see how things went, but the idea was to help businesses take some first steps towards becoming sustainable. The scheme also aimed to help them prepare for joining a VisitBritain endorsed scheme (at the time only the Green Tourism Business Scheme was available). Businesses were offered a range of possible changes to make from nine different areas of their business including energy management, transport or purchasing. The actions included things such as:

- Install water-saving toilets (Reduce)
- Reuse materials where possible (Reuse)
- Recycle waste (Recycle)
- Make sure they meet energy efficiency standards
- Insulate lofts.

There was no formal verification by an assessor of actions taken, but businesses had to supply evidence on their self-assessment form. Once a minimum number of criteria had been reached a strapline (Working Towards Green Tourism) was shown on the VisitBritain suite of websites. VisitScotland have their own scheme called 'Going Green'.

The Green Tourism Business Scheme

The Green Tourism Business Scheme is the national sustainable tourism certification scheme for the UK. Businesses can apply to join

Case Study – Sustainable water and tourism

There are over 120 areas in which The Green Tourism Business Scheme measures sustainability, including energy, waste, transport, wildlife and water.

'Water is the vital component for life and important for health, refreshment, cleansing and sanitation. It should not be wasted or polluted. Drinking water in particular should not be squandered as it uses considerable chemical and energy inputs to make it fit for human consumption – yet we literally flush it down the toilet every day. The water section [of the scheme] assesses a wide range of water efficiency measures as well as using alternative sources to the mains. It also covers measures aimed at reducing pollutions arising from cleaning and wastewater disposal. Examples of the water assessment criteria include:

- Water-efficient showers, taps and toilets
- Washing machines and dishwashers
- Harvesting rainwater and **grey water** or using off-mains sources
- Chlorine and phosphate-free cleaners
- Natural-based cleaners and methods
- Ecological wastewater treatments.'

(Source: The Green Tourism Business Scheme)

the scheme and, in return for improving their environmental, economic and social practices to set standards, receive a bronze, silver or gold award. This helps leisure and tourism customers choose businesses that are helping to minimise their impact on the environment.

Here are some other things leisure and tourism businesses can do to help towards a Green Tourism Business Scheme Award:

- Green training for new employees.
- Free staff travel passes to encourage use of public transport.
- Providing information and leaflets to customers which raise awareness of green issues.
- Recycling of paper, cardboard, glass, cans and batteries.
- Paperless billing.
- Water- and gas-saving schemes in the kitchens.
- Use of energy-saving light bulbs.

Describe it

Grey water is wastewater from places like people's homes. It could be water that has been used to wash up with, rainwater from the roof or bath water. It is likely to be contaminated with some chemicals and other things (like leaves) but it is not toxic and is safe to use again for things like flushing toilets and gardening.

'White water' is fresh, unpolluted water and is safe to drink. 'Black water' is water that is polluted and contaminated.

Research it

The transport of food to and from different parts of the world is a very important green issue and it affects the leisure and tourism industry. Demand for out-of-season produce, like strawberries, leaves a very big carbon footprint. Some businesses make it a policy to only buy seasonal produce from local sources in order to minimise the carbon footprint.

1. **A hotel has asked you to design a 'low carbon-footprint' meal based on local and seasonal produce to help them achieve Green Tourism accreditation. Research the carbon footprints created by various groceries on a website like the Food Carbon Footprint Calculator. Make a list of items you could use and then design the meal. Perhaps you could work with your school or college technology department to actually make the meal.**

Summary

Reduce, Reuse, Recycle and The Green Tourism Business Scheme are two examples of initiatives that address 'green' issues and affect the leisure and tourism industry.

Research it

Visit The Green Tourism Business Scheme website and follow the 'Criteria' link. You will then find details of the ten categories in which businesses can make changes in order to receive an award (e.g. compulsory minimum standards, energy efficiency measures, sustainable travel).

1. **Read what can be done by a business in each of the ten categories. Which are simple and inexpensive to put into place? Which are more difficult and costly?**
2. **How effective is a scheme where criteria are used in this way?**
3. **Choose a business in the leisure and tourism industry. What could they do in each of the ten categories in order to gain an award?**

EUROPARC FEDERATION
EUROPEAN CHARTER FOR SUSTAINABLE TOURISM IN PROTECTED AREAS

EUROPARC Federation Charter logo

Advantages and disadvantages of award schemes for leisure and tourism organisations and destinations

In this section we will look at the advantages and disadvantages of award schemes like The Green Tourism Business Scheme and the Europarc Federation on organisations and some 'green' destinations.

The Green Tourism Business Scheme

Once accredited, an organisation is given a gold, silver or bronze award depending on the number of points it has gained.

EUROPARC Federation

EUROPARC FEDERATION

The EUROPARC Federation was set up in 1973 to protect the natural beauty of Europe. It is a non-governmental organisation (NGO) and aims to facilitate international co-operation in all aspects of protected area management to further improve and conserve Europe's natural inheritance. It does this in a number of ways but one of its most successful tools is the European Charter for Sustainable Tourism in Protected Areas.

The Charter was created as a contribution to Agenda 21, the sustainable development programme of the United Nations agreed at Rio de Janeiro in 1992. To fulfil the Charter the protected area must bring together all those involved with tourism in the area and set out a shared vision/strategy for tourism development and make a five-year commitment to implement agreed joint actions with their partners. The aim of all Charter projects and activities is the protection of the natural and cultural heritage and the continuous improvement of tourism in the protected area in terms of the environment, local population and businesses as well as the visitors.

The Yorkshire Dales attained Charter status in 2008 and the Cairngorms and Brecon Beacons National Parks are also Charter protected areas. Many destinations abroad have also been awarded the Charter, including Spain's Parque Nacional y Natural de Sierra Nevada and Italy's Parco delle Alpi Marittime. You can find out more by visiting the European Charter website.

Advantages and disadvantages of award schemes to organisations

Advantages

- Participating businesses reduce the impact of tourism on the environment.
- Information enables customers to make informed choices.
- Small businesses gain an important marketing angle or unique selling point.
- Small businesses can save money, making them more competitive.
- Schemes raise awareness of green issues to all stakeholders, staff and customers.
- Organisations are showing that they care for the environment and local communities, which can improve business/community relations.

- Where numbers participating are high, there are advantages of economies of scale in advertising and purchasing.
- Technical help is offered to the accreditation organisation.

Disadvantages

- Too few inspectors and infrequent visits can mean that accredited organisations slip back into old habits.
- Dependence on self-assessment discredits the process.
- When criteria are too basic, it can undermine the quality of the accreditation.
- Some schemes simply have too few businesses in their schemes to provide real choice for consumers.
- When businesses have no increases in customer numbers they tend to fall out of the scheme.
- Many of the criteria are similar between schemes so it can be difficult to see the unique quality of each.
- If a business advertises multiple-award logos, the effect can be to devalue each, making it difficult for customers to identify the unique identity of schemes.
- When awards are given to businesses that might also be seen to operate in non-green ways, the quality assurance of the scheme is put into doubt.

Advantages and disadvantages of award schemes to destinations

As we have read, the Yorkshire Dales was awarded the European Charter for Sustainable Tourism in Protected Areas by the Europarc Federation in 2008. The Yorkshire Dales National Park Authority said:

'It will mean a higher profile nationally and across Europe for the area, as well as new links to organisations in the tourism sector at local regional and national level, as well as opportunities for exchange of expertise and experience.'

It was realised that the charter will raise people's awareness of the destination and probably increase visitor numbers. The Park Authority was also looking forward to sharing information with and learning from other organisations, which could improve the conservation work carried out there.

One disadvantage is that a very large amount of work is needed to achieve and maintain the award, which may outweigh the benefits. It may also mean that some other tasks or parts of the Yorkshire Dales are neglected because of this extra work.

Assessment tip

We have already looked at the roles of organisations that promote tourism (see pages 138–143). Don't forget that they also promote sustainable tourism – make sure you know how.

Research it

Organisers of the London Olympics in 2012 have said they will be the 'greenest Games ever!' Visit the official Games website and find out how they are hoping to achieve this.

Summary

- Award schemes, such as those run by the Green Tourism Business Scheme and The EUROPARC Federation, reward good practice and progress in meeting green targets.
- There are advantages and disadvantages of the award schemes for both the organisation itself and tourist destinations.

Unit 3 Make the Grade

There are four sections in Unit 3 and the unit is worth 20% of the GCSE Double Award. The unit is assessed via a one-hour-long exam which covers all the topics. All questions will need to be answered, of which there are three types: multiple choice, short-answer and extended-answer.

Understanding assessment language – command words

For both short- and extended-answer questions, you need to be aware of the command word in the question and you must also know what it means. It will probably be one of those shown in the table.

Command words	Triggers to help you answer
Identify, list, name	Use a word from leisure and tourism vocabulary or a place name.
Describe	Tell the examiner what the word means, or what the place is like.
Explain	Use the word 'because' as a trigger.
Analyse, evaluate, assess	Look at each part of the question and balance your comments using connective words like whereas, but and similarly.

Topic 3.1 A Dynamic Industry

The key concept in this topic is 'change'. For both leisure and tourism you need to know about:

- technological change
- consumer trends
- unforeseen events.

You should expect to spend about 12–13 minutes on this section of the exam paper.

Multiple-choice questions

You will be asked a question and have to choose an answer from those given. Read all the answers, even if you think you know the correct one straight away. They are not trick questions and if you have revised you should be able to answer them. If you are not sure which answer is right, eliminate the answers that are wrong and go for the one that seems most likely. Here's an example:

Q1 Recent technological developments have influenced the tourist industry. Which of the following is **not** a technological development? (1 mark)

☐ Audio trails

☐ Geocaching

☐ Online booking

☑ Orienteering

Short-answer questions

Some of these questions will only be worth one mark and will require you to name or identify something. Try not to write more than is needed – you can't gain any more than one mark no matter how much you write. An example is:

Q2 Name one factor that can cause change in the leisure and tourism industry. (1 mark)

Answer: Unforeseen events.

Other types of short-answer questions will ask you to 'describe' or 'explain' something and will be worth more marks, for example:

Q3 Describe what airlines mean by electronic ticketing. (2 marks)

Answer: Travellers can book their tickets online, print off their details and the airline will not have to send a paper ticket.

Q4 Explain how advances in technology have changed home-based leisure during the last 20 years. (6 marks)

Answer: Computers have become less expensive and there are more computers in each household. (2 marks) Social networking sites such as Bebo and Facebook have developed bigger client groups. (2 marks) Young people spend more of their home-based leisure time communicating on the Internet. (2 marks)

Extended-answer questions

'Analyse' is a word often used in extended-answer questions, so you have to analyse the question, for example:

Q5 Analyse the possible impacts of exchange rates changing. You should make reference to both travellers and leisure and tourism companies. (8 marks)

In your answer you will need to think:

- What is the exchange rate?
- What happens to travellers in the UK who want to go abroad and to companies when the pound goes up?
- What happens to travellers in the UK who want to go abroad and to companies when the pound goes down?
- What happens in the UK?

Answer: Exchange rates are about how much foreign money we get for our pounds sterling (1 mark). If the pound is weak against another currency, it is bad for the traveller because they get less foreign money and can spend less abroad (1 mark). So a weak pound means fewer people travelling abroad (1 mark), which is bad for companies that deal with foreign holidays (1 mark). When the pound is strong, British travellers can get a lot for their pound sterling (1 mark), so many people want to travel abroad from Britain (1 mark), which makes holiday companies happy because people book more holidays (1 mark). However, when the pound is weak, companies that organise holidays in the UK are likely to get more customers, whilst when the pound is strong they suffer because people want to go abroad (1 mark).

The first mark shows you know what an exchange rate is. The second mark says what happens if the pound is weak. The third mark explains the consequence for the traveller. The fourth mark links the consequence to the traveller to the consequences for companies. The fifth mark shows you know what happens if the pound is strong. The sixth mark links the strong pound to the response of the travelling public. The seventh mark links to how companies might react and the eighth mark shows an extension to the effect of the exchange rate to UK tourism companies.

Topic 3.2 UK Tourist Destinations

The key concept in this topic is location. You need to know the location of certain UK destinations on a map and also for some of them:

- The tourist boards and agencies that promote them
- The people they appeal to
- The features that attract these people.

There will be location questions based on maps and knowledge of the locations of destinations. In addition, there will be a question that asks you to explain and perhaps link aspects of the leisure and tourism industry to those places. You should expect to take 12–13 minutes out of the hour to complete this section of the exam.

For any of the places listed in the exam specification you might need to know the county, the home country or the tourist board or agency that promotes them. This is easy marks for people who enjoy lists and facts!

Look at the map and match the places to the names. You need to be able to describe where the places are too. The CD, if you have it, enables you to practise moving the place names to the correct places on the map. You can do it – just keep practising!

Short-answer questions

There are likely to be just one or two 'explain' questions here. Look at this one which is worth four marks.

Q1 Built attractions and transport services and links are features of tourist destinations. Explain why each of these features is important in giving appeal to the theme park Alton Towers Resort. (4 marks)

The first part of the question tells you to divide your answer into two parts:

- Built attractions
- Transport services and links.

The last part of the question tells you that you should apply it to Alton Towers Resort.

Answer: Alton Towers Resort built rides, cafés, restaurants, toilets, roads and gardens (1 mark) because they needed to attract people to a new destination (1 mark). It is easy to get to Alton Towers Resort by car from places like Birmingham (1 mark) because it is just off the M6 (1 mark)

Question 1 linked the built environment, transport links and Alton Towers Resort. There are ten places you need to know about in detail and themes that could be linked to them. You could complete the table below and on page 179 or use them as a revision checklist to help you make these links. Tick the boxes for each destination to indicate which of the headings are relevant.

	Climate	Natural attractions	Built attractions	Events	Food, drink and entertainment	Transport	Accommodation
Blackpool							
Newquay							
Glasgow							
York							
Belfast							
Birmingham							
Aviemore							
Alton Towers							
Chester							
Bath							

	Families	Groups	Couples	Families with young children	Individuals	Business travellers	Visitors with specific needs
Blackpool							
Newquay							
Glasgow							
York							
Belfast							
Birmingham							
Aviemore							
Alton Towers							
Chester							
Bath							

Topic 3.3 The Impacts of Tourism

You may find it easier to think about this topic in the following way:

Positive impacts of tourism on the environment	Negative impacts of tourism on the environment
Positive impacts of tourism on communities	Negative impacts of tourism on communities
	Strategies to reduce the impact of tourism on communities

In the exam, you may be asked questions about balancing advantages against disadvantages. You should expect to take 12–13 minutes out of the hour to complete this section of the exam.

Short-answer questions

Q1 What might the advantages be of a hotel offering reindeer rides in December? (2 marks)

While this question might tempt you to say something like, 'Because it would be fun', notice that there are two marks for this question and you will need to write a more detailed sentence or two.

Answer: Hotels are often quiet in early December. The advantage of reindeer rides would be to attract people to visit who then might also stay to eat a meal.

Extended-answer questions

These questions will be more complex questions. Read the question below and look at the words in **bold**, which have been picked out as the important parts of the question – they will tell you what is wanted in the answer.

Q2 **Analyse** the impacts of the tourism on a **tourist town or city** you have studied. You should include both **positive and negative impacts**. In your answer you could make reference to the **local community** and the **environment**. (8 marks)

'Analyse' is the command word and tells you to compare and contrast. Good words to use in an answer that asks you to analyse are 'whereas' and 'however'. A tourist town or city you have studied should be taken from the list in the specification to be safe. Tell the examiner you know its tourist board and its appeal. You should then talk about the positive and negative impacts on the local community and the positive and negative impacts on the environment.

Answer: I have studied York, which is a tourist city in the English Tourist Board's North Country region. York has a small medieval centre with a Minster, which is the main appeal to tourists. One negative impact on the community is congestion, which tourists create in the summer season. A positive impact of these people is income for the local tourism workers. (2 marks) A second negative impact is the seasonality. Most tourists visit in the summer season and people in the local community are under-employed in the winter. However, seasonality gives those who are not dependent on tourism a chance to enjoy their own cultural activities without visitors interrupting. (2 marks)

Income from tourists has a positive effect on the environment because the money generated is used in the upkeep of the crumbling medieval buildings. However, the tourists themselves have a negative impact on the environment – their cars create pollution and the chewing gum they drop makes the medieval paving unsightly. (2 marks)

Noise is an environmental issue. Tourists disturb the people who live and work in the city. However, this is offset by the positive impact on the community who can enjoy the facilities in York and might stop them moving away. (2 marks)

Topic 3.4 The Issue of Sustainability

This topic is about sustainable tourism. You need to think about what sustainability is in terms of:

- Development
- Transport
- 'Green' issues.

A simple way to think about sustainability is: how can we live our lives without having a bad effect on the planet?

There may be quite a lot of 'source material' to work with in this section of the exam, so it is important to read all of this very carefully. You should expect to take 12–13 minutes out of the hour to complete this section of the exam.

Short-answer questions

Often there is a statement. Read this carefully as it tells you what the examiner wants you to write about, for example:

Q1 Energy is one measure for sustainability given in The Green Tourism Business Scheme (GTBS). Explain two ways in which a leisure and tourism organisation could meet the GTBS criteria for energy. (4 marks)

Answer: Leisure and tourism organisations can switch to energy-saving light bulbs because they use less electricity and last longer. (2 marks) They could also consider installing a wind turbine if this is possible because turbines use renewable energy (the wind) rather than fossil fuels. (2 marks)

Extended-answer questions

There may be some more complex questions here. They are marked with levels.

- Level 1 (one or two marks) – the answer could be notes or bullet points.
- Level 2 (three or four marks) – the answer will be in good English with mainly correct spellings and balanced arguments.
- Level 3 (five or more marks) – a logical argument is given with good English and few spelling and grammar mistakes.

Q2 Evaluate the value to a leisure and tourism organisation of gaining an award under The Green Tourism Business Award Scheme. In your answer you should consider both advantages and disadvantages. (6 marks)

Answer: The Green Business Award Scheme gives gold, silver and bronze awards to organisations that meet their 'green' criteria. The good publicity and improved image that the award offers can attract increased custom, however increased costs associated with meeting the criteria, such as installing a wind turbine, may reduce the economic advantage.

The advantages gained by being seen as technologically up-to-date and sustainable for criteria such as recycling needs to be balanced by the costs of staff training and increased employment. Whilst there is no guarantee that an organisation will generate more business by being in the scheme, it is unlikely to lose business. A unique selling point, such as a heat pump, may be the deciding factor in a customer's choice.

I have studied Hadrian's Wall in Northumberland. An advantage for this site of being in the scheme is that an award adds to the area's substantial number of other awards, such as World Heritage Status. It also reminds the organisers to balance their need for visitor numbers with the need to preserve the environment. A disadvantage is that having the award might attract more visitors and make it more difficult to protect the natural environment. (Level 3)

Revising

It is important that you know how to revise effectively for your exam and make good use of your time. Firstly, don't panic! You will need to plan ahead, which means revising about eight weeks before your first exam.

When you are revising:

- Make sure you have somewhere comfortable to work
- Prepare the area you are going to work in (e.g. make a clear space, move distracting things, get a supply of pens, paper, highlighters etc.)
- Make sure your notes are in order
- Tell people you are revising so they don't disturb you
- Make sure you have plenty of water to drink
- Try to get peace and quiet – don't fool yourself by trying to revise with the television or music on. Turn your mobile phone off too!

Revision methods

Revise for 20 minutes or so and then go and tell someone what you have learned to see how much you can remember. You could tell someone you live with, a friend, the cat, the dog, even the mirror! Have your notes to hand so that the person you are telling can check what you tell them (or if doing this by yourself, check them afterwards).

Revise together in groups. Talk through a topic and see how much you can remember and think of ways to help you learn. This method only works if the group stays focused and works well together.

Simply re-reading your notes or a book is not the most effective way to revise. Find different ways to present the information you need to learn: make mind maps, pictures, charts, tables, bullet lists or even voice recordings or a video. Whichever works best for you.

Unit 4: Customers and Employment in Leisure and Tourism

The Eiffel Tower in Paris attracts huge numbers of visitors

In this unit you will learn about visitor attractions, customer service and employment opportunities in the leisure and tourism industry. You will build on Unit 1 and elements of the other units. This unit is optional for the GCSE Leisure and Tourism Single Award qualification, as you must complete Unit 1 and either this unit or Unit 2. This unit is compulsory if you are completing the Double Award.

This unit covers the following topics:

4.1 Visitor Attractions, Leisure Facilities and Tourist Destinations
4.2 Customer Choice
4.3 Providing Service for Differing Customer Types and Needs
4.4 Employment Opportunities in Leisure and Tourism

This unit will cover all these areas so that you can build up your knowledge and tackle the controlled assessment with confidence.

In the first part of this unit, you will develop an understanding of visitor attractions, leisure facilities and tourist destinations. We will look at examples from both the UK and abroad. You will look at the products and services offered by them, their trends, appeal and popularity. Through the various activities (such as Research it, Case study and Talk about it) you will increase your awareness of the attractions, facilities and destinations that exist. You will then have to choose one on which to base your assessment task. This task is set by Edexcel and your teacher will give you this once you have completed your research folder so that you can apply all of your learning.

By the end of this section, you should be familiar with at least two of the following categories and, to complete topic 4.1, you will need to choose one of these categories on which to base your work:

Visitor attraction in the UK	Leisure facility in the UK	Tourism destination in the UK
Visitor attraction overseas	Leisure facility overseas	Tourism destination overseas

For example, you may base your assessment task for topic 4.1 on Alton Towers (visitor attraction in the UK).

Topic 4.2 will look at the factors which influence how people choose to spend their leisure time. Again, the assessment task will be provided by your teacher and will be based on a different category from the selection used in topic 4.1.

The third part of the unit, topic 4.3, will look at differing types of leisure and tourism customers and their needs. You will also investigate the importance of the health and safety of customers to leisure and tourism facilities. You will base this on one of the categories used so far in topic 4.1 or 4.2, as you should now be very familiar with them.

Finally, section 4.4 looks at employment opportunities in leisure and tourism. Again, you will complete your research folder before beginning your assessed task. This will be based on the category you have not used twice so far in completing this assignment.

Therefore, the categories of study you may have undertaken may appear as follows:

Visitor attraction in the UK *Alton Towers* *Topics 4.1 and 4.3*	Leisure facility in the UK	Tourism destination in the UK
Visitor attraction overseas	Leisure facility overseas	Tourism destination overseas *Benidorm* *Topics 4.2 and 4.4*

When selecting your categories, choose one that you know a lot about and enjoy researching. Do not be influenced by what your peers are basing their assessment task on as this task will be completed individually.

Talk about it

If you won a prize to go anywhere for an all-expenses-paid weekend, where would you go and what would be your itinerary for the weekend?

How you will be assessed

You will carry out research with your teacher and build up a research folder under very limited supervision. This will take about 30 hours. You will then use the research folder to complete your final assessment task. This will be completed in controlled conditions in the classroom and your teacher will collect it at the end of each lesson. You will not have access to your research folder or controlled assessment task outside the classroom. The controlled assessment tasks will take 15 hours to complete so you will have to use your time well to get the grade you deserve.

4.1 Visitor Attractions, Leisure Facilities and Tourist Destinations

Every town in the UK has leisure facilities such as sports centres, ice rinks, cinemas, night clubs, and bowling alleys. Visitor attractions, on the other hand, are major attractions for both domestic and incoming tourists. Often, though not always, these are visited on a one-off basis during holidays, or as a treat to celebrate special occasions. Of course, not everyone's home town can be the birthplace of William Shakespeare, accommodate a theme park or be the site of a historic battle. This is why Stratford-upon-Avon is popular with domestic and international visitors, Alton Towers pulls in thrill-seekers and adrenaline junkies, and Normandy appeals to those interested in learning more about D-Day.

In this section we will explore visitor attractions, leisure facilities and tourist destinations both in the UK and overseas. You will learn about the different types of destinations, their products and services and their suitability for different customers. In your controlled assessment task you will need to be able to talk about their appeal.

With increasing leisure time, a wide range of leisure facilities, visitor attractions and tourist destinations have emerged to cater for the needs of customers. This has created thousands of jobs in the leisure and tourism industry, a fast-growing sector in the UK. Increasingly, people are also willing to travel abroad to enjoy new experiences.

Research it

Gather information on Stratford-upon-Avon, Alton Towers and the D-Day landing sites in Normandy. Whom would they appeal to, and what can visitors do when they're there?

Talk about it

Not that long ago foreign travel was a privilege enjoyed only by the wealthy elite. In your group, discuss the places abroad that you and your families have been to, or would like to go to.

Apply it

Photocopy a map of the world and mark off the locations that you have been to, or would like to visit in the future.

Take it further

Are there many destinations and countries you do not know the location of? Are you confident that your geographical knowledge of the world is good? Try the activity on the Test your Geography Knowledge website. Select a quiz from Europe through to the world. How does your score compare with that of your classmates?

Visitor attractions

As we read in Unit 1, visitor attractions are a key component of both the leisure and the tourism industry. A visitor attraction is a place that offers 'amusement, enjoyment, entertainment and education'. As such, they draw visitors to that place.

Attractions can be visited from home (this makes them part of the leisure industry), or while on holiday in the UK or overseas (this makes them part of the tourism industry). We will look at examples of each.

Leisure facilities

Leisure facilities include:

- Purpose-built buildings, e.g. ice rinks or velodromes
- Multi-purpose buildings, e.g. community centres
- Natural landscapes, e.g. rivers, caves or cliffs.

There are two types of leisure facility.

1. Places where leisure activities take place, such as leisure centres or pools.
2. Organisations that support or provide equipment for leisure activities, such as DVD rental shops or ski hire shops.

Tourist destinations

A tourist destination combines travel with facilities and attractions that appeal to tourists. Employees in the tourism industry need to know where the tourist destinations are, to whom they are suited and the main attractions.

Apply it

Write your own description of the difference between leisure facilities, visitor attractions and tourist destinations.

Research it

VisitBritain is often the first organisation people refer to when they are planning a leisure visit in the UK. Have a look at the website and decide how valuable it is as a resource for helping people decide where to go.

UK visitor attractions

Visitor attractions are vital to the leisure and tourism industry. The UK has a wide range of visitor attractions that appeal to both domestic and incoming tourists. Some of these have historical appeal, such as Goodrich Castle and the Roman Baths in Bath, whilst others are cultural or modern varieties of entertainment, such as the Tate Modern and the Snow Dome. We will now look at two of the UK's most popular visitor attractions: Alton Towers and the Tower of London.

Case study – Alton Towers

Since 1990, when Alton Towers was acquired by the Tussaud's Group, the park's fortunes have soared, and it is now widely considered to be the number one theme park in the UK. The resort comprises a range of facilities that make it 'one amazing event location'. These include:

- an award-winning conference centre
- two uniquely themed hotels providing 391 bedrooms
- two restaurants and five bars
- one of Europe's largest water parks with both indoor and outdoor rides, slides and hot tubs
- a luxurious spa
- two nine-hole adventure golf courses themed around the park's quirky rides and attractions
- 'white knuckle' rides and other entertainments.

Unlike some attractions where one visit is enough, Alton Towers enjoys a lot of repeat business and customer loyalty. This is not just due to the quality of the rides but because of the intelligent marketing that Alton Towers carries out. At various times of the year the park has special events for Halloween, Bonfire Night and Christmas, to name but a few, which offer something new to visitors.

Talk about it

According to British Tourist Authority research, 85% of people are only willing to travel a maximum of two hours on a day trip to a visitor attraction. What services does Alton Towers provide that helps it overcome this problem and attract people from all over the UK?

Research it

Have a look at the Alton Towers website and identify all of the different groups of customers it appeals to. Rate the appeal of the park to each of the types of customer you identify; for example, families, couples, etc.

Look at other theme parks in the UK. Are there any goods and services that Alton Towers could offer that they don't at present?

Case study – The Tower of London

This World Heritage Site is the number one fee-paying attraction in the UK and is likely to be on most incoming tourist's itinerary when visiting the capital. An awesome fortress, which William the Conqueror began the construction of in the early 1080s, it has a rich history which makes for a compelling visit.

With its four distinctive turrets at the centre of the Tower of London overlooking the River Thames, the infamous White Tower was built to strike fear into the unruly citizens of London. It is now an iconic symbol of London and Britain, and one of the world's premier tourist attractions luring visitors with its unique character and place in UK history.

To capitalise on its appeal, the Tower of London website provides essential information such as how to get there, even by river! Opening times, prices, top ten things to see and do, and visitor access for those with specific needs such as mobility difficulties and visual impairment are all identified so that tourists can visit confident that their needs will be met and they will enjoy their visit. You can even hire the Tower and 'dine in the King's Greta Hall, wondering at the thought of those who have dined here before you through the centuries'.

Take it further

1 What goods and services can visitor attractions provide to extend the **dwell time** at their attractions?

2 Think back to some of the visitor attractions that you have been to and calculate their dwell time. Which attraction do you think represented the best value for money in terms of dwell time?

Research it

Find out what other World Heritage Sites there are in the UK. To whom do they appeal, and how successful are they?

Apply it

Your pen pal, Pepe, lives in Barcelona and would like to visit you for two weeks in the summer holiday. It is his dream to visit the following places:

- Stratford
- Blackpool
- Edinburgh castle
- Madam Tussaud's
- Buckingham Palace.

Write an itinerary for his visit so that he can see all of these places over the course of the two weeks. You must consider the advantages and disadvantages of the transport available: air, rail, sea and road. Choose the transport that is most suited to your needs.

As your pen friend is a student, you must try to keep the cost down. If there is time, add some more destinations that you would think would enhance his visit. They could be local leisure attractions that would be relatively inexpensive.

Remember it

Dwell time is an important concept that helps people decide on value for money. Dwell time is the entry fee divided by time spent at the attraction. For example, if a visitor attraction cost £10 and customers typically spend two hours there, the dwell time would be £5 per hour.

Summary

You will need to know about examples of both UK and international visitor attractions for your controlled assessment task. Choosing local examples will mean that you can gain firsthand experience of them.

UK leisure facilities

Leisure facilities are key creators of jobs in the UK, catering for the needs of the local population as well as tourists. Leisure facilities can be purpose-built, such as football stadiums, cinemas or heritage centres. Premiership football clubs have fantastic stadiums that not only cater for home matches but also enable the club to become a 24/7 business. As well as the core activity of hosting football matches, they provide conference rooms which can be used for business during the day and for social events during the evening and at weekends, such as weddings, parties and tribute nights. Catering facilities are often utilised by the public during the week and some clubs even have adjoining hotels.

Natural leisure facilities are those such as the Lake District. Lake Coniston, for example, provides a natural landscape that can cater for an extensive range of leisure activities including sailing, canoeing, rock climbing, abseiling, orienteering, gorge walking and many more.

Manchester Velodrome

The Velodrome is a purpose-built indoor venue built to help Manchester stage the Commonwealth games in 2002. The multi-million pound facility has been used extensively since, and was the base for the British Olympic Cycling team, who raced to glory in the Beijing Olympics in 2008.

Take it further

Look at the Manchester Velodrome website and list all the other activities it can stage.

National Indoor Arena

The National Indoor Arena (NIA) is a multi-purpose venue built in the centre of Birmingham as part of the local council's ambitious plans to regenerate the centre of Birmingham, and to enhance its appeal to tourists from around the UK and abroad. The NIA has hosted a multitude of events including:

- World Indoor Athletics Championships
- Disney on Ice
- Pop concerts, such as Elton John.

Research it

Find out how many different events the NIA has staged. Do you think it was a good investment by the city?

Gower Peninsula

Visitors to Wales enjoy extensive areas of unspoilt beauty. The natural beauty of the Gower Peninsula helped it become the first place in Britain to be designated as an Area of Outstanding Natural Beauty (AONB) by the Countryside Agency on behalf of the UK government. It remains one of only five in Wales.

The peninsula is home to some of the richest wildlife and varied habitats in the UK. Castles and prehistoric standing stones are scattered across the landscape and contribute to a memorable experience for visitors to the area.

Research it

Find out more about tourism opportunities in the Gower Peninsula. If you were to go there for a weekend, what would you like to do? How much of your weekend would be spent at manmade leisure facilities compared to natural ones?

Take it further

Find out where the other AONBs are.

If you could visit any of these which would you visit?

The NIA in Birmingham hosts lots of different events

Talk about it

Do you think staging international sporting events is a good thing for the host city?

What are the advantages and disadvantages of staging an international sporting event?

Research it

Use the Internet to assess the value of tourism generated through sporting events both in the UK and internationally.

Apply it

Using a blank copy of a map of the UK, devise a key for the following components and show where three nationally significant examples are on the map. Include:

- theatres
- museums
- sports venues
- theme parks
- visitor attractions
- historic sites.

Write a presentation on one of the nationally significant facilities from each component, explaining why it is so important.

Summary

You will need to know examples of both UK and international leisure facilities. Remember: a leisure facility can be a natural landscape as well as a purpose-built facility, such as an ice rink or swimming pool.

Remember it

Domestic tourists are tourists who travel within their own country; for example, someone from London travelling to Stratford for the weekend.

Incoming tourists are tourists that arrive from outside that country; for example, US tourists visiting the UK.

Outgoing tourists are travelling out of their own country; for example, UK tourists travelling to Prague.

UK tourist destinations

Some visitor attractions lure tourists for just a single day out. However, some areas have many visitor attractions, and so tourists will go for a weekend break or holiday with the intention of seeing as many things as possible. These areas are called tourist destinations. Growing affluence and the increasing popularity of short breaks throughout the year, as opposed to the traditional two-week summer holiday, are benefiting the UK as tourists home in on the many tourist destinations. Two UK destinations that have benefited enormously from tourism are Stratford-upon-Avon and European City of Culture 2008, Liverpool.

Liverpool

Case study – Stratford-upon-Avon

Stratford is most famous for being the birthplace of William Shakespeare. Every year, thousands of domestic and **incoming tourists** descend on the town to enjoy its extensive range of leisure opportunities. The area has the transport links, facilities and attractions needed to make it a superb tourist destination. With a wealth of accommodation and catering, including caravans, bed-and-breakfasts and hotels, the town is a popular year-round destination.

For those interested in finding out more about Shakespeare's origins there are a range of attractions, the importance of which is shown by the attention given to them by the VisitBritain website.

Shakespeare was born in Stratford-upon-Avon in 1564 and died there in 1616. There are five houses in and around the town that are linked to Shakespeare and his family, giving you an idea of what life was like in Shakespeare's time. In the centre of Stratford, visit Shakespeare's Birthplace and Exhibition, and see Shakespeare's home as it would have been when he was a boy. A short walk from his birthplace is Nash's House, which belonged to Shakespeare's granddaughter, Elizabeth Hall, and her husband, Thomas Nash. Next to this house is the garden of New Place, site of the house that Shakespeare bought and where he later retired and died. A short walk from here is Hall's Croft, the family home of Shakespeare's eldest daughter, Susanna, and her physician husband, John Hall.

Just out of town, in Shottery, is Anne Hathaway's Cottage, which was the home of Shakespeare's wife. Mary Arden was Shakespeare's mother, and you can visit her farmhouse home and learn about rural life in Shakespeare's time by visiting Mary Arden's House and The Countryside Museum in Wilmcote, three miles from Stratford.

1. **There is much more to do in Stratford-Upon-Avon than we have looked at here. Carry out some research on the Internet to find out the full range of attractions on offer in Stratford-upon-Avon.**
2. **Devise a weekend itinerary in Stratford-upon-Avon for a young couple enjoying a romantic break, and a couple taking their two young children away.**

The Albert Dock in Liverpool

Liverpool was European City of Culture in 2008. After a period of decline, its main industry, shipping, experienced a downturn throughout the latter twentieth century, and so the city has had to change direction in order to revive its fortunes. It is now enjoying a renaissance.

Liverpool has many attractions to tempt visitors. With good links by road, rail and air, the city has seen a surge in tourism. Popular attractions include the Beatles Story, the Albert Dock and the Chinese Quarter. Concert Square offers a lively range of bars and clubs, while Matthew Street offers an extensive range of pubs, including the legendary Cavern Club, where the Beatles first performed.

Take it further

Produce a guide to a city of your choice. Identify:

- The main transport routes to the city
- The main attractions
- Who the city would be ideal for.

Remember it

Secondary spend refers to money spent by visitors once they have paid for the core activity (usually the entrance fee). What secondary spend opportunities do you think there would be at the Beatles Story?

Think of a visitor attraction you have been to recently. How much did you spend during your visit on top of the entrance fee?

Research it

How does a city go about becoming European City of Culture?

What benefits does this status have for the host city?

Summary

You will need to know about examples of tourist destinations both in the UK and overseas.

International tourist destinations and visitor attractions

Foreign travel has increased enormously in recent years, particularly with the emergence of budget airlines, which have made travel abroad affordable to many.

Sorrento

Sorrento, on the beautiful Amalfi coastline in south-west Italy, has long been a popular holiday destination, and the home to and inspiration, for many artists and writers. Today, tourists are drawn to its relaxed, cosmopolitan lifestyle. Sorrento is a great base to explore nearby attractions such as Pompeii, Herculaneum, Vesuvius, Sulfatara and Capri.

Mount Vesuvius and Pompeii

Mount Vesuvius stands tall over the Bay of Naples. The volcano, which last erupted in 1944, is most famous for its destruction of Pompeii. A half-hour climb to the summit offers majestic views over the bay.

Pompeii was entombed in lava following the devastating eruption of Vesuvius in 79AD. The excavated and preserved town allows tourists a fascinating insight into Roman life.

The ancient ruins of Pompeii are full of history

Research it

To whom would the following destinations appeal?

- Paris
- Berlin
- Krakov
- Prague.

Research it

Find a budget airline's website and choose one of their destinations. If you travelled there for a weekend, what attractions would you visit?

Take it further

Find out the top ten countries that tourists from the UK visit.

Research it

Visit the Viator website. Where else would you like to go in Naples?

Take it further

Italy has long been a favourite destination for short breaks. Which four other Italian cities would you recommend for a couple wanting:

- A romantic break
- An insight into Roman culture and history
- A vacation with a focus on art
- A shopping break?

Normandy

Normandy lies in northern France. In recent years, many UK residents have chosen to move to the region having holidayed there previously. Relaxed and famous for its good food and drink, the area is a great tourist destination. Normandy can be reached easily by ferry via the numerous ports in the south-east. Accommodation is plentiful, including hotels, guest houses and gîtes (French holiday homes available to rent).

The area is famous for the Normandy Landings of 1944 when Allied troops descended on the Normandy beaches and managed to pierce the Atlantic wall that the Nazis had hoped would repel the allied invasion. The region has a wealth of visitor attractions highlighting the epic struggle that unfolded in June 1944. Numerous museums bring to life the struggle that unfolded, while the war cemeteries are a poignant reminder of the bloodshed.

Normandy, France

Take it further

What do you think would be the best way of getting to Normandy?

Research it

Italy and France are in the European Union (EU), which was created to improve relations between member countries and promote trade. What other counties are in the EU?

Research it

How well do UK attractions provide for foreign tourists?

Summary

You will need to know about examples of tourist destinations from overseas. Perhaps you could research a location you have visited on holiday or with a school trip. Alternatively, you may have researched a destination with your teacher and looked at websites, brochures, etc. Whichever you decide upon, choose a destination that you are interested in and know well.

International visitor attractions

The Eiffel Tower

The Eiffel Tower is perhaps one of the world's most iconic buildings. Gustave Eiffel's design beat off the other 700 proposals in a design competition. Subsequently, the Eiffel Tower was built for the International Exhibition of Paris of 1889, commemorating the centenary of the French Revolution. It was not accepted by all at first, and a petition of 300 names protested its construction. Despite these initial misgivings, it is now synonymous with Paris. Standing at 300 metres, it was the world's tallest building until 1930. It was almost torn down in 1909, but was saved because of its antenna, used for telegraphy at that time.

Talk about it

When we think of France, the Eiffel Tower is usually one of the first things to come to mind (see photo on page 182). It is a unique selling point for French tourism and, as such, is usually a must-see attraction for tourists. When you think of other outbound destinations such as Spain, Germany and Russia, what do you think is their unique selling point?

The Sphinx

Standing majestically at guard at the entrance to the Great Pyramids of Giza, the human-headed, lion-bodied Sphinx is the oldest of all Egypt's stone sculptures. The Sphinx epitomises Egypt's past power and success. Created from a gigantic piece of limestone bedrock, it was covered in plaster and paint in its prime. However, over time, the winds, waters and sands have taken their toll. The Great Sphinx once also wore a Pharaoh's royal beard. Part of it is in the Egyptian Museum in Cairo and the other part is in the British Museum in London.

Visitors are attracted to the Sphinx and Pyramids in Egypt by the history and legends

Talk about it

When the value of the pound against the Euro falls, holidays outside the Eurozone grow in popularity. What are the advantages and disadvantages of taking your holiday in the Eurozone?

Talk about it

What would be your top five international visitor attractions? Why?

Apply it

There is a great variety of tourism destinations abroad that are popular with visitors from the UK.

1 Mind-map the reasons people visit tourist destinations.

2 Complete the table below, providing three examples of each type.

Type of tourism destination	Examples		
Coastal area	St Tropez		
Countryside area			
Tourist towns and cities		Barcelona	
Sporting venues			
Theme parks			
Places of historic interest			Lourdes

Summary

You will need to know about examples of visitor attractions overseas. Make sure that you choose ones that you know a lot about and would be enthusiastic about researching further.

Products and services offered by visitor attractions, leisure facilities and tourist destinations

In section 1.4 we were introduced to products and services. These play an important role in helping people enjoy their leisure experience, and provide an important source of revenue for the leisure and tourism industry. **Products** (also known as goods) are tangible. This means that they can be picked up and taken away. **Services**, unlike products, are intangible and cannot be touched or taken away.

Some goods can be described as perishable goods as they decay over time. For example, leisure centres sell items such as swimming goggles (non-perishable goods) and refreshments such as drinks and sandwiches (perishable goods).

Leisure and tourism is a very competitive industry and in order to do well an organisation has to identify its customers' needs and then provide goods and services they want. Hotels are a good example of an area of the industry that has had to be responsive to customer needs. In the last ten years, many have introduced Wi-Fi, provided docking stations for iPods and adapted their facilities to cater for people with various physical needs.

Remember it

Products (goods) are tangible whereas **services** are intangible.

Apply it

With a partner, produce a mind map of all the different products and services offered by a leisure and tourism facility of your choice.

Talk about it

Theme parks rely on secondary spend to help them generate a profit that can be used to reinvest in new rides. Discuss the products that you can buy at theme parks.

Take it further

Products are often more expensive when purchased within the leisure facility than when they are purchased elsewhere. Why do you think this is?

Apply it

Select a leisure and tourism facility that you are familiar with – perhaps one that you have visited before. As well as this firsthand knowledge, try to use as many sources as you can and make a list of products and services available at this facility.

1 Compile this information in a table.

Name of leisure facility	Products available	Services available	How do they appeal to customers

2 Describe the ways the facility currently measures customer satisfaction and include any evidence it may have produced.

3 Are there any other ways it could measure customer satisfaction that it does not use?

4 Give the organisation a rating out of 10 and describe any ways it could improve its products and services.

Apply it

Select a facility that you are familiar with and find out the following information.

1 Draw a detailed map of the area or facility, labelling it to show what is there.

2 Describe the key features. For example, hard-court tennis courts surrounded by fencing, cafeteria, etc.

3 List the type of staff who work there. For each, explain briefly what they do.

4 List the products and services available and the prices. Make sure you know the difference between a product and a service.

Copy the table below and fill in the gaps. Add any other client groups that may use the facility.

Client group	Product/Service	Why suited to client group
Children		
Adolescents		
Males		
Females		
OAPs		

Summary

The leisure and tourism industry is very competitive. The organisations that provide excellent customer service and meet the needs of customers by providing products and services the customer wants will be those that succeed. Organisations should always keep up to date with new technology and the latest trends, products and services so that they can offer them. This will not only enhance the customers' leisure experience but also give them a competitive edge.

Trends, appeal and popularity of visitor attractions, leisure facilities and tourist destinations

Apply it

Read the definition on the right and then try to write your own definition. Remember, although a visitor attraction can be fee-paying, many are free to enter.

Talk about it

1 Which categories in the table below registered the biggest increase and decrease? Do any of these results surprise you?

2 According to VisitBritain, in 2006 the Tower of London was the most popular fee-paying visitor attraction in the UK. What do you think is the most popular free visitor attraction in the UK?

VisitBritain produces an annual report presenting the findings of the survey of visits to visitor attractions in England. This report provides a comprehensive England-wide analysis of trends, plus visit data for individual attractions. Separate reports are also produced by the national tourist organisations of Scotland, Wales and Northern Ireland. For the purposes of the survey, VisitBritain defines a visitor attraction as:

'..an attraction where it is feasible to charge admission for the sole purpose of sightseeing. The attraction must be a permanently established excursion destination, a primary purpose of which is to allow access for entertainment, interest or education, rather than being primarily a retail outlet or a venue for sporting, theatrical, or film performances. It must be open to the public, without prior booking, for published periods each year, and should be capable of attracting day visitors or tourists as well as local residents. In addition, the attraction must be a single business, under a single management, so that it is capable of answering the economic questions on revenue, employment etc.'

The categories of visitor attraction can be summarised in the table below, which shows visit trends in England during 2006–2007 by attraction.

Category	Attractions sample	Increase	No change	Decrease	% Change 07/06
Country parks	(44)	36%	36%	27%	+8
Farms	(33)	67%	12%	21%	+5
Gardens	(93)	59%	6%	34%	+5
Historic houses/castles	(290)	54%	3%	42%	+1
Other historic properties	(81)	44%	11%	44%	-3
Leisure/theme parks	(33)	58%	15%	27%	+3
Museums/art galleries	(415)	49%	6%	44%	+3
Steam/heritage railways	(38)	50%	13%	37%	-1
Visitor/heritage centres	(46)	72%	7%	22%	+12
Wildlife attractions/zoos	(67)	55%	13%	31%	+4
Workplaces	(48)	42%	21%	38%	-24
Places of worship	(88)	43%	25%	32%	-*
Other	(72)	46%	14%	40%	+1
England	**(1348)**	**51%**	**10%**	**39%**	**+3**

Source: VisitBritain/TNS

Measuring customer satisfaction can be achieved in many ways. Mystery shopper customers provide valuable feedback by pretending to be a normal customer and completing a report on the standard of customer service they received. Even whether a receptionist greeted the customer or said goodbye can help determine the organisation's final mark! This is a mystery shopper report on a visit to a bowling alley.

SOUND LEVELS

	Excellent	Good	Fair	Poor
1. Were the music levels suitable at the lanes?	✓			
2. Were the music levels suitable in all other areas of the building?		✓		
3. Was the choice of music playing appropriate for the time of day and the number of people in the building?		✓		
4. Was the level of sound in the Gaming machines area agreeable?			✓	

STAFF NOMINATIONS

Please nominate any member/s of staff who added to your experience through exceptional service
(N.B. Please make sure you ACCURATELY note the staff's name as shown on their name badge.)

Name and where they were working:

The man with black hair at Reception.

OVERALL FEELINGS

Using your own words, please describe how you felt about your visit overall:

The man at reception who was doing everything did really well. Perhaps more staff would have eased his work load. The children had a great time and we would return.

COMMENTS

Comments for BOOKING

Friendly, helpful and polite on the telephone.

Comments for EXTERIOR/CAR PARK

A nice complex with lots to look at and be interested in.

Comments for RECEPTION/SHOE COLLECTION

There was only one member of staff working hard to cover everything. He did well but did not acknowledge my children.

Comments for AT THE LANES

We had a good time at the lanes but none of the staff checked on us or offered food/drink.

Comments for AMUSEMENT

Appeared a good selection available.

Comments for FOOD

The order was freshly prepared and tasted good.

Comments for BAR

The bar was quiet. The person who served me asked if I wanted anything else.

A mystery shopper report

Most successful organisations regularly get customer feedback to help them improve their goods and services.

Research it

Find out the top ten fee-paying and non-fee-paying attractions in the UK.

Take it further

Looking at your list, find out how this list may have changed over the last ten years.

Apply it

With your peers, look at your lists of top ten visitor attractions. Do they match? Individually, produce a presentation describing your favourite visitor attraction in the UK. Use images and make it as interesting as possible, showing fully what the attraction offers, to whom it is suited and why it is your favourite.

Talk about it

Have you ever taken part in market research or been asked your views on the quality of service you have received?

4.2 Customer Choice

Apply it

Think about the factors that influence your choice of leisure activities and make a list of them.

There are many factors that influence how people choose to spend their leisure time. In this section you will learn how people's choices and decisions about what to do in their leisure time can be influenced.

You will also gain an understanding of the reasons why people use leisure and tourism facilities, and the factors influencing these choices.

Talk about it

Can you think of any other activities that some people may consider leisure while others may consider a chore?

What is leisure time?

As we read in Unit 1, leisure time is defined as 'time free from the demands of work or duty when you can rest or enjoy hobbies or sports'. The amount of leisure time each person has will vary, and what some people consider work or duty, others may consider leisure. For example, some people enjoy DIY, whereas others would consider it a chore and far from a leisure activity.

Apply it

Copy the table below into your books and complete the gaps, showing what you do in each of the slots. Once you have done this, add up the amount of leisure time you actually have each day before finally working out your weekly total.

TIME	MON	TUES	WED	THURS	FRI	SAT	SUN
7–9am							
9.00–11.00							
11.00am–1.00pm			Dinner				
1–3							
3–5		Football practice				Watch football match	
5–7			Homework	Help mum shopping			
7–9	Visit gran				Ice skating		
9pm					babysitting		

Take it further

Do you think you have enough leisure time? Complete the table on page 200 again, this time showing what your parents or guardians do. How do your tables compare?

Research it

A wide range of activities have been developed to cater for people's increasing leisure time. Using your research skills, complete an A–Z list of leisure activities.

Talk about it

Can you think of any leisure activities that someone short on leisure time may struggle to participate in?

Why do people have more leisure time?

Generally speaking, we in the UK now have more leisure time than ever before. Several reasons are put forward to explain this:

- People have shorter working weeks and new work patterns, such as flexible working and home-working.
- Holiday entitlement has increased, along with the number of bank holidays.
- With careful planning, earlier retirement is now possible for many people.
- Improvements in transport networks and mobility have increased leisure time. Faster transport and better transport facilities allow many people to spend less time travelling to and from work, leaving more time for leisure.
- Labour-saving devices such as washing machines, dishwashers and microwaves have freed up more time for leisure pursuits.

Summary

We are lucky to enjoy much more leisure time than previous generations. The reasons for the increase are varied, and the effect has helped the leisure and tourism industry become one the most important and lucrative for many areas and countries.

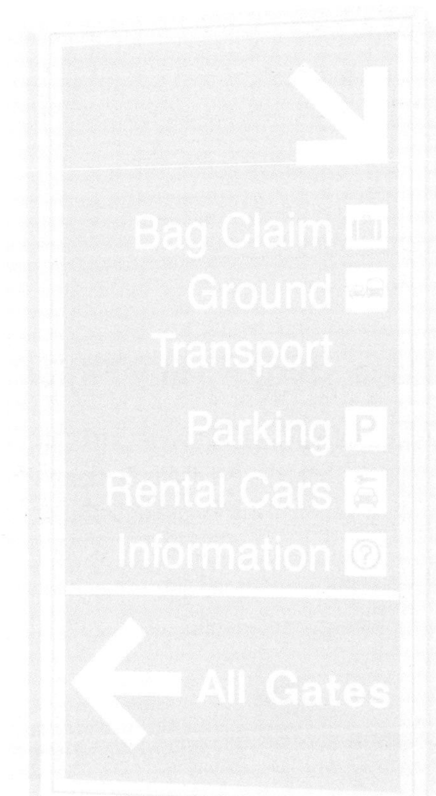

Personal factors that influence leisure time

Personal factors are specific to individuals and are a result of their personal circumstances. It is important that leisure and tourism organisations and staff understand these factors and cater for them in order to attract customers. The mind map below shows some of the most important personal factors.

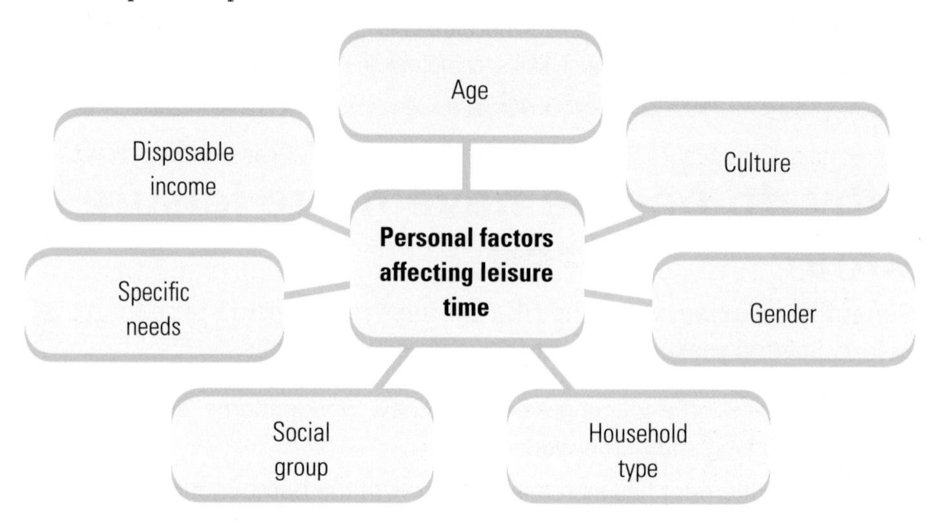

Personal factors influencing leisure choices

Talk about it

How do your leisure choices differ from your parents' and grandparents' choices? Why is this?

Age

Age is a very significant factor in leisure choices. Our preferences for leisure change over time due to physical changes and changing personal circumstances.

Case study – Nifty Fifties

North Solihull Leisure Centre is a public-sector leisure facility designed to serve the needs of its community. It comprises a pool, sports hall, dance studio, cafeteria, health club, dance studio and running track. On weekday mornings, the 'Nifty Fifties' have use of the sports hall and over 100 people aged 50-plus play table tennis, badminton and bowls. Member Edwin Copson says, 'The sessions are great fun. We take part in low-intensity activities like table tennis that keep us fit and provide us with hours of fun. Afterwards we can socialise in the cafeteria and relax. The leisure centre is happy to accommodate us as we use the facility during off-peak hours when many people are working and the facility is quiet.'

Remember it

Programming is a term used for the process whereby leisure and tourism managers decide on an activities schedule (**programme**) during the week.

Apply it

Are there any other activities that could be added to the Nifty Fifties' activities **programme**? Think about the facilities available and write a memo to the Nifty Fifties organising committee outlining your proposals. For each activity, give your reasoning why you feel it would be successful. For example, you may feel the pool could be used for aqua-aerobics as this is a low-impact activity ideal for older people.

Apply it

Copy the table below and match each person with the home-based leisure activities listed below that are most suited to them.

Crafts
DIY
Watching videos
Gardening
Cooking
Internet use
Reading newspapers
Sewing
Watching sport on television
Takeaway meals
Ordering goods on a shopping channel
Aerobics videos
Walking the dog
Watching soaps on television
Listening to the charts
Reading novels
Computer games
Playing board games
Painting
Darts game
Open University course

Person	Activities		
7 year-old boy			
14 year-old girl			
16 year-old boy			
Married couple who have just moved home			
High-flying young female executive			
Middle-aged woman			
Retired man in his sixties			

1 Choose one activity you have allocated to each person and explain why it is suited to them.

Talk about it

With a partner, copy and complete the table below. List the leisure activities that tend to be carried out by each age group, explaining why. For example, young people are energetic and like to be active, while senior citizens prefer low-intensity, relaxing pursuits and the chance to socialise.

Age group	Activities	Why they choose these activities
Toddlers		
Young children		
Teenagers		
18–35		
35–60		
Senior citizens		

Research it

Collect some holiday brochures or look at the websites of Butlins, Club 18-30 and SAGA. What age group are each suited to and how do their products and services appeal to their target markets?

Take it further

Many leisure and tourism organisations focus on capturing the imaginations of children. By capitalising on 'Pester Power' they hope to attract families. So important is this target market that some even survey children's views with brief questionnaires that have smiley and unhappy faces to get a snapshot of their goods and services, and work out how to improve accordingly. Can you identify the different ways that these organisations try to harness 'Pester Power'?

Talk about it

How do your local leisure and tourism facilities meet the needs of different cultures?

Research it

Look at different religions and ethnic groups and assess how their needs can influence their choice of leisure activity.

Culture

The United Kingdom is a multi-cultural society, and different ethnic groups may have cultural beliefs and practices that influence their leisure activities. It is essential that leisure and tourism providers understand their customers' specific needs and cater for them if they are to attract them to their organisation.

For example, Muslims have certain cultural beliefs and traditions that influence their leisure, such as Ramadan. Ramadan is the ninth month of the year in the Islamic calendar, during which Muslims fast from sunrise to sunset. They also have dietary requirements, such as halal meat.

Women's football is becoming more and more popular

Gender

Gender plays a big role in some leisure activities. The line between traditional male and female leisure activities is not as distinct as it once was. For example, football was once a male preserve. However, women's football is now the fastest-growing sport in the UK, while in the US its popularity eclipses that of men's football. However, some differences do remain in provision of leisure activities for different genders.

Household type

As people grow older their circumstances change and this has an impact on leisure preferences. Families with young children are limited in the range of things they can do due to the demands of bringing up small children, and they may prefer the convenience and low cost of home-based leisure. Meanwhile, families with older children may begin to have more freedom in their choice. Working young adults living at home may have lots of disposable income as they do not yet have to pay living costs, such as a mortgage.

Research it

Visit your local health club or gym and find if there are any gender-specific activities.

Remember it

Disposable income is the money left after all of the necessities in life have been paid for, which you can 'dispose' of as you wish.

Take it further

People can be categorised into different groups that share certain characteristics. Often these groups are named so as to reflect their circumstances, as in the case of 'empty nesters' (couples whose children have grown up and left home), while some are given an acronym, which is a memorable sounding word. For example, couples with no children are referred to DINKYs (Double Income No Kids Yet), while young, upwardly mobile professionals are referred to as YUPPIES.

1 How would these groups' leisure choices differ?

2 Can you think of any more categories?

Research it

ACORN stands for 'A Classification of Residential Neighbourhoods'. According to its website, ACORN is the leading geodemographic tool used to identify and understand the UK population and the demand for products and services. Businesses use the information ACORN provides to improve their understanding of customers, target markets and to determine where to locate operations.

Informed decisions can also be made on where direct marketing and advertising campaigns will be most effective, where branches should be opened or closed, or where sites are located, including retail outlets, leisure facilities and public services.

ACORN categorises all 1.9 million UK postcodes, which have been described using over 125 demographic statistics within England, Scotland, Wales and Northern Ireland, and 287 lifestyle variables.

1 Look at the ACORN website and find out how many ways it classifies people into different groups.

Talk about it

Imagine that you have just started work and moved into your own home. What new expenses would you have and how would they affect your leisure choices?

Case study – **Household types**

Falkirk Council has carried out a study of its household types according to the Scottish ACORN groupings.

Scottish ACORN Group		Falkirk		Scotland
		No.	%	%
A	Affluent families	7,094	10.5	7.6
B	Older prosperity	6,545	9.7	11.6
C	Settled families	4,726	7.0	6.4
D	Rural areas	1,190	1.8	5.7
E	City lifestyle	1,244	1.8	8.9
F	Young workers	4,034	6.0	6.9
G	Traditionally comfortable	15,892	23.6	19.3
H	Developing families	15,088	22.4	13.2
I	Poor old age	9,584	14.2	9.9
J	Struggling singles	1,974	2.9	10.2
	Total	**67,371**		

Source: CACI

1 How would this information help Falkirk Council with providing leisure and tourism services for local residents?

Social group

People can be categorised into social groups with other people who share certain characteristics. In determining social groups, occupation is the key factor. Whereas once people were considered to belong to the upper, middle or lower classes, the National Readership Survey (NRS) produces social grade definitions to recognise divisions within these that have been in use for decades. The NRS definitions have become established as a generic reference series for classifying and describing social classes, especially for consumer targeting and market research.

Social grade	Social status	Occupation
A	Upper middle class	Higher managerial, administrative or professional
B	Middle class	Intermediate managerial, administrative or professional
C1	Lower middle class	Supervisory or clerical, junior managerial, administrative or professional
C2	Skilled working class	Skilled manual workers
D	Working class	Semi- and unskilled manual workers
E	Those at lowest level of subsistence	State pensioners or widows (no other earner), casual or lowest grade workers

Source: National Readership Survey

Take it further

Do you think the NRS classifications of occupations still hold true in this hierarchy of income, or should some jobs belong to a different social group?

Apply it

Imagine you are a travel agent and you have been asked to research a suitable holiday for each of the social groups in the above table. Present your findings and give reasons for your choices.

Specific needs

Specific needs are also known as special needs. This can include people with sight and hearing impairment, people with mobility problems, and people with young children. We will look again at some of these people in topic 4.3.

Disposable income/finance

Disposable income is the money left after all of your necessities have been paid for that you can dispose of as you wish. This is a very important factor when it comes to choice of leisure activities. People on low incomes may need to work more overtime to afford the leisure activities they prefer, whereas a self-employed person with plenty of disposable income may be able to take time off to enjoy their leisure pursuits.

Unemployed people and people on benefits have very little disposable income. Local councils often help provide leisure opportunities for them through concessions. They are also more likely to visit attractions that do not charge an admission fee.

Premier League football is very important to lots of people in the UK

Take it further

Premier League attendances have been on the increase since the inception of the Premiership in 1992. How are supporters who have lots of disposable income catered for?

Research it

During the recession that began in 2008, many people lost their jobs as companies struggled to pay their bills. Research the recession and find out how many different ways people in the UK were affected and ended up with reduced disposable incomes as a result.

Apply it

The recession in 2008/9 dramatically reduced many people's disposable income. Leisure and tourism is one of the first industries to be affected adversely in times of economic downturn as people save their money or spend it on more important things such as bills.

1 Imagine you are the manager of a visitor attraction of your choice. How could you alter the way you run your attraction to cater for the fall in disposable incomes?

Talk about it

What life events can occur that will reduce someone's disposable income?

Research it

The Football Premier League has grown enormously in popularity in recent years. Calculate how much it would cost for a family of two adults and two children to go to see your local club in action using public transport from where you live. The parents would like their children to really enjoy the game so would like to get them refreshments and a programme at the match too.

Summary

You must understand and be able to evaluate the factors that influence people's leisure time. Remember, personal factors include:

- Age
- Culture
- Gender
- Household type
- Social group
- Specific needs
- Disposable income.

External factors that influence leisure time

While personal factors are very important, external factors also have a big impact on leisure choices. External factors are those outside of an individual's immediate control. Some of the most important external factors are shown in the mind map (left).

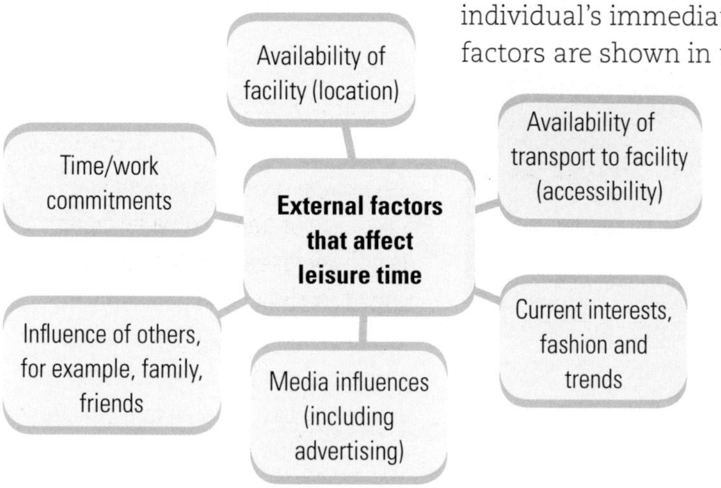

External factors that affect leisure time

- Availability of facility (location)
- Availability of transport to facility (accessibility)
- Current interests, fashion and trends
- Media influences (including advertising)
- Influence of others, for example, family, friends
- Time/work commitments

External factors influencing leisure choices

Location

Location is a key factor influencing what people may do and where they go. For example, for people living in the Lake District, countryside recreation and outdoor pursuits are on their doorstep and easily accessible, increasing the likelihood of their taking part in these activities. Conversely, people living in inner-city London are unlikely to take part in these activities as a regular part of their leisure habits.

Talk about it

Debate still rages in some quarters about the new Wembley Stadium. Built upon the original site, the impressive stadium has staged international sport and pop concerts. Do you think it was the right decision to rebuild the stadium in London, or should other locations have been considered?

Apply it

Sketch an outline map of your local area or photocopy a map. Below are some examples of sports facilities. Add them to your map along with any other facilities that may feature in your locality.

Rate their location on a scale of 1–10 (10 being excellent).

Facility:	**Local example:**
Sport and leisure centres	______________
Park and recreational grounds	______________
Tennis courts	______________
Bowling greens	______________
______________	______________
______________	______________
______________	______________
______________	______________
______________	______________

Availability of transport

This is a vital factor in influencing leisure choices. While a good location in urban areas is often essential for a successful leisure and tourism organisation, making sure the attraction is accessible by as many forms of transport as possible is equally important. The main forms of transport are:

- Road
- Rail
- Air
- Sea.

Apply it

Each form of transport has its advantages and disadvantages in terms of cost, convenience and availability. For example, rail transport is ideal for business people who can either relax or complete work during the journey. Many trains offer working space and some have power sources for laptops. However, delays and high costs in some instances can be disadvantageous.

1 Copy and complete the table below to show that you fully understand the different methods of travel.

Method of travel	Suitable for	Advantages	Disadvantages
Air			
Rail			
Sea			
Bus			
Coach			
Car			
Taxi			

Talk about it

How good are the transport links to your closest city centre?

Could they be improved?

Talk about it

Discuss the factors that influence the choice of transport when going on holiday for each of the following type of tourist:

- Single parent with baby
- Wealthy couple
- Family with older children.

Take it further

The Internet is rapidly becoming a major influence in leisure, used for finding out about tourist destinations, how to get there, and even booking online. Some websites can help people plan journeys. The AA site, for example, is very good. Explore the site and find out how long it would take to get to the following destinations by car from your home address:

- Blackpool
- St Ives
- Eastbourne
- London.
- Newquay
- Cardiff
- Edinburgh

1 How long would it take to get to the above destinations by other forms of transport?

2 For one of the destinations, investigate what it has to offer and describe to whom it would appeal.

3 A new local coach operator has started trading and has asked you to suggest destinations it could run excursions to. Write a memo to the manager explaining:

- **the attractions at each destination**
- **who the target market is**
- **the main motorways used for the journey to each destination and the time it would take to get there.**

Take it further

You are a travel clerk involved in promoting UK tourism, helping people organise the most suitable form of transport to meet their needs. The transport you recommend normally includes:

- Air
- Rail
- Sea
- Road (bus, coach, car, taxi).

It may also involve a combination, for example air then taxi.

You work from home and get enquiries e-mailed to you. This suits you as you can use the Internet to access all the information you need. You use search engines to find information on flights, hotels, maps etc.

You then send them a report on your recommended route. If the customer uses your route you receive commission from the travel companies involved, so you want to make it good! Therefore you need to include:

- Details of the travel company/companies involved
- Times: departure, arrival and length of journey
- Costs
- If staying overnight, details of suitable accommodation
- Advantages of that form of travel.

Today you have received the following enquiries to which you need to reply quickly with your recommendation.

- Pensioners Mr and Mrs Smith would like to go to London for a day of shopping. They have lived in Manchester all their lives and would like to go for one day before Christmas. They are not too concerned about what day or time they go, provided it is cheap!
- Glasgow-based businessman, Mr McIntyre, would like to attend a trade fair for two days at the Birmingham NEC to sell his products, and wants to stay for one night. He is a very busy man and is prepared to spend quite a lot of money to make sure his journey is quick and hassle free. He has a tendency to get stressed if anything goes wrong and has a fierce temper!
- Fifteen-year-old Mark would like to visit his sister at Liverpool University. He lives in Bristol and would like to go for the weekend, leaving Friday afternoon after school and returning Sunday afternoon. He doesn't need accommodation as his sister will put him up. As he is a student he does not have much disposable income!
- Mr Dugarry would like to visit London. He lives in Arromanche, Normandy, and would like to bring his girlfriend to London to watch a play or similar performance. Also, he plans to propose to her! As this is so important to him, he is willing to spend quite a lot of money, although he is scared of flying. He would like to impress his future wife by staying in a nice hotel.

Take it further

The London Marathon was started in 1981. Since then it is estimated that over £200 million has been raised for charity.

1 Find out how participant numbers have increased. Why do you think the marathon has become so popular?

2 Are there other marathons that you think would be good to compete in?

Current interest, fashion and trends

As in all aspects of life, fashion and trends have a big impact on leisure interests and facilities. For example, keeping fit is now seen as an essential leisure activity by many people and has led to the emergence of a multitude of health clubs throughout the UK. However, it was not until the 1980s that its popularity began to grow.

Talk about it

What are the most popular leisure activities and places to go at the moment? Why is this?

Apply it

It is hard to believe that football in the UK was ever in decline. Its popularity was lowest in the 1980s, as attendances dwindled to record lows and the game was plagued by hooliganism and poor facilities for fans. It is now enjoying a resurgence, buoyed by massive investment through Sky and foreign ownership, which has led to the best players in the world flocking to the Premiership.

1 Look at other sports and assess how their popularity has changed over the years. Why is this?

Media Influences

The media plays an important role in shaping our views as we are bombarded with messages from an ever-increasing range of sources, including TV, radio, the Internet and newspapers. With the emergence of wireless technology and mobile Internet media, exposure is now 24/7.

Talk about it

Can you think of examples where media coverage has affected leisure and tourism? For example, ITV's celebrity ice-skating programme 'Dancing on Ice' has led to a massive resurgence of interest in ice skating. Equally, a favourable review on one of the many holiday programmes can boost visitor numbers enormously.

Take it further

Films can have a profound effect on the popularity of destinations. The Greek island of Kefalonia was widely considered to be a quiet, relaxing destination for older couples. However, all that changed with the release of *Captain Corelli's Mandolin* in 2001, in which Nicholas Cage and Penelope Cruz's romance against the beautiful Greek backdrop led to a boom in visitors. This effect has been replicated with the portrayal of an idyllic Greek island in *Mamma Mia!*, and Australia's popularity is set to have a shot in the arm with Nicole Kidman's 2008 film of the same name.

1 Research how effectively these films have boosted tourism in the destinations in which they were shot. Are there any drawbacks of the influence of these films?

The media can influence our leisure habits and choices, both positively and negatively. It can also have a detrimental effect on tourism by highlighting events as they unfold. Following the terrorist attacks of 11 September 2001, tourism in New York City plummeted, causing massive losses in a sector which employed thousands and generated millions of dollars for the local economy. The 2005 terrorist bombings in London had a similarly devastating effect on tourism, as did the 2008 terrorist attacks in Mumbai.

Talk about it

Holiday resorts aimed at the 18–30 market have experienced massive ups and downs over the last 20 years, as hotspots emerge only to face a media frenzy with stories of binge drinking, violence and general social disorder. The resort of Laganas in Zakynthos, Greece, once a sleepy fishing village, was the focus of the media spotlight in the summer of 2008, and followed in the footsteps of Falaraki and Malia in Greece, and San Antonio and Magaluf in Spain in receiving adverse publicity. What effect do you think this publicity has? Is it entirely negative?

Just having a laugh or giving Brits a bad name and ruining it for everyone else?

Influence of others

The influence others, such as family and friends, is undoubtedly a major factor in determining leisure choices. Often interests in adulthood will be started in one's youth, as parents introduce their children to sports and leisure activities that often stay with them for life. Many top sportspeople and entertainers have begun developing their talents shortly after holidaying!

Friends have a profound impact on leisure choices, particularly in adolescence where the desire to be seen as 'in with the in crowd' is at its strongest. Indeed, many providers try to make their products as appealing to this age group as possible to capitalise on peer pressure. Organisations may also try to encourage a positive perception by getting top celebrities to endorse or associate themselves with the organisation.

Time/work commitments

Time/work commitments are an important external factor. Many high-flying workers are cash-rich and time-poor. Their leisure choices are heavily influenced by time. As a result, many organisations, such as health clubs, open for longer hours and provide a range of services that satisfy their needs. For example, many health clubs not only allow customers to work out but enable them to eat, shower and even get their dry cleaning done! Many health clubs are established in city centres so that fitness regimes can be arranged around customers' work.

People with families are often deprived of time too and they may well choose a takeaway and DVD over a night out. Conversely, those groups with few time commitments, such as the retired and students during school/university holidays, have a wealth of opportunities available to them.

Summary

You must understand and be able to evaluate the external factors that influence people's leisure time. Remember, external factors include:

- Availability of facility (location)
- Availability of transport to facility (accessibility)
- Current interests, fashion and trends
- Media influences (including advertising)
- Influence of others, for example, family, friends
- Time/work commitments.

4.3 Providing Service for Differing Customer Types and Needs

In this section we will look at how customer service is provided in order to meet the needs of a variety of customer types. Failure to meet customer expectations can have a devastating effect through negative publicity.

Customer types and their needs

Internal and external customers

Customers do not come in one size. As we will see, there is a wide range of different customer types, each with their own specific needs. 'Customers' does not simply mean customers visiting a facility. Staff working for an organisation also need looking after, as their satisfaction will reflect on the organisation. Staff are called 'internal customers', and organisations which look after their needs and develop their skills and knowledge help to ensure the success of the business.

Individuals

The most important individuals to any business in any industry are the staff. Without good, conscientious staff, the chances of the organisation meeting and exceeding customer needs are slim.

There are different ways that individuals can be looked after. Many organisations provide staff with free membership or free usage of the facility. Alternatively, they may be given discounted rates. For example, many of the top hotel chains provide a 'Friends and Family scheme' whereby employees can book accommodation at a reduced price. This is a valuable perk and one that could be a strong incentive for staff to remain with the business.

As with most industries, it is now common for staff to enjoy bonuses, paid holidays and flexible hours, where possible. Staff may also receive a regular newsletter updating them on the organisation and its latest products and services.

It is important that staff feel valued by their employers. One way that organisations do this is through appraisals. This is where staff members meet their managers and discuss progress made over the last year. Managers can give employees feedback on their progress and identify areas for improvement that will make them more effective. This can then be used as evidence to help secure promotion within the business and apply for training courses that will help them perform their jobs better.

Staff working in leisure and tourism facilities are often very well placed to recognise ways that the organisation can improve its services. To encourage this, some have suggestion boxes where the best suggestion of the month may be implemented and rewarded. 'Employee of the month' schemes are also very successful in helping motivate staff and are based on either customer or staff feedback.

Apply it

All staff at Sea Life Centres are given a handbook outlining basic information on the sea life they have. This allows them to deal with customers' questions straight way, without having to refer them to other people.

1 For a leisure and tourism organisation of your choice, make a list of the most important things that all members of staff should know.

Talk about it

Think of a local leisure and tourism business that you know a lot about. If you were an employee, what would be your suggestion to improve customer service? How would this benefit both internal and external customers?

Case study – Solihull Ice Rink staff appraisal

1. **Why do you think employees receive an appraisal?**
2. **How could the findings of this appraisal form help the employee?**
3. **Appraisal forms are sometimes used to help decide whether employees should receive a bonus. Why do some organisations pay part of the salary in a bonus?**

Blue Ice Solihull Rink

Staff Appraisal Form

Employee Name: ______________________ Job Title: ______________________

Appraising Manager: ______________________ Date: ______________________

This appraisal form is to be completed by the appraising manager during a 1:1 meeting with the employee. As part of this performance review, a Personal Development Plan will be produced to set personal objectives, which will then be reviewed periodically over the next 12 months.

Performance to Key Responsibilities Within Role		
Score: 5. Excellent 4. Good 3. Average 2. Poor 1. Unacceptable		
Key Responsibility	*Score*	*Supporting Comments*
• Attendance • Timekeeping • Customer service • Application to the role • Conduct/attitude to work • Planning/organisation • Team player		

Key Achievements Within the last 12 Months
Detail what the employee feels they have achieved during the past year. Include any training received along with involvement the employee has had in projects/objectives that the business has undertaken.

Areas for Development & Training

Appraiser Comments

Employee Comments

Signed (Appraiser) ______________________ Signed (Employee) ______________________

Date: ______________________

Research it

Trainee managers at JD Wetherspoon, one of the largest pub chains in the UK, are offered a bonus scheme. Look at other leisure and tourism employees to see what benefits they receive.

Some organisations, such as McDonald's, have received the Investor in People Award, which is given in recognition of an organisation's commitment to looking after its employees. By looking after and developing employees, the award has been shown to improve employee productivity, motivation and retention, as well as customer satisfaction.

Talk about it

Why is maintaining employee motivation and good staff retention levels so important in leisure and tourism?

Groups

Groups are welcomed by organisations as they generate significant admission and secondary revenue. Provided they enjoy their visit, it can also lead to positive word of mouth publicity and more customers in the future.

To encourage group visits, organisations often provide concessions if the group exceeds a certain size. For example, The Brighton Sea Life Centre offers special group rates for ten or more people if booked in advance.

To cater for very large groups, extra staff are often laid on, while the attraction can even be tailored to the group's needs.

Research it

Look at the websites of some visitor attractions and note how they encourage groups to book.

Case study – The Landing Museum, Arromanche

In 1944, Normandy in France was the setting for the greatest seaborne invasion the world has ever seen. Many thousands of Allied troops left the relative safety of the English coastline to try and break the Atlantic Wall, which the Nazis had developed to repel any invasion. The Landing Museum was inaugurated in 1954 and, using exhibitions such as a scale model and a film, explains how the landings unfolded and how the formidable technical challenge of the Arromanche artificial harbour was managed.

The museum caters for all visitors. Often, large groups dramatically increase the numbers within the facility. Many of these groups are schoolchildren or war veterans. To accommodate the groups, an expert speaks to the group as a whole and watches a video of the landings with them, rather than waiting with other visitors.

1. **What might be the challenges facing staff when groups of schoolchildren and war veterans visit?**
2. **Find out what other visitor attractions are in Normandy. Which ones appeal to you and why?**
3. **If you were to visit Normandy, find out the different ways that you could travel there. What if you were part of a large group?**

Modern hen and stag parties also provide participants with the opportunity to travel and see new places. These groups are often specifically catered for by the leisure and tourism industry. City breaks in the UK have been popular for many years now with such groups, while the emergence of budget airlines has opened up many destinations abroad. Groups can book seats together on transportation, and many leisure facilities will provide them with activities such as go-karting, clay pigeon shooting and paintball. Some companies have developed that specialise just in catering for the needs of these groups and have developed packages to cater for all their needs including transport, accommodation and activities.

Take it further

Using the Internet, look at the activities available and places to go for hen and stag parties. Imagine that you are putting together a weekend package for a hen or stag party in the UK or overseas.

How might the package vary for different social groups, such as A or C2 (see page 206)?

People of different ages

Children and pensioners have less disposable income than other age groups and are therefore often charged differently. For example, football clubs often charge young people and pensioners considerably less.

Organisations will try to provide products that are attractive to different age groups. Often, for example, they have a specific children's menu. They may even carry out market research to find out what the children liked and disliked, such is their value to leisure and tourism organisations. Surveys will be simplistic and allow them to circle happy, content or sad faces, rather than requiring lots of writing.

Apply it

Design a questionnaire aimed at children for a leisure and tourism organisation of your choice.

1 How could you encourage them to complete it?

2 Why is it so important to cater and adapt to the needs of children in leisure and tourism?

Talk about it

Apart from the fact that children and pensioners have less disposable income, why else might they be charged less?

Take it further

'Pester Power' is a term given to the effect organisations hope to achieve when children want to visit an attraction and 'pester' their parents to take them. How do organisations achieve Pester Power? Think about where and how they advertise.

People from different cultures

As we saw in topic 4.2, organisations need to respond to the diverse needs of people from different cultures. It is important to understand what those needs are and to address them through effective customer service. Some of these cultural considerations are shown in the mind map below.

Talk about it

Looking at the mind map on the right, discuss how these considerations may affect people working in leisure and tourism. For example, the dress code associated with some cultures may conflict with the dress code enforced by some organisations.

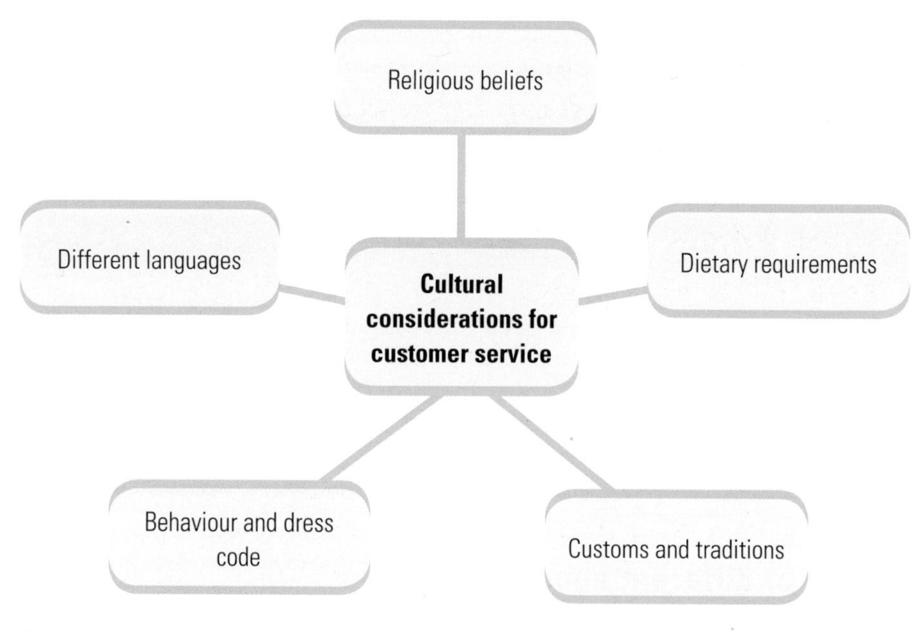

Cultural considerations for customer service

Research it

Find out about the religious beliefs of some different communities in the UK.

How might they affect the leisure and tourism industry?

It is important to Muslims that they pray at certain times of the day

Religious beliefs

Star City is a multi-million pound leisure development in inner-city Birmingham designed to regenerate the surrounding area. The area is multicultural in nature, and the development provides employment and leisure opportunities for the community.

At certain periods of the year, staffing requires careful consideration. For example, during Ramadan, when Muslims fast, catering provision does not need to be great. However, the festival of Eid puts Star City under pressure as thousands of revellers celebrate the end of Ramadan.

Customs and traditions

Staff may have to pray at certain times, and this will affect staffing. For example, though Muslims can pray to God at any time or place, and in any language, there are five prayers they are obligated to perform throughout the day. They follow the same pattern so everyone can follow in congregation, and set prayers are always recited in Arabic. Some hotels provide compass directions to show where south east is to help Muslims pray.

Dietary requirements

Talk about it

According to Visit London, London's culturally diverse population – as well as its visitors from all corners of the globe – mean that many specialist restaurants, takeaways and food shops offer halal and kosher food to Muslim and Jewish people respectively.

1 What is halal and kosher food?

2 Do you know of any visitor attractions or leisure facilities that sell food prepared in this way?

Behaviour and dress code

The Employment Equality (Religion or Belief) Regulations 2003 prohibit direct discrimination, indirect discrimination and discrimination by way of victimisation or harassment in the workplace by reason of 'any religion, religious belief or similar philosophical belief'.

Devout Muslim women will not reveal themselves to men in public, and this creates difficulties participating in some leisure activities. To cater to these needs, some swimming pools have women-only sessions, while some facilities are hired out in their entirety to Muslim groups.

Employing staff from different faiths can help organisations in terms of understanding different religious groups' needs and can also help overcome language and cultural differences.

Talk about it

Where possible, religious behaviour and dress code should be accommodated. Can you think of cultural behaviour and dress codes that may not be appropriate for customers and employees?

Case study – Prayer Room, John Lennon Airport

Perhaps one of the most used leisure and tourism facilities that have to cater for a diverse range of customers are airports.

The 24-hour Prayer Room of John Lennon Airport in Liverpool provides a multi-faith sacred space for travellers. It includes features such as a prayer tree, bookcases of holy books and articles of faith, and a rainbow garden. It aims to provide 'a quiet space in which to pray, to reflect or simply to be still, collect thoughts and find a moment's peace'.

Research it

Look at Liverpool John Lennon Airport's official website. How well does it cater to different customer needs?

Non-English speakers

Ensuring customers understand how to use facilities is essential not only for the enjoyment of their leisure experience but also to guarantee their safety. There are many ways this can be achieved and one of these is signage. Signs should be located where they can be seen, and adhere to internationally accepted meanings.

Some universal signs found in leisure and tourism attractions around the world. Do you know what they mean?

Staff can help non-English speakers by speaking slowly and using simple terms. Hand gestures can be very helpful in clarifying meaning. Staff can also help by using the 'feedback loop', where they repeat back what they have been asked to confirm that they have understood. Staff at Tenpin are trained extensively in this, as the extract from its training booklet below demonstrates.

Customer Service Training Manual

Be repetitive and confirm their requirements

"In all areas of the business you need to repeat all of our customers requirements back to them"

For example:

- **Repeat booking details**
- **Confirm food requirements**
- **Repeat bowling requirements**

Extract from Tenpin staff training book

Some hotels employ people who can speak other languages. To save time and for the convenience of customers, staff may wear badges showing the flags of the countries whose language they speak. In major tourist cities like London, their skills are called upon on a regular basis. As an alternative, hotels may also provide staff with simple phrase books for common customer enquiries.

People with specific needs

The phrase 'specific needs' covers an extensive range of needs. In this section we will look at the specific needs you may encounter in the leisure and tourism industry.

People with children

Organisations can cater for people with young children by providing changing rooms, high chairs, bottle-warming facilities and family parking spaces. Crèches are sometimes provided so that parents can leave their children with qualified staff while they enjoy their leisure experience.

Case study – David Lloyd

David Lloyd is a national chain of health clubs that offers a multitude of leisure pursuits. To attract members with young children, they have linked up with Asquith Nurseries to provide nurseries and crèches.

1 Do you think this gives them an advantage over rival clubs who do not have child care facilities?

2 What activities might be provided within the crèche?

3 Ball pools are very popular with young children. Design a crèche that would keep young children happy and occupied.

Research it

Look at the advice for caterers on the Vegetarian Society's website and find out what vegetarians do and do not want. How does this compare to provision for vegetarians in your school and local leisure and tourist organisations?

Vegetarians

Vegetarians do not eat any meat, poultry, game, fish, shellfish or crustacea, or slaughter by-products. According to the Vegetarian Society, in the last 10 years, the number of vegetarians in the UK has practically doubled, and about 5% of the adult population is now vegetarian. As a result, vegetarian options feature on most menus. Catering staff must provide options to meet their needs.

Those with sensory and physical assistance needs

Sensory needs include those with hearing and visual impairments. Those in wheelchairs or those who have other mobility difficulties have physical assistance needs. Some of the measures for providing for people with sensory and physical needs are outlined in the mind maps opposite.

Case study – The Bullring

The Bullring in Birmingham has revitalised England's 'second city' with its state-of-the-art shopping centre. Its website boasts that 'from the minute you walk through our doors we've got people on hand and a range of services available to ensure your day at Bullring is enjoyable, hassle-free and the best it can be'.

1 Look at the website for the Bullring and investigate how it caters for people with sensory and physical needs. How well does it ensure their day is indeed enjoyable and hassle-free?

Providing for people with sensory needs

There are numerous ways that organisations can ensure that they comply with the DDA. Organisations like the Royal National Institute for the Blind (RNIB) offer information, support and advice to over two million people with sight loss. They provide DDA training that enables organisations to learn how this legislation affects them and how to ensure they comply with the act. Thanks to their work, people with visual problems can now enjoy activities like the cinema, theatre and football.

Medical conditions

Organisations should cater for the needs of those with medical conditions. There should be some staff trained in first aid. For both internal and external customers, refrigeration should be provided for medication, as well as privacy for self-medication. Organisations should have clear policies on medical conditions and make these available to the public.

Business people

Business people make up an important customer type for leisure and tourism organisations. Often they lead pressurised lifestyles, and are cash-rich but time-poor.

To help them cope with the stress of their jobs, they often wish to make the most of their leisure time through, for example, exercise or relaxation.

Remember it

In 1995 the Disability Discrimination Act (DDA) came into force. This means that all providers must make reasonable adjustments to ensure that their services are accessible to disabled people. Since 2004, it has been a legal requirement to make physical adjustments to buildings to allow access for all.

Hotlink

Look at the RNIB website to see how they are helping improve leisure and tourism opportunities for the visually impaired.

Research it

The RNIB has greatly helped visually impaired people. How do other charities help improve access to leisure and tourism for people with special needs?

Talk about it

Ice rinks can cater for wheelchair users by having skis that can be attached to the wheelchair and helpers who guide them around.

How can other leisure and tourism organisations help provide for people with specific needs?

Talk about it

Business people often work long and changeable hours. How can leisure and tourism organisations meet their needs?

Take it further

For each type of customer, write an evaluation of how well you believe they are provided for at a leisure and tourism facility of your choice. If provision could be better, describe how.

Talk about it

Think of the health and safety risks and hazards that could be posed to internal and external customers at a leisure centre, a football ground and a hotel. How can the organisations minimise these risks and hazards?

Research it

What are the most common causes of food poisoning? How can these be avoided?

Apply it

New food hygiene laws have applied in the UK since 2006. Have a look at the new food hygiene laws outlined on the Food Standards Agency website.

At a leisure and tourism organisation of your choice, decide on the critical points which would need to be considered in the business.

Health and safety of leisure and tourism facilities

The Heath and Safety at Work etc Act 1974 was passed in order to ensure the health and safety of people at work. This applies to both internal and external customers.

In the leisure and tourism industry, as in other industries, safeguarding the welfare of customers is essential. Over recent years, 'no win no fee' lawyers and litigation for personal injury have increased enormously, and accidents in leisure and tourism organisations are as liable for litigation as other industries.

Food and drink hygiene

With secondary spend through food and drink sales contributing extensively to the revenue raised by leisure and tourism organisations, organisations are extremely keen to promote sales of these products. However, in their efforts to increase output and sales, organisations must also ensure that immaculate standards of hygiene are in force. Failure to do so could lead to food poisoning and loss of customer confidence.

Aside from the threat of the food hygiene legislation, it is in the organisation's best interest to ensure excellent food hygiene as customers now have access to food hygiene ratings through the 'Scores On The Doors' rating system. Visit the Scores On The Doors website and find out more.

Case study – Environmental health

A recent report in *The Oxford Student* remarked on how restaurants around Oxford are breaching dozens of environmental health regulations. In a series of inspections carried out by Oxford City Council, numerous restaurants were found to be in contravention of the Food Safety Act (1990). Reports ranging from dirty chopping boards in Maxwell's to serious insect infestations have shocked diners across the University, the report said.

The inspections, carried out without warning over an 18-month period found 15 restaurants in Oxford that 'pose a considerable risk to the health of customers'. At Chopsticks restaurant on Cowley Road, the infestation of pharaoh ants was so severe that the inspector ordered that it be removed by a pest control expert. The management at Chopsticks refused to comment on the issue.

Some restaurants had failed to perform a risk assessment or COSHH (Control of Substances Hazardous to Health) report. The latter is required by law and premises that do not comply risk immediate prosecution and closure. At La Cucina, the inspection discovered ice cream stored next to raw prawns, risking cross contamination. It was also noted that raw produce was being stored in the original cardboard packaging, risking it being impregnated with cockroach eggs, which would cause an infestation.

Aziz Restaurant, an award-winning establishment, was criticised for storing potentially lethal cleaning chemicals alongside food products. The restaurant was also criticised for having no sanitiser in its kitchen and no inlet ventilation in the cooking area. Mario's Pizzeria was found to have left the chemical cupboard open to customers during the inspection. Joe's Café on Cowley Road was found to have no ventilation in the toilets, resulting in an unpleasant smell.

Source: Mood Food Magazine

Importance of regular maintenance checks

Regular maintenance checks will identify items that may require repairs at an early stage. In this way, the need to spend large amounts of money on repairs can be avoided. Perhaps of more importance is the fact that if the fabric of a building or piece of equipment breaks down it could endanger internal and external employees and break health and safety laws. At Alton Towers, for example, every ride is tested daily prior to the public having access.

Setting and practising emergency procedures

Emergency procedures should be in place so that staff are well trained and can deal with emergencies efficiently and effectively. Procedures should be established to cover all eventualities.

Talk about it

Check out your favourite restaurant's rating on the Scores On The Doors website.

1. **What effect do you think the Scores On The Doors scheme will have on restaurants?**
2. **Do you think the scheme is a good idea? Why?**

Take it further

Write a list of the maintenance checks that would need to be carried out at a leisure centre. Which checks would need to be made on a regular basis?

Case study – Emergency procedures

Staffordshire Council have produced the following guidance on developing an emergency procedure:

STAFFORDSHIRE COUNTY COUNCIL –
C&LL DIRECTORATE

Guidance on developing Swimming Pool Operating Procedures.

The following checklist is intended to help head teachers and/or premise managers to develop a written Pool Operating Procedure.

Emergency Action Plan

Action to be taken in the event of a foreseeable emergency, for example:

1.1 Overcrowding
1.2 Disorderly behaviour
1.3 Lack of water clarity
1.4 Outbreak of fire (or sounding of alarm to evacuate the building)
1.5 Bomb threat
1.6 Lighting failure
1.7 Emission of toxic gases
1.8 Serious injury to one or more bathers
1.9 Discovery of a casualty in the water.

The procedure should make clear how, if it is necessary to clear the water or to evacuate the building, this is to be done.

1. **In the event of 1.8 occurring, serious injury to a bather, what sequence of events would you expect the lifeguards to carry out?**

Importance of staff training concerning health, safety and security of customers

Staff training is essential, so that if problems do arise the organisation can prove that they have prepared their staff adequately. Such training can include practice fire alarms and food hygiene training and official certification. Documentation should be kept accurately and monitored so that all staff are up to date with the latest training for their field of work and are aware of what is expected of them.

Talk about it

Have you ever been involved in an emergency at a leisure and tourism facility? If so, how well did the staff handle the situation? Could you tell if they were well rehearsed in this emergency operating procedure?

Customer service

Customer service includes any contact with the customer, whether it is face to face, over the telephone or through correspondence. Customer service is concerned with meeting and exceeding the needs of customers. Excellent customer service is vital to give an organisation the edge over its rivals in a competitive industry.

Apply it

The passage below describes the scene when a young woman interested in booking a holiday visits her local travel agent.

Rewrite the passage below and insert in the gaps the correct emotion from the following: **confusion; happy; disinterested; unhappy; bored; excitement; shock; annoyance; anger**

A woman walks into a travel agency, looking very upbeat ( ). She looks at a travel brochure, and is thrilled at the prospect of booking a holiday ( ). As she shuts the door she turns to see two travel agents sitting at their desks. One of them is talking on the phone twirling her hair while yawning ( ), while the other is staring blankly at the screen and looks upset ( ). The customer begins to step towards them but decides not to and instead looks at some of the promotional offers on the wall. She looks over her shoulder to see one of the staff put the phone down, before turning to her partner who now sits back, swings round in her chair and begins tapping her pen on the desk while talking. As she turns, she makes brief eye contact with the customer before looking away and resuming her conversation with her colleague. The customer's mouth drops open briefly, incredulous at their conduct ( ). The customer starts to step forwards then rocks back on her heels. She proceeds to gaze around the room arms folded across her chest ( ).

Finally she gets increasingly annoyed, coughing with her hand to her mouth to try and get their attention ( ). She begins tapping her feet, tension begins to build up in her face before she storms out slamming the door in the process ( ). Only then do the two travel agents look up and shrug their shoulders as if to ask what was up with her ( ).

The ways in which customer service can be used to meet the needs of a wide variety of customers

Now that we have looked at the different customer types and needs, let us look at how customer service can be provided.

Providing information

Leisure and tourism organisations provide information by including their details in, for example, directories and on the web. Staff can talk face to face to customers, while on-site TV screens, posters and PA systems provide quick information. Leaflets and direct marketing to existing customers can help achieve this too.

Talk about it

Have you experienced very good or very bad customer service? Describe what happened and how it made you feel.

Remember it

A dissatisfied customer will often tell several friends, who in turn will tell their friends. This is known as the **multiplier effect**, and something that excellent customer service can eliminate.

Apply it

Write down your own definition of customer service.

Research it

Welcome Host is an established customer service training programme that provides an introduction to the essentials of great customer service. On its website it claims to put customer service training at the heart of an organisation by allowing an organisation to:

- stand head and shoulders above the competition
- amaze your customers and win more repeat business
- gain more business through word of mouth recommendation
- attract higher quality staff and improve staff retention.

1 Look at its training programme. Are there any parts of the programme that would interest you further?

Talk about it

Providing information is one way customer service is supplied. What ways can you think of to provide information and give advice?

Giving advice

Giving advice is different to providing information. It is about helping customers make a decision. For example, at a cinema it could be about helping customers decide what film would suit them, or at a restaurant it could be making a recommendation based on the customers' preferences.

Receiving and passing on messages

Messages can be communicated in many ways such as email, two-way radios or telephone. It is essential that messages are passed on accurately.

Keeping records

Accurate records are needed to ensure that mistakes are not made. Furthermore, many organisations keep a database of customers' financial details, and this data must be secure and retained as long as is necessary according to the Data Protection Act.

Providing assistance

This can be achieved by staff circulating around the facility, helping where necessary.

Dealing with problems

Problems should be resolved quickly and efficiently. If one member of staff cannot help, the problem should be referred to a manager.

Dealing with dissatisfied customers

This is potentially one of the most difficult activities for staff to undertake. However, with the right training and commitment to dealing with complaints correctly, staff should be able to resolve problems.

It is vital that the customer leaves with a positive perception of the organisation. Key rules are:

- Stay calm
- Listen
- Use positive body language
- Be sympathetic
- Sit down in a neutral area and perhaps offer a drink.

In the case of genuine failings on the part of the organisation, as a final effort to appease the customer, the organisation may, at the discretion of the manager, offer compensation of some form. Rarely will this take the form of financial compensation. More often than not, products or services will be offered that will help bring the customer back and provide the organisation with the opportunity to impress the customer once more. Another benefit of this approach is that the cost is relatively small to the organisation. For example, at Ramada Hotels, if a customer is dissatisfied in some way, they may be offered a complimentary bottle of wine or champagne. Although the champagne would be perceived by the customer as costing a considerable amount, Ramada will be buying it at the cost price, significantly less that the retail price the customer would have to pay.

Apply it

Think of a message that may need to be passed on to another member of staff in a leisure and tourism organisation. Write your message down and pass it on to someone else. Did they understand your message?

How could you ensure the message is passed on exactly as you intended?

Research it

Find out what the Data Protection Act is and how it affects organisations and the way they keep customer details.

Apply it

1 With a partner, play the roles of dissatisfied customer and customer service manager. Act out a situation as realistically as you can.

Once complete, give each other feedback highlighting how well each of you did and how you could do better next time.

2 As an expert in customer service, you have been asked to write a beginner's guide to dealing with complaints. It should include:

- a definition of customer service
- why complaints must be dealt with effectively
- the correct procedure for dealing with a dissatisfied customer.

Apply it

Now we have learnt how organisations provide customer service, let's see if you can apply this knowledge to a leisure and tourism facility of your choice.

Using the following headings, describe how an organisation you have chosen provides customer service:

- Providing information
- Giving advice
- Receiving and passing on messages
- Keeping records
- Providing assistance
- Dealing with problems
- Dealing with dissatisfied customers
- Offering extra services.

Offering extra services

Customer service is not simply concerned with meeting customer needs; it should aspire to exceed them. In offering extra services, organisations may look to meet every customer's needs and desires by offering extras such as:

- vending machines
- taxi-booking service
- first aid
- restaurants
- online booking
- newspapers, magazines and televisions in reception.

Apply it

Read the examples of customer service provision in the right-hand column below.

1 Draw a line between the headings and the examples to show the most suitable match.

Providing information	Keeping your fitness programme and card secure
Giving advice	Providing an ATM inside the facility
Receiving and passing on messages	Sending emails to customers informing them of the latest offers
Keeping records	Offering a complimentary meal if customers are unhappy with the onea they received
Providing assistance	Having CCTV so staff can monitor what is going on within the facility
Dealing with problems	Discussing what product is most suitable for a customer
Dealing with dissatisfied customers	Staff helping a disabled person get out of the swimming pool
Offering extra services	Announcing that a parked car is blocking access and the driver must make their way to reception

2 Design an activity like the one above, but think of new examples for the right-hand column.

The overall importance of customer service

As we have learned, poor customer service is the primary reason why organisations lose custom. There are many other benefits of good customer service.

Benefits to organisations which provide excellent customer service to external customers (customers who use the organisation's facilities) include:

- increased sales
- satisfied customers
- more customers through repeat business and recommendations
- a better public image
- an edge over the competition.

Internal customers (employees that work at the organisation) will benefit from good customer service in the following ways:

- a more pleasant place to work in
- a happier and more efficient workforce
- improved job satisfaction
- improved chances of promotion within the organisation.

Apply it

Design an A4-sized poster that could be put up in a staff room to remind employees of the benefits of effective customer service.

Entertainers can work on cruise liners or holiday camps

4.4 Employment Opportunities in Leisure and Tourism

In Unit 1 we discovered how the leisure and tourism industry is now one of the major employers in the world, and looked at a range of jobs in the industry. In this section we will look at the skills, qualities and responsibilities of staff working in the leisure and tourism industry. Many of these attributes can be applied to more than one job role.

Roles, responsibilities and main duties of jobs in the leisure and tourism industry

With such an extensive range of jobs in the leisure and tourism industry, ranging from directors and managers through to casual employees, the list of roles, responsibilities and main duties is almost endless. We will now look at some of the jobs available, the skills and qualities required to get your foot in the door, and the CV and interview skills needed to help to secure the job.

What are the main areas of work?

There are many areas within leisure and tourism to choose from and a variety of career paths as, for example, targetjobs.co.uk illustrates below.

Adventure tourism: plan and oversee adventurous expeditions of all kinds and in all areas. You could run treks going deep into the jungle or hikes up mountains in Wales.

Bars, clubs and pubs: entertainment venues need people to manage them – doing tasks such as bar work, PR, accounts and purchasing – to make sure things run to plan and everyone has a good time.

Conferences and events: events and conferences have to be planned in great detail to make sure that everything runs smoothly. You could focus on client invitations and registration, venue logistics, budgeting or even staffing.

Cruise liners: sail the seas and earn while you travel – sounds perfect, so what's the catch? Its glamorous image makes cruise work very competitive and you will have to work hard, but there's a huge variety of jobs and it's a great way to see the world.

Entertainment and leisure: management, marketing and working with people are just some of the options if you work in entertainment. There are opportunities to work in venues ranging from holiday camps to bingo halls.

Foodservice management: all sorts of organisations need food provided, keeping costs low and nutritional content high. You could oversee operations at schools, hospitals, large businesses or entertainment venues.

Health and fitness: sport and leisure is a thriving sector with opportunities ranging from hands-on fitness trainer to leisure centre manager. You don't have to work at a fitness centre – there are also positions in hotels and housing developments.

Heritage: Britain's heritage is known worldwide and you could be involved in its management, protection and visitor interactions. The essential requirement is a passion for heritage.

Hotels: as a hotel manager, you could be in charge of the day-to-day running of a small establishment and have frequent customer contact, or oversee one area (such as finance or health and safety) of a large hotel from behind the scenes.

Public sector: hospitality services are required by most public sector organisations, including hospitals, schools and the armed forces. Catering is the most common service required but there are also opportunities to work in events or facilities.

Restaurants: there are restaurants ranging from national chains to independent haute-cuisine establishments – and they all need staff. You could manage a whole restaurant or focus on one aspect at a larger place.

Tour operators: organising package holidays involves buying accommodation and transport, and arranging leisure activities during the trip. Managers oversee the whole process, planning new packages, negotiating rates and setting up reservations.

Visitor attractions: you could work anywhere from a museum to a theme park. Managers may be in charge of a whole venue or just one aspect of the attraction, such as operations or human resources.

Source: targetjobs.co.uk, February 2009

Career progression

The leisure and tourism industry offers employment opportunities straight from school through to degree level. Within the industry there is great scope for promotion from operative, to supervisory through to management (see table below). Experience, allied to the right skills and qualities can help employees progress through the levels.

Operative	Supervisory	Management
Hotel receptionist	Front of house manager	Hotel manager
Recreation assistant	Duty manager	Centre manager

Being a personal fitness trainer can be a rewarding career

One of the attractions of working in this industry is the scope for moving around the country or even internationally, flexible hours and the opportunity to work with a wide range of people.

When searching for employment opportunities, job descriptions and personal specifications are an important source of information identifying the roles and responsibilities.

Talk about it

What attracts people to work in the leisure and tourism industry?

Take it further

Can you think of any more examples of career progress from operative through to management in the leisure and tourism industry (see table left)?

Take it further

Search the Internet to identify career progression in a component of the leisure and tourism industry that appeals to you.

Skills and qualities required by staff in the leisure and tourism industry

What do you consider to be the most important skills and qualities required by staff in the leisure and tourism industry?

Skills

Communication

In a people-orientated business, good communication skills are essential. These can be both written and oral (speaking). Communication is equally important for internal customers as it is for external customers and is vital to ensure good customer service. Failure to communicate well and get your point across could lead to great difficulties.

Talk about it

How might employees adapt their communication for different internal and external customers types?

Inaccurate written communications could lead to double bookings, amongst other mistakes. What problems could this cause?

Information Technology

In the past, most records were maintained by hand and filed away, and communication was done by phone, letter or fax. The growth of information technology (IT) has greatly changed the way we communicate and enhanced the speed and effectiveness of customer service.

Records are now routinely kept on computer and updated quickly and efficiently. Data can be backed up and securely maintained. Examples of records that can be recorded using IT include:

- bookings
- membership records
- financial expenditure.

Technology has helped communication by allowing swift interaction and a cost effective way of sending documents. Examples include emails, scanners, projectors, swipe cards, websites, computerised electronic point of sale and video conferencing.

Take it further

List all the different ways that IT can be used in a leisure and tourism organisation to maintain effective customer service.

It is hard to see how employees could work efficiently without a grasp of IT, and computer literacy is an important skill to develop.

Foreign languages

As we saw earlier in the chapter, in order to accommodate the needs of incoming tourists from different countries, foreign languages can be a very desirable skill to have. Hotels in particular may benefit from staff that can converse with guests in their native language and enhance customer service. Even a basic knowledge of a foreign language can be useful in dealing with foreign customers, so it is worth focusing in language lessons!

Problem-solving skills

An inquisitive, problem-solving mind is advantageous in this industry. In a hectic work environment, not everything always goes to plan. Problem-solving skills can be essential in order to resolve problems quickly and efficiently.

Questioning and listening skills

Listening and asking the right questions, to establish what customers want, is essential in order to provide good customer service.

This is the case in all aspects of leisure and tourism, from a hotel trying to provide the right accommodation, through to tourist information centre staff recommending appropriate attractions for visitors. When dealing with problems, being attentive and asking questions to establish the root of the problem can put customers at ease and help come to a successful resolution of the problem.

Physical skills

For some jobs, certain physical skills are a prerequisite. For example, a lifeguard needs to be a competent swimmer, and a rugby coach needs to be a relatively competent rugby player if they are to demonstrate the skills. There are many qualifications available that will show potential employers your capabilities. Football coaches, for example, can take their Football Level 1 and then progress all the way to UEFA Licence.

Research it

What other jobs are there in leisure and tourism in which physical skills are essential?

Talk about it

Can you think of problems that may arise at school, college or work where quick problem solving could reduce the impact of the problem and help avoid negative publicity?

Case study – Selling skills

Here is an example of how you, as a travel agent, can use different methods to meet some customers' needs for a Greek holiday. The customers are a family who are looking for a summer holiday in August, flying from Birmingham. They really enjoyed Greece in the past, particularly Corfu, but would like to try somewhere different. They visited Crete last year but felt it was too hot for them.

In any sales situation it is vital to be positive Don't apply too much pressure. Once a positive rapport has been created the sales process can begin.

Ask open questions to establish needs

Open questions rather than closed questions will allow the customer to fully express their needs.

Switch sell

If you know that their request may not be the best one, switch their attention to a more suitable product. They will appreciate it and enjoy their product more.

For example, if the family wanted a nice resort where they can relax together and have things for the children to do, you could switch sell them from Kefalonia to Kos Town.

You could suggest an alternative along the following lines:

'Well although Kefalonia is a very nice destination, as you wanted lots of things to do, I feel you may find it a little quiet. Kos on the other hand is an idyllic island that enjoys a similar climate. However, as well as being a great place to find relaxing spots for peace and quiet, it also offers lots of fun things to see and do.'

Sell up

Highlight a higher specification or even other products to maximise the sale. For example, you could suggest additions to their booking: 'Have you thought about car hire? We can book your car hire for both weeks so you don't have to worry about booking it when you get there and you can see all the local sights.'

Other opportunities to sell up could include insurance, currency, car parking at the airport, or a hotel at the airport.

Turn features into benefits

Highlight any features of the product that are important to the customer and explain how the feature of the product meets their needs.

For example, if a hotel has a health club and the opportunity to work out on holiday had been mentioned, you can highlight how this would enhance their stay.

'The hotel is in the middle of town, so you won't miss any of the attractions and you will save a lot of money on taxis. Furthermore, I know you wanted a pool if possible, and this has both a children's pool and adult's pool, so you can swim in peace while the children have fun. There is even a gym in the complex that you can use completely free. It really is fabulous accommodation.'

Overcome objections

This is where you use your persuasive skills. It could be that you have not fully understood their needs and need to ask more questions, or that they need reassurance that the product is suited to their needs.

'Admittedly, it is not actually on the beach front. However, you are only a short walk from the beach and this hotel has its own pool. It has enjoyed some excellent customer feedback.'

Close sale

Thank them and use the feedback loop to ensure both parties are fully aware of the precise details of the sale.

'I will book that for you now, no problem whatsoever. So, just to confirm, we are booking a two-week stay at Hotel Grandiose in Kos Town between the 14th and 28th August for £540 per person. Is that correct?'

Take it further

Look at the selling skills flowchart below.

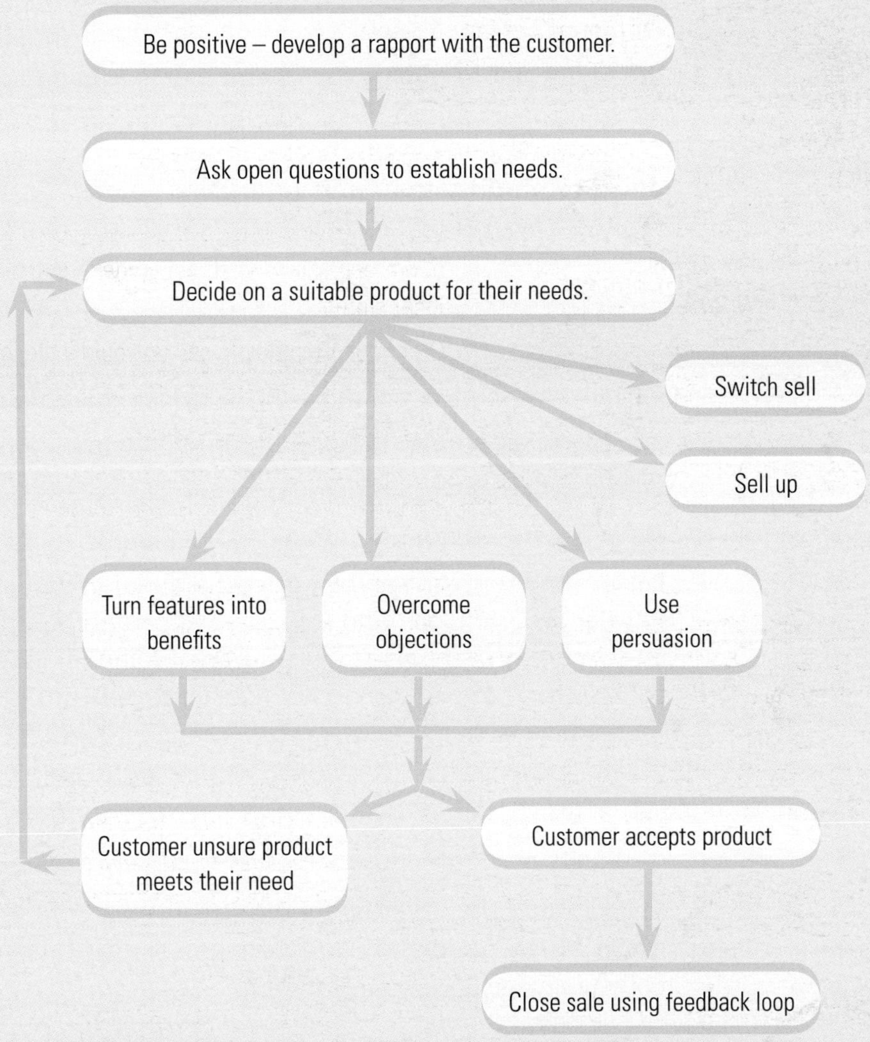

1 Imagine that you work for a top travel and tourism organisation and have been asked to produce a guide to personal selling for distribution to sales staff. You must create a flowchart showing the stages of personal selling and a breakdown of each stage. For each stage you must provide an example relevant to a sales situation within your organisation. For example, a member of the sales staff at a hotel may to try sell up and persuade a room-only customer to switch to dinner and bed and breakfast or a more expensive room by utilising their sales skills and powers of persuasion.

Remember it

Direct communication is either face to face or over the telephone. **Indirect communication** is not face to face, such as email or written correspondence.

Qualities

In a people-orientated industry, personal qualities are essential if you are to be successful.

Outgoing personality

While it is not necessary for all employees to be extreme extroverts, an outgoing personality and willingness to be proactive and approach customers and fellow employees is very desirable. Many jobs require **direct communication**, and enthusiastic interaction will provide a positive image of the organisation.

Confidence

Projecting confidence will put the customer at ease and give a good impression. The better prepared you are, the more confident you will be at meeting the demands of the tasks you face. Professionalism and thorough preparation will increase your confidence and ability to inspire others around you.

Calm under pressure

Leisure and tourism can be a stressful and demanding environment to work in. Often, demand is focused at certain periods, such as Friday and Saturday evenings at a restaurant, or bank holidays at theme parks. Being calm is essential if you are to perform effectively and professionally.

Friendly and welcoming attitude

Many leisure and tourism organisations go to great lengths to ensure that their staff are friendly and welcoming. Often, they will employ mystery shoppers to evaluate the effectiveness of their staff. Staff can even be marked down for failing to greet or say farewell to customers. Body language is very important in dealing positively with customers.

Take it further

Did you know that body language plays a bigger part in the message we are conveying than either the words we use or our tone of voice?

With a partner, try to show the emotions below through your body language and see if your partner can select the correct one.

- Annoyance
- Happiness
- Unhappiness
- Shock
- Excitement
- Confusion
- Boredom
- Anger.

Which do you think should be avoided at all costs in a leisure and tourism environment?

How to prepare for employment

When searching for work, it is essential to read person specifications and job descriptions before you begin an application. These can normally be acquired from the employer or through a recruitment website. The person specification focuses on the personal qualities required, and the job description focuses on the responsibilities.

Person specification

A person specification describes the requirements a job holder needs to be able to perform the job satisfactorily. These are likely to include:

- education and qualifications
- training and experience
- personal attributes/qualities.

Employers increasingly use what are known as 'competencies' to design the person specification. These are classified as either 'essential' or 'desirable'.

Competencies may include some or all of the following:

- physical attributes (e.g. state of health, height, speech)
- attainments (e.g. highest level of education completed, relevant occupational experience, ability to supervise/manage)
- aptitudes (e.g. verbal reasoning, numeracy, ability to drive, ability to speak a second language)
- interests (e.g. social activities, sporting activities)
- personal circumstances (e.g. ability to work shifts or away from home, full- or part-time hours).

Person specifications have to be prepared and used with great care, as if not applied appropriately, the specification of particular competencies may lead to unlawful discrimination against potential employees.

Case study – Person specification

PERSON SPECIFICATION: FITNESS INSTRUCTOR

EDUCATION AND QUALIFICATONS

- Recognised fitness qualification
- Current First Aid Certificate.
- Coaching qualifications wet and/or dry.
- GCSE subjects (Grade C and over) or be able to pass a Numeracy and literacy test.
- Circuit training qualification.
- Exercise to music qualification.

EXPERIENCE RELEVANT TO THE JOB

- Experience in dealing with the general public.
- Demonstrable experience of working in a leisure centre or similar environment.
- Demonstrated experience of working within a fitness centre.
- Experience in undertaking clerical tasks.

ABILITIES AND SKILLS

- Interpersonal skills, including friendly, outgoing personality who likes to meet different people.
- Ability to work as part of a team working to a defined quality level and common objectives.
- Willingness to work when most people are enjoying their leisure time.
- High standards of personal presentation and appearance.
- Ability to liase with all users.
- Ability to provide a customer-orientated service.
- Flexible and helpful.
- Effective written and oral communication skills.
- Ability to instruct people with differing abilities.
- Ability to instruct people with disabilities.
- Ability to keep records.
- Ability to work on own initiative.
- Ability to pursue further training opportunities.

KNOWLEDGE AND AWARENESS

- An affinity with sport and an understanding of the needs of customers of sports and leisure facilities.
- Knowledge of equal opportunities.
- Knowledge of customer care.
- Awareness of promoting and marketing fitness facilities.
- Awareness of health and safety policies, practices and procedures.
- Knowledge of the fitness industry.

OTHER

- Satisfactory enhanced level disclosure check.

Source: Wigan Leisure & Culture Trust

Job description

A job description sets out the purpose of a job, where the job fits into the organisation structure, the main accountabilities and responsibilities of the job, and the key tasks to be performed.

The main contents of a job description are normally:

- job title and department
- job purpose: the main duties involved in the role
- responsibilities: establishing who the job holder is responsible to and all the responsibilities of that post
- physical conditions: where the work is performed
- salary range
- prospects for future promotion and training.

Case study – Job description

JOB DESCRIPTION

POST: Fitness Instructor

VAC REF/POST NO: 0219/SHL105

GRADE: £15,524 per annum. No other enhancements/allowances will be paid.

HOURS: 37 hours

REPORTS TO: Duty Manager/Duty Supervisor

RESPONSIBLE FOR: All customers using fitness facilities

BASE: Robin Park Indoor Sports Centre. Employees may be required to work at any other location as and when needed.

JOB PURPOSE

1. To work as one of a team to ensure to the satisfaction of the Duty Manager/Duty Supervisor the safe and efficient day to day operation of the Fitness Suite through effective use of resources and compliance with operational procedures.

MAIN DUTIES AND RESPONSIBILITIES

1. To have a sound understanding of the safe use of all equipment in the Fitness Suite.
2. To ensure that all persons using the fitness equipment receives instructions in the safe use of the equipment.
3. To advise and provide customers with appropriate training programmes.
4. To provide, after training, a competent Fitness Testing Service and to ensure that all customers using the Fitness Suite undergo a Fitness Test before using the equipment.
5. To positively assist with the marketing initiatives implemented for the Fitness Suite to ensure that the annual attendance level targets are achieved.
6. To assist with the development and operation of fitness initiatives within the centre and within the specified outreach area of the centre.
7. To ensure that all equipment in the Fitness Suite is maintained to the specified standard.
8. To ensure that the area and equipment is maintained to the specified level of cleanliness and hygiene.
9. To ensure that all persons using the Fitness Suite are in possession of a valid receipt, fitness induction card and, if relevant, Fitness Pass.
10. Safety and control of customers in accordance with the Code of Conduct and other relevant guidelines, policies and procedures as provided, to prevent injury, misuse and damage to facilities in all areas.
11. To work in co-ordination with the Active Living Team to ensure the success of any Active Living Initiatives.
12. To attend meetings and training days relevant to fitness facilities.
13. To maintain records.
14. To promote the Trust's Equal Opportunities Policy in terms of employment and delivery of service.

OTHER DUTIES AND RESPONSIBILITIES

1. The above requirements of the job are intended as a basic outline. There will be other tasks related to ensuring customer satisfaction and the care and safety of customers and Fitness Instructors will be expected to adopt a flexible and helpful approach.
2. All Fitness Instructors will be expected to ensure they remain in possession of valid qualification certificates issued by the appropriate governing body.
3. In addition to these responsibilities, Fitness Instructors will be expected to conform to the Codes of Conduct for all Active Life Services staff and will be expected to comply with the Scheme of Conditions of Service for APT and C Staff relating to conduct and confidentiality and with the Authority's procedures, policies and processes.
4. To undertake any other duties as and when required by management.

Source: Wigan Leisure & Culture Trust

Applying for the position

Once you have analysed the person specification and job description and decided you have the necessary skills and qualities to fulfil the position, it is time to apply. A Curriculum Vitae (CV) and covering letter should be sent in good time. A covering letter should always be sent too and this should include further information on your suitability that is not included on your CV. If there are many applicants for the position, the letter of application could help get the potential employer's attention. A poorly written letter of application could well lead to them not even reading the CV! Therefore, the letter of application should be word processed and proofread to ensure there are no careless mistakes.

Curriculum Vitae (CV)

A CV is a record of yourself and an essential marketing tool for you as an individual. It should be concise but highlight all of your skills and qualities to help you stand out from other applicants.

A CV should always include:

- Personal information: name, address, contact details
- Education and qualifications
- Employment history: previous employment with dates
- Skills: such as the ability to drive, speak a foreign language, IT skills, etc.
- Referees: two independent people who can give the potential employer a reference showing your suitability for the role.

Take it further

Produce a CV for yourself using the headings to the right. Ask one of your peers to give you feedback on the quality of the CV.

Interviews

Should your CV reflect your ability to meet the requirements of the person specification and job description, you may be called to interview.

The interview is the final opportunity to secure the job and, as such, you should prepare yourself as well as you can to maximise your chances of success. To do this you should consider the following.

- **Personal presentation:** Personal appearance is very important and, as such, interviewees should dress smartly, avoid showing any piercings (except earrings) or tattoos as some organisations do not allow them. Clothing should be pressed neatly and body language should be positive.
- **Be punctual:** Failure to turn up for the interview on time might give the impression that you can't turn up on time for the job! Arrive early so that you can relax and prepare yourself.
- **Research the organisation:** Find out about the organisation. Where does it operate? How successful is it? What opportunities are there for promotion? Should you be asked about the organisation, this awareness will reflect very favourably on you.
- **Prepare questions:** Most interviews finish with the opportunity to ask questions. A good interviewee will have some, and this is your opportunity to show you have thought carefully about the job and are enthusiastic about the position.

Remember it

Questions can be classed as **quantitative** or **qualitative**. Quantitative questions are closed questions that demand a simple answer such as 'Yes' or 'No'. Qualitative questions are open-ended and demand more than a one-word response. An example of a qualitative question could be, 'Tell me about yourself' or 'What makes you suitable for the job?'

Take it further

Write down ten questions that you might face in an interview. Note whether they are quantitative or qualitative questions. Practise likely questions and rehearse your answers. Practise with a friend, ideally someone who has been through an interview themselves. This will reduce the chances of your facing an awkward question you may struggle to answer.

Talk about it

What would your answer be if you were asked what your weaknesses are or where you see yourself in five years? An ill-thought-through response to either could affect your chances of success. What other questions do you think you could be asked and what would your responses be?

Take it further

With a partner, each download a job description and person specification for a job that you are interested in. Analyse them and prepare some questions to evaluate your partner's suitability. Take it in turns as the interviewee and interviewer before giving them feedback on their performance.

Case study – Career progression

The leisure and tourism industry provides incredible opportunities for young people to establish themselves and pursue a stimulating career. The industry rewards effort and success, as reflected by Suzi Marshall's progression at Pizza Hut. Work hard and you too could establish a successful career!

Suzi Marshall, Regional Director of Operations, talks us through her 20-year, and counting, career at Pizza Hut.

Restaurant Management

I left college with a qualification in Hotel Management and Institutional Catering and wanted to get into the restaurant business. When I was aged 15 I worked at Pizza Hut, cleaning tables at weekends in a restaurant in Edinburgh. I'd had a great time so it seemed the obvious place to begin. I joined what, at the time, was Edinburgh's busiest restaurant as an Assistant Manager and here's how quickly things moved. Within a year I'd been promoted to Deputy Manager, with responsibility for a team of 45 people. Two years later, and with a lot of training under my belt, I was running my own restaurant. And just a couple of years after that I was back in Edinburgh, running the restaurant where it all started. That's the thing about Pizza Hut, hard work and initiative never goes unnoticed.

New Restaurant Opening

Next up came the chance to manage a new restaurant opening, and being an ambitious person I jumped at it. I had to recruit and train up my team, get involved planning the design and layout of the restaurant, and for the next 18 months I had a great time running the place. But there's always something new around the corner. This time, Pizza Hut's Development Centre designed a course to give restaurant General Managers the skills to take them to the next level.

Area Management

The next level was responsibility for six restaurants across the north of Scotland. That number quickly grew to 13. I was only 29 years old and I felt like I'd achieved so much – I'd even won 'Area of the Year' two years running. But things didn't stop there. I was given responsibility for supporting three other Area Managers in a role that also gave me exposure to a number of our Board Directors – and that opened up new avenues.

Regional Director of Operations

Twenty years in and my patch now includes 93 Restaurants in 10 areas stretching from Liverpool to the top of Scotland. I'm kept busy moving between locations spreading our vision of being the number one casual dining experience to each of our teams, making sure our menu is hero and our people are passionate about what they do.

The Future

It could be a move into a different brand or even abroad. Who knows? All I do know is that every few years I feel like I'm part of a whole new business – and that's what keeps me motivated and loving what I do.

Source: Pizza Hut

Unit 4 Make the Grade

The controlled assessment will always consist of four activities.

Marks are awarded for each section as follows:

- Topic 4.1 Visitor Attractions, Leisure Facilities and Tourist Destinations (12 marks)
- Topic 4.2 Customer Choice (18 marks)
- Topic 4.3 Providing Service for Differing Customer Types and Needs (12 marks)
- Topic 4.4 Employment Opportunities in Leisure and Tourism (18 marks)

The assessment tasks will be completed under controlled conditions and are set by Edexcel. There will be some choice in the case studies selected and your teacher will help you select what companies or organisations you can base your work on. Research is carried out under limited supervision; all other work must be carried out under informal supervision. You will not be able to take your work home. To learn more about the controlled assessment, see the Make the Grade section for Unit 2 (pages 116–121). The assessment criteria will always remain the same, and for Activity 1 (for Topic 4.1), marks will be awarded for planning, research and presenting information. Let us now look at a sample of some student work that has been completed for Topic 4.1.

Practice question

Activity 1

At one visitor attraction/tourist destination/ leisure facility, investigate the range and appeal of products/services it provides for its customers.

For this you should consider the following:

- Range of products/services it provides.
- Customer needs.
- Measuring customer satisfaction.
- Overall importance of customer service in terms of reputation, repeat business and customer satisfaction.

A sample student response is shown on pages 243–247. What mark do you think Chris' response would get? To help you, the table below shows the guidelines your teacher will use. A moderator will also refer to these to check that your teacher's mark is accurate.

Criteria	Descriptor	Mark range
a) Plan and research	No plan submitted or research evident.	0
	A basic plan with little detail or breakdown of activities to be undertaken or timescales. Information is collected from a single source with little selectivity or relevance to the task. Needs support and guidance to carry out the task.	1–2
	A plan with some breakdown of activities and timescales for the task. Information is collected from more than one source with some selectivity and relevance to the task. Some guidance needed.	3–4
	A detailed plan with activities and timescales clearly indicated for all parts of the task. Information is collected from different sources with a high degree of selectivity and relevance to the task. High level of independent work shown.	5–6

b) Present information	No attempt to present the information researched.	0
	Some information is presented with limited organisation in a generally unstructured way. Basic use of spelling, punctuation and grammar with noticeable errors. Terminology may not be used accurately or appropriately. The information is incomplete.	1–2
	Most information is presented clearly with satisfactory organisation and structure. Spelling, punctuation and grammar used with general accuracy, although spelling errors may still be found. Some terminology is used accurately and appropriately. Many aspects of the information are well presented.	3–4
	Information is presented in a well-structured, logical and clear way with high levels of detail. Spelling, punctuation and grammar used with considerable accuracy, spelling errors are unusual. There is good use of accurate and appropriate terminology. The information has been presented comprehensively.	5–6

Assessment criteria – Activity 1 (12 marks)

Chris's answer

What do I have to do?

For this piece of coursework I need to investigate one visitor attraction, and the range and appeal of goods and services that it provides for its customers. This is worth 12 marks. To get a good mark I need to plan carefully what I need to do and work out how I will get the information. I have limited time to complete this so I will need to decide on some deadlines.

I have decided to investigate Cadbury World.

- I need to find out the range of products and services that Cadbury World provides.
- I need to find out the needs of different types of customers.
- I need to learn how they measure customer satisfaction (how happy they are with the service) and why this is important.
- I need to describe all the products, goods and services that Cadbury World offer.
- I need to describe the appeal of these goods and services and how they appeal to different customers.
- I also need to evaluate how they measure customer satisfaction and how this helps them decide what products/services they offer.
- Finally, I need to explain why it is important for Cadbury World to meet their customers' needs and provide good customer service.

How am I going to do it?

We will be visiting Cadbury World on a class trip and before we go I will listen carefully to my teacher who will introduce this unit and explain what everything means.

We are also having a visit to the school next week from a representative of the marketing department at Cadbury World, which should tell me more about how Cadbury World markets itself. My teacher has said that they provide an excellent talk and it is highly recommended, so I should be able to get lots of information.

During the visit I will go around the attraction and look carefully at all of the different goods and services on offer, making notes and asking questions if I need to know more.

Information I need:

- Products/services that they provide
- Customer needs
- How they measure customer satisfaction
- Importance of customer satisfaction.

Research sources:

- Educational visit and presentation by Cadbury World staff
- Photographs taken during our visit
- Leaflets I collect

- Examples of questionnaires they may use
- Cadbury World website (www.cadburyworld.co.uk)
- Cadbury World case study.

GCSE Leisure and Tourism Coursework

UNIT 4: Customers and employment in leisure and tourism

Products/services Cadbury World provides

Products can be goods or services. Goods are tangible, which means that you can pick them up and take them away. Services are intangible and cannot be taken away. Services are experienced. Cadbury World provides a big range of goods and services to help customers enjoy their visit.

According to their website, Cadbury World is the place 'where chocolate comes to life'. Cadbury World is a tourist attraction which offers lots of information on how Cadbury chocolate is made. People pay to go around the exhibition and discover everything about Cadbury, such as the origin of the business in Victorian Birmingham, and the Quaker ethics and principles that led to the creation of the Bournville Village and the 'factory in a garden'. Visitors can move through the exhibition to discover how some of Cadbury's popular brands are made, including Cadbury Dairy Milk, and watch chocolatiers make chocolate products that can be bought in the shop. Free chocolate is given to the visitor at intervals in the tour.

Aimed at lots of different age groups, Cadbury World appears to have something for everybody. Whilst the Cadabra ride might be more suited to a younger audience, the interactive exhibits within the Purple Planet zone would appeal to a teenage age group, and the Bournville Experience, which is full of history and heritage, may be of greater interest to an older group.

The goods – tangible things

The company has lots of chocolate products which they sell. Some of these products include:

- Cadbury Creme Egg
- Wispa
- Cadbury Dairy Milk
- Double Decker
- Crunchie
- Heroes
- Picnic
- Milk Tray.

The company also has a wide range of products in its shop which you can purchase as souvenirs or gifts. Some of these things include:

- tops
- bags
- books
- pens
- pencils
- teddy bears
- cups, glasses and mugs
- aprons
- ornaments.

As with the exhibition, the Cadbury World merchandise is aimed at all ages. Cadbury World sells a souvenir brochure that explains the history of Cadbury chocolate and has a section on Cadbury World. There are also history books available and I think that this sort of product is aimed at an older generation. The little tops and teddy bears may be aimed more at younger people. The chocolate though is obviously aimed at everybody, regardless of age. The goods are of a high quality and many of them can only be purchased at Cadbury World, which makes them more appealing to buy.

The services – intangible things

The whole Cadbury World experience is a service. Everything that the public could want to learn about Cadbury and its products since it first opened is a service because it is something that can't be taken away.

The education area where students have their talk is interesting for your coursework. It helps a lot. Obviously this bit of the Cadbury World experience is only aimed at students. There are elements of these talks which would be of interest to everybody, although only students can attend. Cadbury World offers talks across all the five key stages and various subjects to support the national curriculum. This is a very good service as we were given all the information we needed and it was made really interesting. Rather than just talking to us, slide show presentations and video clips helped us understand it better and keep us motivated.

Cadbury World currently has 14 zones, each themed and dealing with an individual aspect, whether this is the history, the products, or simply opportunities to have fun based on chocolate.

- The Aztec Forest and the Cadbury Story are aimed, in my opinion, at the older generation who are interested in the history of the cocoa bean, its journey to Europe, the first steps of Cadbury and how it all became what it is today.
- The next zones deal with the manufacturing process. The Making Chocolate zone allows the visitor to experience 'life as a cocoa bean' as it makes its way from Ghana through to the Cadbury Factory. In Manufacturing, the 'Professor' talks about how various Cadbury products are made, including Fry's Turkish Delight and Crunchie. The Packaging Plant includes a walk past the original factory where you can see boxes of product making their way along the conveyor belt on their way to shop.
- Whilst probably more aimed at children, the Cadabra ride lets visitors jump aboard bean mobiles (small cars) as they drive through a magical land of Chuckle beans (the Cadbury World cocoa bean mascot). The ride is one of the most popular areas of Cadbury World and the visitor can buy a souvenir photograph of their journey, which is a nice memento.
- The demonstration area is aimed at any generation really as it just shows how certain things are done. A Cadbury World employee shows the crowds the various stages chocolate used to go through before mass-manufacturing methods were introduced. The area also shows various products being made that can only be bought in the Cadbury World shop.
- The play area/playground is aimed at little children, something for them to do when they have filled themselves up on chocolate and need a way to burn all their energy off. This is good for parents as it extends their visit and helps Cadbury World offer good dwell time and value for money.
- Purple Planet is aimed at early teens and children as it has activities that you can enjoy for free. These are based on the various chocolate processes or things that represent Cadbury, including playing with chocolate rain, chasing Cadbury Creme Eggs or growing a cocoa bean tree. An illuminated globe has touch-screen pads at the sides and shows various Cadbury sites and ingredients from around the world, along with how the company works with communities.
- The shop and café are aimed at parents and older people as it's most probably their money which will be spent there. They offer many goods for the public and customers to buy as souvenirs or to have there and then. The shop has won an award in the past for its quality and I like the illuminated ceiling in Cadbury brand colours, which if you follow will take you around the entire shop so you don't miss anything.

The other zones in Cadbury World include Advertising (including old Cadbury TV commercials), Essence (a fun take on how Cadbury Dairy Milk came to life where the visitor can try warm liquid chocolate with their own choice of sweet in it), and the Bournville Experience (a museum about how the village was made). Cadbury World also has ancillary services which help visitors enjoy the main services, such as restaurants, toilets, car parking and disabled access.

Customer needs

Different customers have different needs. Following my visit, I can say that Cadbury World seems to have something for everyone.

Young children like being active and have a limited concentration span. They would really like Cadabra. They are not that aware of danger so everything needs to be safe. Older children prefer more stimulating challenges and also like hands-on tasks. The opportunity to make our own chocolate and draw our name in chocolate really appealed to us. We also needed to find things out for our controlled assessment and they do this really well. I would recommend Cadbury World to all students as the talk is very good.

School children are an increasingly important group for leisure and tourism organisations to target. With the growth in qualifications such as GCSE Leisure and Tourism, GCSE Business and GCSE PE, organisations can provide learning opportunities outside the classroom to make learning more relevant and real-life. This benefits the attraction in many ways. Clearly, Monday to Friday in school time is a quiet period for leisure and tourism attractions. By catering for students, the organisation can increase its visitor numbers. There is also the added benefit that, provided the students really enjoy their visit, they could then encourage their parents to go. This is known as 'pester power'. Finally, these students may return in their own time and may one day bring their families. Cadbury World caters for young people's needs so well that it has a Council for Learning Outside the Classroom (LOtC) Quality badge award. LOtC badges are for:

'...all organisations and venues that provide learning outside the classroom and experiences for children and young people aged 0–19 where they are:

- *offering high-quality teaching and learning experiences*
- *safe (i.e. managing risk effectively).'*

This is a really important aspect of customer service. During our visit, all our needs were met and we really enjoyed learning about chocolate's history and how it is made. We also found out how Cadbury World markets itself in order to achieve high visitor numbers. By getting an LOtC award, there are more chances of teachers and youth clubs visiting these attractions as they have proved that they are suitable and safe. Cadbury World was one of the first organisations to achieve this award.

It can be quite expensive for parents to take their children to some attractions so they must be good value for money and have plenty to do. 'Dwell time' helps us decide whether an attraction is good value for money. Dwell time is when you work out how long an average customer is going to stop at the organisation and then divide it by the entry fee. This is a mini-evaluation of whether or not the entry fee is set at the right price. The number they work out would determine what the price is for each hour. The dwell time for adults in Cadbury World is £4.33 (time spent (three hours) divided by price (£13)). The dwell time for children at Cadbury World is £3.22 (time spent three hours; price £9.95). The dwell time for senior citizens would be £3.33. This represents good value for money and the range of services means most people would be happy.

Older people enjoy Cadbury World because a lot of it is about the history of chocolate and there is nothing too physically demanding. There is also a concessionary rate and it runs promotional offers aimed at older age groups, such as entry and a meal.

Measuring customer satisfaction

It is important that Cadbury World measure customer satisfaction as there may be room for improvement. Also, dissatisfied customers are very bad for business as it is estimated that unhappy customers tell seven people, who in turn tell seven other people. It is therefore important that customers enjoy their visit. According to Cadbury World, 30% of their customers are repeat customers, so they must be doing something right. During our talk we were told how they measure customer satisfaction using a variety of methods, which shows how important they consider customer satisfaction to be. One of these is an annual visitor survey where they ask 300 people a year what they think. An extract of the survey is shown opposite.

Thinking about everything you have seen and done during your visit to Cadbury World today, what, if anything, did you particularly **like** about it?

____

____

____

And is there anything that you **disliked** about your visit? (Probe fully)

____

____

____

This is an example of a questionnaire to assess customer satisfaction. The last question is a very good question because if a lot of people all dislike the same thing Cadbury World can change it and keep the things people like.

Cadbury World has also just introduced another way of getting feedback: a touch-screen questionnaire. This is good because someone may be embarrassed to complain and not tell anyone if they are unhappy. As this machine is quick to use and does not involve staff they can give honest answers. Finally, staff in the attraction ask you if you are okay during your visit.

By providing excellent goods and services for all customers and measuring customer satisfaction Cadbury World achieve a very good level of customer service. This has many benefits, the main one being that customers will go away happy. This can create the multiplier effect where they will tell lots of people positive things, and they will tell others also in turn.

Comments on Chris' answer:

Criteria a) Plan and research

A plan has been completed with a fairly detailed breakdown of activities. There is some detail about what information needs to be investigated and researched and Chris has identified how information will be collected from different sources.

The information that is presented shows some selectivity and is relevant to the task. The tasks show the different types of information Chris needs to collect with some specific examples. There is no timescale and this could be why Chris has not fully explained the overall importance of customer satisfaction. This section is worth 3 marks out of a possible 6.

Criteria b) Present information

There is a very detailed investigation of a range of goods and services and how they appeal to different customers. Customer needs are also described in detail, particularly the needs of young people. Chris has clearly listened well to the presentation at Cadbury World and knows how customer satisfaction is measured. He also included a good example form the visitor survey and identified advantages of the touch-screen console for collecting customer views and ultimately working out levels of satisfaction. However, Chris did not describe how the mystery shopper service can help identify examples of poor customer service, which can lead to customer dissatisfaction. Chris did, however, correctly identify the need to avoid negative word of mouth promotion. Unfortunately, Chris did not explain the benefits of excellent customer service in terms of repeat business and enhanced reputation, despite previously mentioning the LOtC award Cadbury World has received, which would give the attraction a competitive advantage over rivals. This section gained 5 marks out of 6.

Overall, Chris' work would be awarded 8 marks out of a possible 12 marks.

Author acknowledgements

Thanks to my long suffering husband, who cooked while I wrote!

Stella Douglas

I would like to thank my family, Mark, Andrew and Emily, for their patience and understanding whilst I researched and wrote this book. Thank you also to my editors for your valuable advice.

Pauline Morris

Photos

The authors and publisher would like to thank the following individuals and organisations for their permission to reproduce photographs.

p10, Fantasticable; p14, Shutterstock/Galyna Andrushko; p19, Thomas Cook; p20, Pauline Morris; p23 (left), Fancy/Veer/Corbis; p23 (right), Press Association Images/John Birdsall; p27, Xscape; p29, Corbis/Standard RF; p31, Phil Rees/Rex Features Ltd; p42, Shutterstock/Edwin Verin; p45, Butlins; p49, Lindsay Lewis; p56, Patrick Durand/Corbis; p60, Virgin; p63, Sipa Press/Rex Features; p64, Whitakes/Dreamstime; p66, Shutterstock/David Hughes; p69, D. Buerkel/Still Pictures; p78, Margo Silver/Getty; p80, Rex Features/Image Source; p85, easyJet; p90, Tom Stewart/Corbis; p91, Peter Dench/Corbis; p92, Press Association Images/John Birdsall; p93, Tauseef Mustafa/Getty Images; p100, David Robertson/Alamy; p103, Thomas Cook; p105, Alton Towers Resort; p107, David Fisher/Rex Features; p108, Press Association Images/Sang Tan/AP; p111, NITSmartserve; p112 Corbis/Fancy/Veer; p115, Jacon Van Essen/Corbis; p122, Corbis/Jon Hicks; p124, Bettman/Corbis; p125, Getty/AFP; p126, PA Photos/Chuck Stoody; p127, Oyster Card; p129, Zorbing South UK Ltd; p132, Nicholas Bailey/Rex Features Ltd; p134, Ho New/Reuters; p139, See Glasgow; p142, VisitPeakDistrict.com; p143, Roman Baths, Bath and North-East Somerset Council; p145, Shutterstock/Brian Busovicki; p146 (top), South of England Agricultural Show; p146 (bottom), The Bupa Great North Run; p148 Royal Caribbean Cruises Ltd; p150, Glastonbury Festival; p151, VisitEngland; p153, Jlindsay/Dreamstime; p156, Soundsnaps/Dreamstime; p163, Karina Moreton; p166, Shutterstock/Clara; p182, Shutterstock/Thomas Sztanek; p186, Alton Towers Resort; p187, iStockphoto/Photo75; p189, Tom Upton, The NEC Group; p190, Shutterstock/Rachelle Burnside; p191, The Mersey Partnership; p192, Shutterstock/Sailorr; p193, Shutterstock/Olga Langerova; p194, Shutterstock/Maksym Gorpenyuk; p204, Brendon Thorne/Stringer/Getty Images; p207, Liverpool FC; p212, Llo Musto/Rex Features Ltd; p216, Sipa Press/Rex Features Ltd; p218, Corbis/Estelle Klawitter/Zefa; p222, Anthony Walker/View Pictures/Rex Features Ltd; p230, Thomas Cook; p231, Image Source/Rex Features Ltd; p234, Thomas Cook.

Background photos used throughout book, with page number each first appears on:

p11, Shutterstock/Magna; p14 Pearson Education Ltd/Naki Photography; p17, Shutterstock/Natalia Bratslavsky; p21, Shutterstock/James M Phelps Jr; p25, Shutterstock/Chad McDermott; p37, Creatas; p44, Shutterstock/Styve Reineck.

Index